REVOLUTION IN THE STREET

Revolution in the Street

Women, Workers, and Urban Protest in Veracruz
1870–1927

Andrew Grant Wood

A Scholarly Resources Inc. Imprint
Wilmington, Delaware

Scholarly Resources Inc.
104 Greenhill Avenue
Wilmington, DE 19805-1897
www.scholarly.com

Library of Congress Cataloging-in-Publication Data

Wood, Andrew Grant, 1958–
    Revolution in the street : women, workers, and urban protest in
Veracruz, 1870–1927 / Andrew Grant Wood.
        p. cm. — (Latin American silhouettes : studies in history and
    culture)
    Includes bibliographical references and index.
    ISBN 0-8420-2879-X (alk. paper)
    1. Rent strikes—Mexico—Veracruz (Veracruz)—History. 2. Rental
housing—Mexico—Veracruz (Veracruz)—History. 3. Urban poor—
Mexico—Veracruz (Veracruz)—Political activity. I. Title. II. Latin
American silhouettes.

HD7288.84.W66 2001
322.4'4'097262—dc21   00-058768

ISBN 0-8420-2880-3

For Monica

Veracruz, pedacito de patria que sabe sufrir y cantar . . .
—Agustín Lara

Contents

Acknowledgments

This project got its start during a trip south from San Francisco to the Pacific beaches of Mexico in August 1990. In what would become the first of many visits to Mexico City—as well as the charming east coast cities of Jalapa and Veracruz—my first walk up the subway stairs into the capital's main plaza, the Zócalo, was an unforgettable experience that left me hungry to learn more about Mexican and Latin American history.

At the University of California, Davis, my advisers, Arnold Bauer and Charles Walker, proved to be not only excellent scholars but also quite wonderful people. Arnie's prize-winning paella and his status in the transnational vitacultural community are exceeded only by his reputation as a man of letters. Likewise, Chuck regularly offered sound advice—often as we made our way to the Davis Coffee House or neighboring Café Roma. John Walton's suggestions on comparative and theoretical issues provided me a solid foundation from which to venture into the archival waters. At the same time, Michael Johns encouraged my interest in urban topics while also taking time to talk jazz. My deepest thanks to you all.

A grant from the University of California Institute for Mexico and the United States (UC MEXUS) made initial research in Mexico possible. Special thanks to Martha Schteingart at the Colegio de México for her sponsorship. Additional support came from the University of California, Davis, History Department and the UC Humanities Research Institute. Time spent as postdoctoral historian at UC MEXUS from April 1998 to June 2000 gave me time to make revisions. For this great opportunity I am indebted to Juan Vicente Palerm, Kathy Vincent, Andrea Kaus, Brian Haley, Travis Dubry, and everyone at UC MEXUS.

In Mexico, Professors Ricardo Corzo Ramírez, María Elena Díaz, Octavio García Mundo, and Olivia Domínguez Pérez at the Universidad Veracruzana in Jalapa as well as my colleagues María Eugenia Terrones and Ariel Rodríguez Kuri in Mexico City all helped orient me to the task of archival research. Doña Teresa Blanco and José Luis Blanco made living in Jalapa a real pleasure, while Helga Baitenmann, Pepe Ochoa, and Miguel Fematt gave me welcome relief from the semi-solitary world of academic research. In Veracruz, Elizabeth Novell and Miguel Angel Montoya welcomed me into their homes with characteristic *jarochan* hospitality. Additionally, the staff at Hotel Rioja in Mexico City provided this *canadiense* researcher with a clean bed, a warm shower, and a lobby *televisión* at an affordable rate.

Assistance by archival staff and librarians has been invaluable. In Mexico, I have been most fortunate to receive the patient attention of many at the AGN, AGEV, and AMV who responded to questions and requests for material during visits in 1992, 1993–94, 1995, 1996, and 1999. The Inter-Library Loan staff at both UC Davis and UC Riverside also supplied many important source materials.

Bill Beezley, Barry Carr, Judith Ewell, and Heather Fowler Salamini read the entire manuscript and offered insightful comments. John Hart, John Lear, Simon Miller, Mauricio Tenorio, Paul Vanderwood, Eric Van Young, and members of the UC Davis Hemispheric Initiative of the Americas all provided helpful advice along the way. Errors of fact and interpretation, of course, are mine alone.

My gratitude goes to Richard Hopper, Linda Pote Musumeci, Sharon Costill, and everyone at Scholarly Resources and to copyeditor Debby Stuart Smith. Lechelle Calderwood provided skillful work on the maps. Thanks also to former teachers, colleagues, and fellow travelers James Baer, David Bailey, James "Moksha" Barnes, Patrick Barr, Diane Bishop, Cynthia Brantley, James Brennan, David Brody, James Brooks, Gordon Finnie, Eitan Ginzberg, Alex Greene, Denny Greenleaf, Darlene Clark Hine, Charles Hale Jr., Ted Hamm, David Kaiser, Michael Kearney, Emilio Kouri, Kathy Kudlick, Glen Kuecker, Piers Lewis, Randy Lewis, Debbie Lyon, Michael Moore, John Mraz, my cats Shish and Allie, Patrice Olsen, Richard Peterson, Jeff Pilcher, Emily and Steve Plesser, Ron "Big Red" Redmon, Harry Reed, Robert Rice, Michelle "Miko" Rice, Ruth Rosen, Anne Rubenstein, Pedro Santoni, Myrna Santiago, Bill Skuban, Michael Snodgrass, Linda Stanford, Norman Stolzoff, Richard Thomas, Clarence Walker, and Glen Wright.

For their love and support over the years, I especially want to thank my parents, Mary (Wendy) Wood and Grant Wood. My gratitude goes to Dave and Libby Wood, who have watched this project develop. In recent years, Cindy and Bob Barczak have warmly welcomed me into their home. Finally, I want to thank Monica Barczak for her companionship, joyous spirit, and beautiful smile. Without her the everyday business of history would indeed be only half the fun.

Abbreviations

AGEV	Archivo General del Estado de Veracruz, Jalapa
AGN	Archivo General de la Nación, Mexico City
AMV	Archivo Municipal de Veracruz
AT	Archivo Tejeda
CGT	Confederación General de Trabajadores
CROM	Confederación Regional Obrera Mexicana
CTRM	Confederación del Trabajo de la Región Mexicana
FLTV	Federación Local de Trabajadores del Puerto de Veracruz
PCM	Partido Comunista Mexicano
PNC	Partido Nacional Cooperatista
RDS	Records of the Department of State relating to the Internal Affairs of Mexico

Introduction

Tenant Protest in Revolutionary Mexico

Even today, the mass historical memory rejects any interpretation of the revolution as a mere defeat of its aspirations, while remaining unshakably suspicious of anyone who presents it as a complete victory for the Mexican people.
—Adolfo Gilly, *The Mexican Revolution*

The activism of the poor is a factor in urban politics since their behavior constitutes an unknown element which is alternatively feared and sought after, depending on the strength and political complexion of the government of the day.
—Brian Roberts, *Cities of Peasants*

In April 1987 residents of Mexico's capital formed a citywide organization dedicated to improving housing conditions in popular neighborhoods. In part, collective action had emerged in the wake of the 1985 Mexico City earthquake, which left more than ten thousand dead. When governmental responses to the disaster proved inadequate, organizers, including the internationally known defender of tenants and scourge of greedy landlords Superbarrio Gómez, began advancing popular demands for better housing.

Just as the struggles of the 1980s reflected the reawakening of civil society and a move toward more democratic politics in Mexico, the social protest many of the urban poor undertook immediately after the revolution of 1910–1917 reflected a new consciousness. This book examines that consciousness and tells the story of one of the most dynamic urban protests in twentieth-century Mexico: the Veracruz tenant movement.

A first wave of tenant mobilization took shape in various Mexican cities as revolutionary elites drafted what would become the new national Constitution of 1917. Then, early in 1922 a group of prostitutes in the Veracruz neighborhood of La Huaca stopped paying their rent. They quickly found many others throughout the city willing to join a housing boycott. Soon, led by the charismatic tailor and anarchist Herón Proal, renters (*inquilinos*) who came out of the crowded Veracruz neighborhoods and off the waterfront docks where workers had been politicized by the writings of the anarchists Ricardo and Enrique Flores Magón, soon founded the Revolutionary Syndicate of Tenants.[1] Within weeks the mobilization had grown to include some forty thousand residents in the port of Veracruz or nearly 75 percent of the city's population.

As thousands refused to pay their landlords, they helped launch a protest that quickly spread to other cities in the state, including Orizaba (and the nearby towns of Río Blanco, Santa Rosa, and Nogales), Córdoba, Soledad de Doblado, Minatitlán, Puerto México (today's Coatzacoalcos), Tierra Blanca, Tuxpan, and the capital, Jalapa. Across Mexico, tenants also organized in Mexico City, Guadalajara, Puebla, San Luis Potosí, Mazatlán, Monterrey, Tampico, Torreón, Durango, and Aguascalientes.

In cities where tenant mobilization took the most dramatic form, nearly equal numbers of male and female renters blocked evictions, participated in marches, and attended open-air meetings. In the port of Veracruz, protesters regularly paraded in the streets, shouting "Death to the Spanish landlords!" and various pro-Communist and anarchist slogans, all the while hanging red-and-black flags in their wake. Strikers targeted landlords, rent collectors, police, and politicians to denounce high rents and substandard conditions. Occupying public plazas, streets, and parks during the early 1920s, tenant protesters captured the attention of the nation.

The history of the Veracruz tenant movement raises a number of important questions about the relationship between state and civil society before, during, and after the revolution. What, for example, were the economic and social conditions that gave rise to the housing crisis? How did the ideals of the revolution and new political leadership help shape popular political attitudes and social organizing? Who participated in the rent protests, and what influence did the movement have on Mexican society?

Memoirs by strike participants Arturo Bolio Trejo, Rafael Ortega, and Rafael "El Negro" García, mayor of Veracruz, provide first-hand accounts of the protest. The 1932 novel *La ciudad roja*, by the Veracruz radical José Mancisidor, portrays the housing protest and stresses proletarian and nationalist themes. Octavio García Mundo presented the first full-length treatment of the protest in 1976.[2] And since then, Manuel Castells and Paco Ignacio Taibo II have discussed the history of the postrevolutionary rent strikes.[3]

Building on these earlier accounts, this book takes a longer view of the movement. I argue that the conditions for tenant organizing first arose with the modernization projects and development of working-class neighborhoods in Mexican cities during the late nineteenth century. Subsequently, elite state-building efforts after the revolution politicized citizens who soon used the discourse of nationalism and workers' rights to frame their grievances over housing. Finally, in contrast to earlier studies, I describe how the protests persisted for almost a decade.

Previous treatments suggest that the movement emerged almost spontaneously, as if protest represented a necessary consequence of accumulated complaints about poor housing conditions, high rents, and Mexico's tenuous position in the world economy.[4] Collective action by tenants, however, did not come as an inevitable eruption of a social "volcano." Instead, the renters' movement emerged when and where it did through the combination of moral outrage and grassroots organizing in conjunction with a widening set of political opportunities created largely "from above" by elites.[5]

Tenant protest took shape because of three factors: an emergent popular political discourse concerned with daily living conditions and matters of social justice, grassroots social networks established by the labor movement that intersected with local neighborhood cultures to provide critical links for the mobilization of both male and female renters, and new political opportunities for grassroots protest that developed because the federal government was weak. Political opportunity eventually proved short-lived, however, as changes on the local, state, and national political scene began to threaten economic and political security, forcing elites to clamp down on striking renters.

Across Mexico the revolution had created a significant "vacuum of sovereignty" in which local and regional groups enjoyed a relative degree of autonomy from the federal government.[6] Once the insurrectionary phase of the revolution (1910–1917) had come to a close, the new government faced an enormous challenge.[7] The vast array of new actors (workers, peasants, and various middle-class groups) who had made their entrance onto the national political stage created a "crisis of participation" for the first postrevolutionary regimes, under Presidents Venustiano Carranza (1916–1920), Alvaro Obregón (1920–1924), and Plutarco Elías Calles (1924–1928), that required their winning significant popular support if federal rule was ever to be successfully established.[8]

Working to extend their control, Carranza, Obregón, and Calles gradually developed a political strategy designed to forge a new social pact with the masses by promising economic redistribution and social justice. Using the rhetoric of Mexican nationalism, these leaders called for the creation of new public works, education initiatives, land reform, and, probably most important for urban popular groups, a bill of rights for workers. As such, Article 123 of the 1917 Constitution provided laborers with basic workplace protections as well as the right to strike. Encouraged by what seemed to be a growing toleration for grassroots collective action, more and more Mexicans joined labor unions and took part in municipal politics and local organizing. Strikes, once largely confined to the workplace, began to occur in urban communities as well.

More specifically, rent protests were first undertaken in the port of Veracruz with the support of Governor Adalberto Tejeda and Workers' Party mayor Rafael García. Inspired by the ideology of revolutionary nationalism, both men had made strong appeals to formerly disenfranchised groups. Their style of postrevolutionary politics, along with other regional and local leaders of the time, provided encouragement for tenant organizing that local militants such as Herón Proal wasted no time in turning to their advantage.

An active and longtime resident of the port, Proal knew the intimate culture of Veracruz well enough to make effective use of social networks established in the popular neighborhoods, production centers, and local hangouts.[9] Then, beginning in early 1922, a new wave of protest by tenants presented a political threat to local, regional, and national elites. Like other urban popular groups in Mexico City, Guadalajara, and several other towns, these protesters forged their own brand of local citizenship in response to incipient revolutionary rule.

What happened in Veracruz during this period is distinctive not only because the tenant movement flourished in the port and in the state's other three major cities of Jalapa, Orizaba, and Córdoba but also because renters' efforts eventually helped influence the passage of Mexico's only significant housing reform legislation during the 1920s. Proposed by the administration of Adalberto Tejeda and approved by the state legislature in early 1923, the Veracruz rent law (Ley de Inquilinato) provided for the reduction of urban rents to approximately 1910 levels, donation of land to be colonized by workers outside the city, and close monitoring of landlord-tenant relations.

Although citizens complained of similar problems in rental housing and in some cases, such as Mexico City and Guadalajara, residents undertook a comparable, although less sustained, mobilization, their protest encouraged little or no legislative action resulting in reform.[10]

Interestingly, precedent for the Veracruz law had been set when leaders in the Gulf states of Campeche and Yucatán had enacted minor urban housing reforms in June 1921 and January 1922, respectively. But, unlike the law in Veracruz, these measures had been decreed "from above" and received relatively little public attention.[11]

To set the stage for an examination of the Veracruz tenant movement, this book discusses a range of transformations related to matters of everyday life in cities before, during, and immediately after the revolution. Chapter 1 considers urbanization in Mexico by focusing on the port of Veracruz. With residents celebrating the completion of new railroad, harbor, and urban facilities around the turn of the century, many believed that a new era of civilization had begun. But not everyone benefited equally from economic growth as Veracruz also saw the haphazard development of urban popular neighborhoods on the city's periphery. As increasing numbers of working-class women and men crowded into local tenements, they hastened the development of various pathologies as well as the establishment of social networks that would later help facilitate popular organizing. Following this period of urban renewal, the 1914 invasion and occupation of the city by North American forces served as a kind of shock therapy that stimulated the development of a new local political consciousness. As the Yankees imposed a new sanitary discipline, they raised expectations regarding public health conditions as well as the ire of Veracruz residents who deeply resented the gringo presence.

When the North Americans eventually ceded control of the city to Constitutionalist forces under Venustiano Carranza in November 1914, many found cause for celebration. Yet after a brief period of euphoria, Chapter 2 describes how for most citizens relief from day-to-day hardships would not be forthcoming. Instead, residents in Veracruz, as well as in several other areas of the nation, suffered greatly during one of the most difficult periods of the revolution as rampant inflation, food shortages, and civil war tore at the fabric of Mexican society.

In response, revolutionary elites began encouraging Mexicans to demand basic rights as citizens and to expect improvements in their day-to-day lives. With a concept of social justice deeply rooted in the ideals of Mexican nationhood, popular interpretations of the Constitution of 1917 helped to stimulate new forms of organizing. In the port of Veracruz, growing resentment initially felt toward North Americans was transferred toward local elites, especially foreign property owners, whom many people viewed with growing suspicion.

Chapter 3 considers how local political culture successfully interacted with the emerging national revolutionary discourse after 1917.

Arguing that the environment in Veracruz was right for collective action, evidence suggests that divisions between elites at the national, regional, and local levels provided new opportunities for tenant organizing. Particularly important in appreciating this situation is the way Veracruz governor Adalberto Tejeda took charge of building his own power base through the use of populist appeals and progressive legislative action.

Chapter 4 begins in early 1922 with an account of how Veracruz renters joined with Herón Proal in founding the Revolutionary Syndicate of Tenants. Over the next few months, protesters—including a dynamic group of female militants—transformed neighborhood tenements into organizational bases for collective contention and anarchist direct action. Chapter 5 continues to describe how the strike developed in the port and then spread to other Veracruz cities. At the same time, protests broke out in areas elsewhere in the republic. As a result, spring 1922 proved to be a remarkable season as striking tenants, property owners, and state officials maneuvered for political position. Soon, Veracruz state lawmakers in Jalapa began work on a housing reform bill that appeared sympathetic to the protesters' point of view.

Chapter 6 examines a fleeting period of popular euphoria felt by tenants and organized labor in the port as well as a deepening fear among elites who believed that a "tyranny of the masses" was placing the political stability of Veracruz at risk. Contributing significantly to the carnivalesque drama in the city at this time were female militants who bullied rent collectors, badgered police, blocked evictions, plastered syndicate propaganda throughout the city, and hounded merchants for lower prices. As clashes between striking tenants, property owners, and police became more intense, federal troops attempted to bring an end to the protest in July 1922. By the time the confrontation had ended, several residents lay dead or injured in the Veracruz streets and police had arrested Herón Proal and nearly one hundred members of the syndicate.

Chapter 7 details how the movement continued after the July repression. Realization of a Veracruz tenant convention in August 1922 as well as frequent public demonstrations the following year eventually helped influence passage of Mexico's only significant state housing reform during the 1920s. Chapter 8 opens with a bang, describing movement supporters tossing firecrackers (*cohetes*) into the streets to celebrate the freeing of Revolutionary Syndicate members in May 1923. With their release, militants pledged to continue their fight for social justice and housing reform. But the state political environment had begun to change as elites grew increasingly divided and subsequently withdrew support from the movement. Sensing a significant change in the Veracruz scene, Proal and his followers began to grow desperate.

The final chapter describes the last months of the movement when infighting among tenant factions, legal action taken by property owners, and pressure by the new president, Plutarco Elías Calles, resulted in the arrest of Herón Proal. Despite the efforts of many tenants in the port, Veracruz renters increasingly grew tired of the strike and began negotiating new contracts with their landlords. By early 1926, state officials had forced Herón Proal and his *compañera* María Luisa Marín to leave Veracruz. With their departure, the independent renters movement led by the Revolutionary Syndicate of Tenants gradually came to an end.

By considering the perspective of those living in cities, *Revolution in the Street* contributes to the new urban history of modern Mexico. In addition to detailing changes in the regional political economy and built environment of Veracruz, this book shows how many people on the margins of revolutionary society struggled for influence in the new revolutionary order taking shape during the 1920s. Although renters largely may have failed to realize their more utopian goals, the history of the Veracruz tenant movement represents an important example of women and men working for a more democratic Mexico after the revolution.

Notes

1. On the Flores Magón brothers and their influence, see Arnoldo Córdova, *La ideología de la revolución mexicana: La formación del nuevo régimen* (Mexico City: Ediciones Era, 1973), 173–87; and W. Dirk Raat, *Revoltosos: Mexico's Rebels in the United States, 1903–1923* (College Station: Texas A&M University Press, 1981). On Mexico and the influence of the Russian Revolution, see Mario Gill, *México y la revolución de octubre (1917)* (Mexico City: Ediciones de Cultura Popular, 1975).

2. Arturo Bolio Trejo, *Rebelión de mujeres: Versión histórica de la revolución inquilinaria de Veracruz* (Veracruz: Editorial "Kada," 1959); Leafar Agetro (Rafael Ortega), *Las luchas proletarias en Veracruz: Historia y autocrítica* (Jalapa: Editorial "Barricada," 1942), 65–93; Rafael García Auli, *La unión de estibadores y jornaleros del puerto de Veracruz: Ante el movimiento obrero nacional e internacional de 1909 a 1977* (Veracruz: Author's edition, 1977), 72–73; José Mancisidor, *La ciudad roja: Novela proletaria* (Jalapa: Editorial Integrales, 1932); Octavio García Mundo, *El movimiento inquilinario de Veracruz, 1922* (Mexico City: Sep-Setentas, 1976). Two contemporary North American observations of the protest are Mildred Champagne Moore, "Veracruz Tenants Rebel, Capture City Government," *New York Times*, July 8, 1923, and Ernest Gruening, *Mexico and Its Heritage* (1928; reprint, New York: Greenwood Press, 1968), 340.

3. Manuel Castells, "The Dependent City and Revolutionary Populism: The Movimiento Inquilinario in Veracruz, Mexico, 1922," in *The City and the Grassroots: A Cross-Cultural Theory of Urban Social Movements* (Berkeley: University of California Press, 1983), 37–48; Paco Ignacio Taibo II, *Bolshevikis: Historia narrativa de los orígenes del comunismo en México, 1919–1925* (Mexico City: Editorial Joaquín Mortiz, 1986), 158–79.

4. Discussion of the Veracruz tenant movement can also be found in Harry Bernstein, "Marxismo en México: 1917–1925," *Historia Mexicana* 7, no. 4 (April–June 1958): 508; Mario Gill, "Veracruz: Revolución y extremismo," *Historia Mexicana* 2, no. 4 (April–May 1953): 618–36; Heather Fowler-Salamini, *Agrarian Radicalism in Veracruz, 1920–30* (Lincoln: University of Nebraska Press, 1971), 29–33; Rosendo Salazar, *Las pugnas de la gleba* (Mexico City: Comisión Nacional Editorial, 1972), 340–42; Moisés González Navarro, *Población y sociedad en México, 1900–1970*, 2 vols. (Mexico City: UNAM, 1974), 180–86; Manuel Perlo Cohen, "Política y vivienda en México, 1910–1952," *Revista Mexicana de Sociología* 41, no. 3 (July–September 1979): 777–84; Erica Berra-Stoppa, "Estoy en huelga y no pago renta," *Habitación* 1, no. 1 (1981): 33–39; Olivia Domínguez Pérez, *Política y movimientos sociales en el tejedismo* (Jalapa: Universidad Veracruzana, 1986), 57–62; Romana Falcón and Soledad García Morales, *La semilla en el surco: Adalberto Tejeda y el radicalismo en Veracruz, 1883–1960* (Mexico City: Colegio de México, 1986), 137–42; Gema Lozano y Nathal, "La negra, loca y anarquista federación local de trabajadores del puerto de Veracruz," *Antropología* 30 (April–June 1990): 10–19; and Bernardo García Díaz, *Puerto de Veracruz* (Jalapa: Archivo General del Estado de Veracruz, 1992), 198–209.

5. Earlier theorizing on the emergence of rural social protest in Mexico includes John Tutino, *From Insurrection to Revolution in Mexico: Social Bases of Agrarian Violence, 1750–1940* (Princeton: Princeton University Press, 1986), esp. 22, and Eric Van Young, "Islands in the Storm: Quiet Cities and Violent Countrysides in the Mexican Independence Era," *Past and Present* 118 (February 1988): 130–55.

6. The term "vacuum of sovereignty" is borrowed from James Scott in his foreword to Gilbert Joseph and Daniel Nugent, eds., *Everyday Forms of State Formation: Revolution and the Negotiation of Rule in Modern Mexico* (Durham: Duke University Press, 1994), ix. Charles Tilly suggests that the time when elites are divided or in a process of realignment represents a condition of "dual sovereignty"; see Charles Tilly, *From Mobilization to Revolution* (Reading, MA: Addison Wesley, 1978). Doug McAdam's *Political Process and the Development of Black Insurgency, 1930–1970* (Chicago: University of Chicago Press, 1982) builds on Tilly's findings that violence in France took place more in conjunction with electoral opportunities than cycles of hardship. For a cogent summary of "political opportunity," see Sidney Tarrow, *Power in Movement: Social Movements, Collective Action, and Politics* (New York: Cambridge University Press, 1994), 85–89.

7. Adolfo Gilly characterizes the rule of President Carranza, followed by those of Presidents Obregón and Calles, as "Bonapartist," suggesting that each regime successfully played opposing sectors of Mexican society against each other in order to establish the domination of the new elite. See Adolfo Gilly, *The Mexican Revolution* (London: Thetford Press, 1983), 357–58.

8. See reports by U.S. State Department officials in Mexico including the U.S. consul in Durango, Theodore Hamm, who wrote in 1911 that "more strikes have taken place in the last two months than in all the history of this district." The U.S. consul in Saltillo added that the strikes "would not have occurred

except for the condition of political unrest" prevalent in Mexico at the time. Both are quoted in Alan Knight, "The Working Class and the Mexican Revolution, 1900–1920," *Journal of Latin American Studies* 16, no. 2 (May 1984): 73. Knight adds that "the 1910 revolution ushered in a phase of political change, popular mobilization, and plebeian optimism—all of which historians have consistently underestimated" (72). The phrase "crisis of participation" is borrowed from Kevin Middlebrook, *The Paradox of Revolution: Labor, the State, and Authoritarianism in Mexico* (Baltimore: Johns Hopkins University Press, 1995), 10.

9. The term "intimate culture" is from Claudio Lomnitz-Adler, *Exits from the Labyrinth: Culture and Ideology in the Mexican National Space* (Berkeley: University of California Press, 1992), 28–29 and passim.

10. On the outcome of tenant protest in Mexico City, see Taibo II, *Bolshevikis*, 176. For Guadalajara, see Jaime Tamayo, "El sindicato revolucionario de inquilinos y la huelga de rentas de 1922," in *Jalisco desde la revolución: Los movimientos sociales, 1917–1929,* ed. Jaime Tamayo (Guadalajara: Universidad de Guadalajara, 1988), 129–40.

11. The text of the Yucatán rent law was published in the *Diario oficial del gobierno socialista del estado libre y soberano de Yucatán* on April 12, 1922. For a discussion of reforms carried out under Governors Salvador Alvarado and Felipe Carrillo Puerto, see Gilbert M. Joseph, *Revolution from Without: Yucatán, Mexico, and the United States, 1880–1924* (Durham: Duke University Press, 1988), 111–227. On the history of Campeche, see José Alberto Abud Flores, *Campeche: Revolución y movimiento social, 1911–1923* (Mexico City: Instituto Nacional de Estudios Históricos de la Revolución Mexicana, 1992).

1

The Process and Politics of Modernity in Veracruz

When these works are completed it is confidently anticipated that Veracruz will rank as the healthiest city on the Mexican Gulf.
—J. R. Southworth, 1900

A stroll through almost any part of the city is sufficient to make a lasting impression on one. The buildings are of stucco or wood, painted mellow colors, and having long overhanging balconies. In the picturesque *barrios* tiny houses of clapboard and tiled roofs are painted unusual shades of pale pink, ochre, salmon, and blue, with red or emerald green doors and wooden grilles. They are set in the midst of small gardens crowded with almond trees, olean-der, bougainvilleas and acacias. . . . [Veracruz] is gay, cosmopoli-tan, and noisy. Its citizens and visitors delight in lolling around the Plaza in the late afternoon, sipping beer or soft drinks and playing dominoes, listening to wandering musicians as well as the town band. The city has no great museums or architectural wonders—its art is simply the art of living.
—*Terry's Guide to Mexico*

With the fall of Emperor Maximilian and the restoration of the republic in 1867, many businessmen and political leaders throughout the country looked forward to "a period of civilizing re-generation" that would grant Mexico a status equal with "the rest of the cultured peoples of the world."[1] In their enthusiastic embrace of modern technologies in communication and transportation, national boosters saw the railroad as the way to overcome Mexico's "backward" status. One politician in the 1870s confidently predicted that railroads would eliminate "all the political, social, and economic questions that the patriotism, self-sacrifice, and blood of two generations have not been able to resolve." Another saw the situation in even starker terms, stating that "without the railway from Mexico [City] to Veracruz we will do nothing, [but] . . . with it we will have everything."[2] The coming of the railroad, in other words, signified Mexico's entry into the modern age.

Central Veracruz, circa 1900. *Courtesy of AGEV, Concepción Díaz Cházaro Collection*

When Porfirio Díaz came to power in 1876 he initiated a development project designed to put the nation on an equal footing with other industrializing countries. In many ways, he succeeded. During the next thirty-four years that Díaz stayed in power, industrial production doubled. Gross national product rose an unprecedented 8 percent annually between 1884 and 1900.[3] Export-oriented output in such areas as mining and agriculture grew dramatically. Production in textiles, paper, glass, soap, shoes, beer, food processing, and other light industries also developed significantly. After José Limantour became minister of finance in spring 1893, international credit increased, improving economic performance in certain sectors even more spectacularly. Thus, between 1876 and 1910 the nation's total trade grew from approximately 50 million pesos to 488 million pesos. Investment incentives and subsidies for transportation, particularly railroads, opened important commercial avenues that further connected Mexico to rapidly expanding Atlantic and North American markets.[4]

Modernization projects began with the transformation of Veracruz, the nation's principal port throughout the colonial period. With a harbor too shallow for the larger steamships that now traveled the Atlantic, many felt that significant changes needed to be made if the city—and by extension, Mexico—was to keep pace with the rest of the industrializing world. The completion of the Mexico City-Veracruz railroad in January 1873, cause for a two-day celebration, ushered in a new era of economic growth. As this chapter will examine, modernization projects in the port helped to make Veracruz a city that reflected Mexico's economic dynamism. At the same time, however, health and housing problems brought on by rapid urbanization aggravated divisions between rich and poor. With the outbreak of revolution, this situation would intensify with the North American invasion of the port of Veracruz in 1914.

A dramatic event marking the transformation of Veracruz took place on July 14, 1880. That morning, a delegation from the City Council headed by Mayor Domingo Bureau and accompanied by a musical band and firemen, volunteers, and prisoners armed with shovels and picks walked to the San Javier bulwark and began demolishing the city wall. Before the work began, Bureau addressed those gathered:

> The 1880 City Council has the glorious satisfaction of initiating the destruction of this wall which, for so many years, has [needlessly] enclosed city residents, preventing their advancement and enrichment. The work that today we begin will eliminate the division between those inside and outside the wall, thus allowing both groups to unite as one. . . . It is time to eliminate the distinction of "outer neighborhoods" [*barrios extramuros*] because our heroic city will now develop as a peaceful, hardworking, and dynamic commercial center. *Veracruzanos: ¡Viva el progreso! ¡Abajo las murallas! ¡Viva el engrandecimiento de Veracruz!*[5]

As the mayor optimistically announced the opening up of Veracruz, the many *porteños* assembled to witness the ceremony must have wondered what the new era would mean for them.

With railroad concessions and the tearing down of the Veracruz city wall also came plans for modernizing the nation's ports. In December 1880, President Díaz approved a plan to renovate the harbor facilities at Veracruz, Tuxpan, Puerto México, Salina Cruz, and Isla del Carmen.[6] Before the renovations began, harbor, dock, and warehouse facilities in Veracruz lay in disrepair while harsh weather, especially during the winter months, made landing there difficult and often dangerous.[7]

In February 1881 members of the Veracruz City Council and Mayor Bureau formed a special commission to study proposed improvements.

Soon, they sent their recommendations to Mexico City and, after contracting two engineering firms, announced that work would begin. A few months later, Mayor Bureau presided over a five-day celebration marked by parades, dances, and banquets. Again, he addressed the city: "Veracruz has entered into a new period: the walls that had once enclosed it, the bulwarks that had defended it, testified to the heroic valor of an earlier time. [Those remnants] have fallen with the blow of the pickax, bringing the city's once separated population together. With this we have embellished the city and improved its health, we have added to the value of the lands on the margins of the city, and Veracruz has lost much of its bellicosity."[8]

After a year of deliberations and false starts, the French firm of Buette Caze and Company received word to go ahead with the project. In 1887 a Jalapa businessman, Agustín Cerdan, picked up where the French had left off. Finally, in 1895, the English firm of Sir Weetman D. Pearson took over and brought a degree of professionalism never before seen in the port. As one observer noted in 1900, "The improvements completed have resulted in making Veracruz one of the finest facilities on the American coast, and the largest vessels are able to enter with safety even in stormy weather."[9]

Between 1895 and the project's completion in early 1902, the Pearson Company erected breakwaters to protect the harbor as well as new walls and docks. They deepened the harbor to thirty-three feet below sea level to accommodate the newer vessels and built three piers designated for freight and one for passengers. Laborers also built large warehouses to accommodate the increased volume of cargo the port would be expected to handle and, just beyond the passenger dock, a new customs house and sanitation inspection area. In the end, tremendous amounts of sand and coral had been removed from the harbor. Workers transported approximately 1.25 million tons of rock from nearby quarries and used over fifty thousand tons of cement, steel, and iron in the construction.

Pearson's company also helped improve public health in the city by augmenting the water supply and sewage systems. They modernized the Veracruz streetcars and installed electricity to illuminate public buildings and the central plazas of the city.[10] During this time, porteños also constructed many new streets, public areas, and buildings including such neoclassical structures as the Customs House, the People's Library, the Mail and Telegraph Building, and the Veracruz railroad terminal and an adjoining hotel. The establishment of the Veracruz Terminal Company in 1906 added nearly two thousand new jobs in the city. Increasingly, offices, stores, small businesses, cafés, and restaurants lined many of the main thoroughfares. Soon, evening walks in the Plaza de Armas, freshly tiled in Italian marble and landscaped with tropical plants, or along the waterfront promenade (*malecón*) became a popular pastime for residents.

Topping off the many changes in turn-of-the-century Veracruz was the official inauguration of the port facility, celebrated with a visit to the city by President Díaz, Veracruz governor Teodoro A. Dehesa, various senators and deputies, and Sir Weetman Pearson on March 6, 1902. The visit began with the official contingent inspecting the harbor aboard the steamer *Nereida*. Back on land, they toured the new maritime customs house, lighthouse, and other auxiliary sites. Then, marking the achievements that had taken nearly a decade to complete, Díaz proclaimed: "Inaugurated today and forever dedicated for public use, the new port has been constructed with funds from the national treasury for the benefit of the nation."[11] Later that afternoon, as the president dined with local leaders, a spirit of optimism prevailed throughout the city, within the salons of the local elite, in the halls of business associations such as the Centro Mercantil and Lonja Mercantil, and at tables in the popular Café Parroquia.

Residents of all social classes felt a sense of jubilation as the celebration continued in the evening. For the elite, city boosters organized an elegant banquet and dance near the customs house. Meantime, some of the workers who had helped build the new port facility invited Pearson to a party at a local tenement, where he danced the *danzón*—to popular Cuban music recently brought to Veracruz by immigrants from the island—while others watched in the crowded patio.

In the wake of the president's visit, the daily newspaper *El Dictamen* proclaimed that Veracruz had joined the modern world as an international city, thanks to the leadership of Díaz, who had inaugurated a "new era of civilization" in the port.[12] Official statistics show population increases in Veracruz and the state's three other main cities in the first three decades of the new century (see Table). Contributing to urban growth were significant numbers who had begun to arrive from overseas—particularly from Spain and Cuba.

The Compañía Trasatlántica Española, established in 1886, helped facilitate a new wave of Spanish immigration around the turn of the century. Single men between the ages of twenty and thirty constituted the majority who traveled to Mexico. Encouraged by what they heard about life in Mexico, some had fled difficult conditions and emigrated, hoping to "make it" in America (*hacer la América*). Many Spaniards opened businesses, especially in the commercial centers of Mexico City and Veracruz, where substantial immigrant populations were already established and newcomers could enjoy the support of family and sympathetic countrymen who helped them get credit, find employment, and make important social contacts.

Population in Veracruz Cities, 1900–1930

City	1900	1910	1921	1930
Veracruz	29,164	48,633	54,255	67,801
Orizaba	32,393	35,263	39,563	50,193
Jalapa	20,388	23,640	27,623	36,812
Córdoba	8,136	10,295	14,744	16,200
State totals	**134,469**	**179, 279**	**211,779**	**261,223**

Sources: Mexican census, 1900, 1910, 1921, 1930.

Different than in Azevedo's story.

Like ordinary Mexicans, however, immigrants faced difficult working conditions and relatively slim chances for social advancement. As one historian writes, "Laborers were abundant, but regrettably, wages and food were not. [Thus,] the age of the Porfiriato generally did not look any more kindly upon the condition of the industrial worker than upon the *campesino*."[13] Soon, problems associated with rapid urbanization began to plague several Mexican cities, including Veracruz.

As the city expanded haphazardly to the northeast and southeast in the years between 1880 and 1910, the number of city blocks nearly doubled.[14] Paved streets, adequate drainage, and sewage disposal remained in short supply. The Veracruz water system that Pearson's engineers had improved did not extend to all areas. In this context of rapid growth, the omnipresent vultures perched along the waterfront testified to the fact that the city, while on the verge of becoming a thriving and progressive center, also remained a site of sad neglect in many ways. Veracruz was a city of contrasts. Or, as one writer put it, "If one could ignore or overlook the filth—and most Mexicans did—life could be pleasant in Veracruz."[15]

The growth of the city's working-class neighborhoods coincided with the modernization projects of the Porfiriato. Areas that had existed just outside the wall of the old city to the south, such as the famous La Huaca neighborhood, experienced a continually growing population after 1870. At the same time, residents of lands to the northeast and southeast hastily built shelters to accommodate the rising tide of migrants to these areas.[16]

By 1895, the state of Veracruz ranked third (after Jalisco and Guanajuato) in the total number of houses under construction.[17] Property owners also reconfigured existing buildings by adding on or subdividing. Those who could not afford to buy their own homes crowded into rooms (*cuartos*) clustered around a common courtyard in tenements known as *patios de vecindad*. Others figured ways to settle on the margins of established lots or improvised add-ons (*accesorías*) between buildings. For a majority of the Mexican working class living in urban areas around the turn of the century, these two modest expressions of local architecture—despite their often crowded, unsanitary conditions—represented the only affordable housing available.[18]

Veracruz street scene, circa 1900. *Courtesy of AGEV, Bernardo García Díaz Collection*

Much of the popular housing in the port had been slapped together with old wood, tin, stone, and other found materials. Often rooms lacked doors and flooring. Some of the larger patios housed as many as two hundred men, women, and children while, on average, sixty or seventy people shared limited facilities.[19] Contemporary reports suggest that, as in other cities in the Americas at the time, it was not unusual to find eight to ten people sharing a dirty room without ventilation.[20]

Veracruz patios opened onto a shared courtyard where residents found space for leisure activities as well as cooking, dining, and bathing.[21] Not surprisingly, the intimate character of residential life forced neighbors (*vecinos*) to accommodate each other daily. Artisans who set up their workshops within the confines of the patio further encouraged social cohesion and cooperation.

Judging from police and newspaper reports of the time, this close proximity also fostered an equal share of conflict within the tenements.

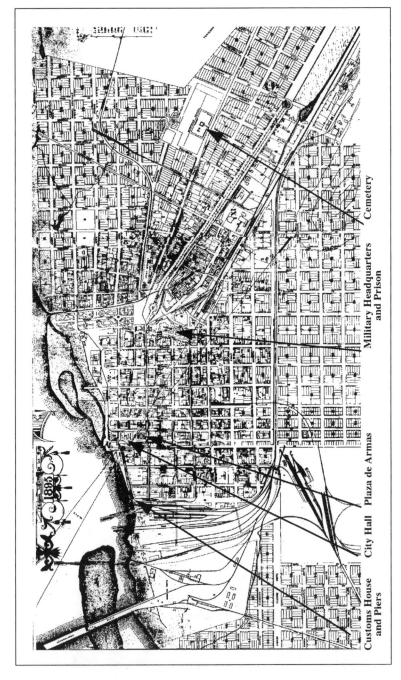

Veracruz in 1895. *Courtesy of Mapoteca Manuel Orozco y Berra*

Customs House and Piers

City Hall   Plaza de Armas

Military Headquarters and Prison

Cemetery

Although the exact number is uncertain, by 1910 dozens of these structures—known by such names as de la Cruz, La Industria, San Antonio, La Angelita, La Palma, de la Concepción, El Paseo, La Lima, Tanitos, and San Salvador—dotted the Veracruz landscape, serving as key geographic coordinates for popular social life in the port.

Throughout the city, porteños living in the patios mingled to fashion new music, cuisine, dances and other recreational activities or to adapt imports, such as the danzón from Cuba. Later, patio residents revived the celebration of Carnival as part of the larger resurgence of regional cultural practices encouraged by the revolution.[22] Thus, though the new popular neighborhoods, with their haphazard constructions and conspicuous lack of sanitation, ungraciously hosted a majority of the city's workers and their families, the culture and social networks that grew out of these areas became the main base from which political grievances would soon be articulated and social resources for popular protest mobilized.

As the city grew, problems resulting from crowding—lack of adequate water, drainage, and ventilation as well as a host of other concerns—increasingly dogged residents. Along the streets of working-class districts, waste of all kinds collected outside people's homes, while gutters, nearby streams, and shores also served as dumping grounds. Domesticated animals roamed freely and sometimes shared living quarters with their owners. Even the inhabitants themselves often referred to the patios as hovels or pigsties.

At a basic level, lack of potable water was probably the most dangerous consequence of rapid population growth because so many digestive ailments could be traced to contaminated water. Hoping to avoid the threat of bodily discomfort or outright disfunction from drinking the available water, some chose instead to consume *pulque*, *aguardiente*, *mescal*, and other alcoholic beverages, but often this practice only generated new problems. Lack of sanitary codes throughout the republic complicated matters by allowing the sale of contaminated food in public markets and streets.

In Veracruz the new water service provided by Pearson's engineers had improved the quality and amount of potable water available to residents living in the city's central districts. Pearson's crew had also provided a basic sewer system that allowed wastewater to be drained. Subsequently, various public health efforts, including a September 1903 campaign against yellow fever headed by Eduardo Liceaga of the Consejo Superior de Salubridad, were undertaken to improve sanitary conditions in the port. Yet while these efforts offered relief, they were not enough. As Veracruz historian Bernardo García Díaz points out, "Before the end of the first decade of the century it became necessary to discuss new projects to add to the [city's water] supply . . . sewage system and other municipal services. . . . By the end of the Porfiriato only the old Spanish core of the city exhibited an attractive quality given the construction of new buildings equipped with electricity. The process of establishing similar services throughout the rest of the city lagged behind, leaving only the central district and thus, a minority of the population to benefit."[23] Despite the modernization of the port and the city's central district during the last years of the nineteenth century, officials found they could not keep pace with the demand for urban services.

Attempting to combat deteriorating conditions in outlying districts, Veracruz elites, including the Porfirian governor, Teodoro Dehesa, established new sanitation codes that they hoped would alleviate problems for many of the port's working-class residents. In conjunction with municipal efforts, state legislators passed new laws that identified popular housing sites as "foci of infection" and required landlords to provide for basic sewage and sanitation. These initial efforts by elites to address the condition of popular housing set an important precedent by acknowledging housing as an item of political concern and identifying the state as an arbiter for reform.

As municipal and state governments sought to promote public health by passing measures to improve water, food, and sewage systems, city boosters put their faith in "everything known to science to improve the health of the population."[24] Earlier in 1892, Eduardo Liceaga had appointed Manuel S. Iglesias to head a new delegation in charge of city sanitation. Soon, they began a coordinated effort designed to confront the problems of public health in ways they hoped would parallel advances in other commercial and technological fields. In conjunction with this and various other local campaigns elsewhere in the state, the Veracruz legislature issued a set of new sanitary codes.[25]

After 1900, local health officials required that property owners submit construction and remodeling plans for their buildings as a way to ensure compliance with new sanitation regulations.[26] In the process, officials reviewed blueprints and visited various tenements. During their inspections, they counted toilets, urinals, sinks, wash areas, barrels, tubs, and drains. Sanitation agents also judged whether ventilation and room dimensions met code requirements. In cases where inspectors cited landlords for noncompliance, they required that improvements be made within a relatively short time.

DQ: Would things have been different had the elites not acknowledged housing as a bore of contention?

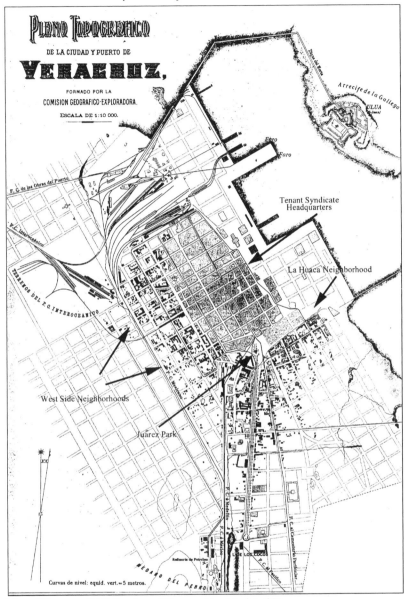

Map of Veracruz, 1907. *Courtesy of Veracruz Municipal Archive*

Generally, the new sanitary codes pressured landlords to establish sufficient drainage and other basic services for their rental properties. Surveying actions taken in 1907 as well as city council records in subsequent years indicate that positive changes—thanks to the prodding of the state—were indeed under way in Veracruz. Still, officials noted that nearly 90 percent of the city's patios would require significant improvements if they were to be brought up to code.[27]

The outbreak of the revolution in 1910 temporarily discontinued almost all efforts to improve popular housing in the port as local sanitary regulation was left largely unenforced and new construction brought to a halt. The next significant effort to modernize the city's built environment would be overseen by an occupying North American military force during the spring and summer of 1914. In an interesting twist, the U.S. invasion would contribute not only to improving the public health of the city but also to something even more important: the reawakening of Veracruz residents as "political subjects."

To Mexicans, Veracruz is the city "four times heroic," a phrase meant to glorify local sacrifices in the name of national sovereignty. Four battles fought on local soil—against the Spaniards in 1825, the French in 1838, and the North Americans in 1847 and again in 1914—distinguish the port as a site of resistance against foreign invaders.[28] The 1914 invasion did more, however, than mark another heroic defense of the nation; collective memories forged during the event awakened a political consciousness in porteños as they struggled to find their place in the new revolutionary order.

In April 1914, friction between U.S. President Woodrow Wilson and counter-revolutionary general Victoriano Huerta led to the bombardment, invasion, and seven-month occupation of the port.[29] On the morning of April 21, the first wave of twelve hundred marines and navy Bluejackets landed in Veracruz. Meeting with little resistance, U.S. forces soon captured the train depot and adjoining hotel, which they then used for barracks. Gradually, the invaders advanced toward the center of the city, supported by a U.S. naval squadron offshore, and surrounded the cable station on Montesinos Street and took possession of it. Then, as the marines moved along Independence Avenue, a group of Mexican soldiers prepared to confront them. Around noon that day, North American forces tangled with the porteño resistance.

Throughout the afternoon and evening, fighting broke out sporadically as the city became a battlefield. The next morning, Rear Admiral Frank F. Fletcher ordered his men to establish order and take control of the entire city. The marines entered the more heavily populated areas of Veracruz, carefully searching each block and rooting out pockets of armed resistance. As one U.S. observer described the scene: "With characteristic precision the leathernecks then moved through the blocks, house by house, hacking their way through adobe walls and clearing each building before entering the next. It was this efficient ruthlessness which caused many of the civilian casualties and the destruction of property."[30] The "efficient ruthlessness" of the North Americans terrified Veracruz residents and intensified their resistance.

North Americans leaving Veracruz, 1914. *Courtesy of AGEV, José Pérez de León Collection*

José Mancisidor, a local writer, later described the invasion through the eyes of a Mexican soldier:

> For Lieutenant Melesio Infante the neighborhood had come alive. From everywhere came men and women to stop the invaders. Their faces, once familiar, now seemed to be animated with hatred and a heartfelt determination. Men and women, risking death, united to keep the Yankee marines at bay. As the fighting grew more heated a quiet intensity enveloped the scene. It seemed as if each of the defenders assumed that victory depended on their effort alone. Soon, however, Lieutenant Melesio Infante could no longer resist the temptation to break the silence. And, as he shouted "Viva Mexico," a thousand once invisible voices from all parts of the neighborhood responded in kind.[31]

Yet despite a spirited porteño resistance, Mexican efforts would eventually prove no match for Yankee firepower.

The invasion had left the city in a shambles, with nearly two hundred dead and three hundred injured. Debris from the shelling could be seen scattered throughout Veracruz. Then, nearly twenty-four hours later, a force of approximately six thousand North Americans moved in and held the port. Shocked and disgusted, many *veracruzanos* decided to remain indoors and refused to cooperate with the invaders.

Soon after taking the city, the North Americans initiated measures designed to further establish their control. They first collected the corpses of dead Mexicans, doused them in kerosene, and set them on fire. Then military officials and Red Cross representatives began coordinating efforts to address North American concerns about public health. The marines saw an urgent need to rectify problems that were the by-products of accumulated waste, inadequate drainage, and constant infestation by flies and mosquitoes. Their interest came, however, less from a concern for the city residents than from a desire to protect themselves from disease. Inhabitants of the city, the occupying force claimed, had left dead animals to rot in streets regularly patrolled by vultures, stray dogs, and rodents. The apparent casual attitude and irregular habits of many porteños suggested to the North Americans that proper maintenance in matters of public health had been neglected for some time. They believed that their sanitation efforts would help "civilize" a city too long left to the savage forces of nature.

Praising the military's efforts, the North American press corps assumed a superior attitude and, like the marines, judged the Mexicans dirty and degenerate. The *New York Times* reported that disease represented a "greater danger to soldiers than bullets and shells" and suggested that while "authorities of Mexico have given considerable attention to the study of sanitation and preventative medicine, little progress has been made, however, in obtaining the cooperation of the people." Viewing local residents as devoid of any concern for their personal health, the author of the article, who seemed to see Mexico as a land inhabited by dirty, uneducated primitives, imagined that "Mexicans [care little about] personal hygiene. [They appear to] submit to attacks of contagious disease as a matter of course [or] have become immune to further attacks of yellow fever and smallpox."[32] He warned Americans against contracting a sickness called *tabardillo*, known locally as *tifo*. This "filthy disease," as he put it, could easily be transmitted through normal contact with "the natives." For this reason, officials advised travelers to "guard against this disease by keep[ing] away from unclean places and persons, [avoiding] crowds and permitting their clothing to brush against that of natives in the streets."

The novelist Jack London echoed many of these same sentiments when he reported from Veracruz in June 1914. Writing that "smallpox appears to be endemic, rather than epidemic while tuberculosis collects a greater toll of death than all the more serious diseases added together," London gives the impression that the very landscape of the city was essentially infected and dangerous.[33] Acting on these kinds of assumptions, the North Americans wasted no time in working to remake Veracruz in the image of a U.S. city.

In late April and early May, a company of one thousand marines began a sanitation campaign in the city. The occupying force endeavored to sweep every street, inspect all residential areas, and collect refuse and transport it to a designated area to be burned. Additionally, troops sealed old wells, dug ditches, drained stagnant pools, and sprayed nearly sixty-nine thousand gallons of petroleum in an attempt to kill off insect larvae. They added public toilets, flytraps, and screens and occasionally repaired broken windows, doors, roofs, walls, and floors. The army quartermaster distributed cans to be used for refuse in hotels, restaurants, and public areas, and every night, sanitation agents rinsed the main streets of the city with seawater. To realize their plan, the North Americans hired hundreds of local laborers.

On May 15 the *New York Times* reported that the U.S. "house and street cleaning department has made a great record." Veracruz, the article states, "to-day is the cleanest place in the tropics as every house has been cleaned; every puddle has been filled; every street and byway have been flushed clear; all refuse has been incinerated, and every mosquito breeding place oiled or abolished." Yet not only did the North Americans cleanse the city, they also imposed strict sanitation regulations—a matter that infuriated many residents. As the paper describes: "Proprietors of hotels and cafés have been told that if their places are not kept clean they will be closed, and fines will be imposed. The scale of punishment provides for permitting refuse to gather without incineration, twenty days in jail; ten days for allowing cesspools to form; and five days for expectoration." Besides hotels, restaurants, and cafés, the public market also received special attention. Here, putting their methods to the test, the North Americans endeavored to improve health conditions in one of the most difficult of all local sites, and there they found vendors unwilling to cooperate. In fact, local resistance in the market hinted at more generalized feelings of resentment toward the occupying force.

Cartoons published in Veracruz newspapers at the time poked fun at the North Americans. One characterized them as overly demanding customers in local taverns. Another, titled "Coming Back to the Ship after a Few Hours in Vera Cruz," depicted U.S. sailors as gullible tourists. Many of the Mexican picture postcards portray "the invaders in command, in positions of authority and as interlopers."[34] One card expresses the disdain many felt toward the foreigners:

They came to show us that in spite of being the thieves of the town, they live in comfortable military tents, on cots beneath netting to ward off the mosquitoes, and at daybreak, instead of getting up to go to work or to exercise, they revive themselves at the wash basin, and after a savory breakfast, they head, satisfied and smiling, for the nearest tavern, where they drink common liquor and joke around, not in the refined language of Lord Byron, but in insulting words, imitating the English that they use in *Yanquilandia*.[35]

Other cards remind their readers of the real damage inflicted by the North Americans. One shows injured men recovering in a local hospital with the words, "Here is what the gringos have done to us." These messages echo resistance demonstrated toward North Americans elsewhere in Mexico at the time. In Guadalajara, for example, citizens burned U.S. flags, harassed North American businessmen, and attacked diplomatic offices. Congressmen in the capital shouted, "Death to the thieves of 1848!" while riots broke out in sections of the city.[36]

Funeral of José Azueta. *Courtesy of AGEV, José Pérez de León Collection*

Throughout Mexico, anti-Americanism after the invasion proved to be short-lived. Yet in Veracruz, a passionate blend of xenophobia, patriotism, and anti-imperialism aroused by the occupation did not die out as quickly. Soon after the incident, residents honored local heroes who had given their life in defense of the city. A young cadet named José Azueta, who had defended the port to the death, was transformed into a local martyr. Residents erected a statue memorializing him near the embattled naval academy. In the wake of the occupation, the press referred to the North American intervention as "barbarous," "savage," and "infamous."[37]

In the years that followed, Mexicans would continue to view the invasion as an imperialist act. Proudly remembering the efforts of veracruzanos in poems, songs, books, street names, newspaper articles, and other forms of tribute, accounts all strongly condemned the North Americans and passionately swore to defend the nation's soil if ever trespassed upon again. Just as important, the event sparked changes in porteño popular consciousness that soon would prove important in the framing and articulation of grievances over housing.

Notes

1. This phrase is borrowed from Arthur P. Schmidt Jr., *The Social and Economic Effect of the Railroad in Puebla and Veracruz, in Mexico, 1867–1911* (New York: Garland, 1987), 1.

2. Ibid., 6.

3. Friedrich Katz, "The Liberal Republic and the Porfiriato," in *Mexico since Independence*, ed. Leslie Bethell (Cambridge: Cambridge University Press, 1991), 74.

4. For a concise summary of Mexico's political economy during the Porfiriato, see Roger D. Hansen, *The Politics of Mexican Development* (Baltimore: Johns Hopkins University Press, 1971), 13–29.

5. Bernardo García Díaz, *Puerto de Veracruz* (Jalapa: Archivo General del Estado de Veracruz, 1992), 79.

6. Olivia Domínguez Pérez, "El puerto de Veracruz: La modernización a finales del siglo XIX," *Anuario* 7 (1990): 87–102. On Mexican exports through Veracruz during this time, see Schmidt, *Social and Economic Effect*, 148–49.

7. As a young boy traveling with his family to Campeche, José Vasconcelos remembered leaving Veracruz during one of the port's infamous winter storms as "one of the most dangerous excursions of our entire journey." José Vasconcelos, *Ulysses criollo: La vida del autor escrita por el mismo* (Mexico City: Ediciones Botas, 1945), 87.

8. Quoted in Domínguez Pérez, "El puerto de Veracruz," 92.

9. John R. Southworth, *El estado de Veracruz-Llave: Su historia, agricultura, comercio e industria en inglés y español* (Jalapa: Gobierno del Estado de Veracruz, 1900), 88.

10. García Díaz, *Puerto de Veracruz*, 91.

11. Quoted in ibid., 126.

12. *El Dictamen*, March 8, 1902.

13. Schmidt, *Social and Economic Effect*, 140.

14. Ibid., 131.

15. Robert E. Quirk, *An Affair of Honor: Woodrow Wilson and the Occupation of Veracruz* (New York: Norton, 1962), 83.

16. Veracruz City Council records dating from 1881 chronicle urban growth through the selling of lots and solicitation of building permits.

17. Secretaría de Economía, Dirección General de Estadística, *Estadísticas sociales del porfiriato, 1877–1910* (Mexico City: Talleres Gráficos de la Nación, 1956), 15.

18. Moisés González Navarro, "El Porfiriato: La vida social," in *Historia moderna de México*, ed. Daniel Cosío Villegas (Mexico City: Editorial Hermes, 1957), 82.

19. Reports on popular housing conditions in Mexico City (January and February 1922) and Veracruz (June 1922) were published by the Department of Labor in their *Boletín Mensual del Departamento de Trabajo*. For an earlier discussion of living conditions and public health issues in Mexico City, see Alberto J. Pani, *La higiene en México* (Mexico City: J. Ballescá, 1916).

20. For housing conditions in Mexico City, see Anthony J. Mazzaferri, "Public Health and Social Revolution in Mexico, 1877–1930" (Ph.D. diss., Kent State University, 1968).

21. On popular housing in Mexico City for the period 1870–1930, see González Navarro, *Población y sociedad en México, 1900–1970* (Mexico City: UNAM, 1974), 1:143–227.

22. During the week before Lent, business in the city would come to a virtual halt as floats, dancers, and "costumed merrymakers" filled the streets. "For days no one [slept] and the streets [were] a vivid labyrinth of *veracruzanos* dancing their *huapangos* and *bambas*, strumming harps and guitars and singing happily." James Norman, *Terry's Guide to Mexico* (Garden City, NY: Doubleday, 1962), 271. On Carnival, see Marta Cortés Rodríguez, "Bailes y carnaval en Veracruz, 1925," *Horizonte: Revista del Instituto Veracruzano de Cultura* 1, no. 1 (March–April 1991): 19–25. On the history of danzón, see Jesús Flores y Escalante, *Imagenes del danzón: Iconografía del danzón en México* (Mexico City: Asociación Mexicana de Estudios Fonográficos, 1994), and Antonio García de León, "Los patios danzoneros," *La Jornada Seminal* 223 (September 19, 1993): 33–40. For accounts of the port's rich cultural history, see Roberto Williams García, *Yo nací con la luna de plata: Antropología e historia de un puerto* (Mexico City: Costa-Amic Editores, 1980), and Anselmo Mancisidor Ortiz, *Jarochilandia* (Veracruz: Author's edition, 1971).

23. García Díaz, *Puerto de Veracruz*, 139.

24. Southworth, *El estado de Veracruz-Llave*, 93–94.

25. Carmen Blázquez Domínguez and Emilio Gidi Villarreal, *El poder legislativo en Veracruz, 1824–1917* (Jalapa: Gobierno del Estado de Veracruz, 1992), 178.

26. AMV, Ayuntamiento 1906–07, box 365, vols. 494–95.

27. Ibid., Ayuntamiento, sala de comisiones, May 4, 1912, box 366, "Ayuntamiento 1912."

28. Leonardo Pasquel, *Biografía integral de la ciudad de Veracruz, 1519–1969: Colección suma Veracruzana* (Mexico City: Editorial Citlaltépetl, 1969), 26–27. Testimonies (many recorded in 1985) by several women who lived in the port during the 1914 North American invasion can be found at the Instituto Nacional de Antropología e Historia, Archivo de la Palabra. On the invasion, see Leonardo Pasquel's *Manuel y José Azueta, padre e hijo, héroes en la gesta de 1914* (Mexico City: Editorial Citlaltépetl, 1967) and *La invasión de Veracruz en 1914* (Mexico City: Editorial Citlaltépetl, 1976). North American appreciation of the defense of Veracruz can be noted more recently in John Hart's dedication of his book "to the martyrs of Veracruz who gave their lives in the defense of national integrity." John Hart, *Revolutionary Mexico: The Coming and Process of the Mexican Revolution* (Berkeley: University of California Press, 1987).

29. Probably the best accounts of the invasion can be found in Quirk, *An Affair of Honor*, and Berta Ulloa, *Veracruz, capital de la nación, 1914–15* (Mexico City: Colegio de México, 1986), 13–45. For treatment of Wilson's foreign policy, see Arthur S. Link, *Woodrow Wilson and the Progressive Era, 1910–1917* (New York: Harper and Row, 1954), and Friedrich Katz, *The Secret War in Mexico: Europe, the United States, and the Mexican Revolution* (Chicago: University of Chicago Press, 1981), 195. For a discussion of Wilson's views of the different revolutionary factions, see Hart, *Revolutionary Mexico*, 294–99. For various correspondence and comment on the evacuation of North Americans from the port during this time, see RDS, reel 161.

30. *New York Times*, April 22, 1914.

31. José Mancisidor, *Frontera junto al mar* (Mexico City: Fondo de Cultura Económica, 1953), 185.

32. *New York Times*, April 26, 1914.

33. Jack London, "Stalking the Pestilence," *Collier's*, June 6, 1914; reprinted in *Jack London Reports: War Correspondence, Sports Articles, and Miscellaneous Writings*, ed. King Hendricks and Irving Shepard (Garden City, NY: Doubleday, 1970), 161.

34. Paul Vanderwood, "The Picture Postcard as Historical Evidence: Veracruz, 1914," *The Americas* 45, no. 2 (October 1988): 223.

35. Quoted in ibid.

36. See Alan Knight, *The Mexican Revolution* (Lincoln: University of Nebraska Press, 1986), 2:158–62.

37. Justino N. Palomares, *La invasión yanqui en 1914* (Mexico City: Author's edition, 1940), 63–67.

2

Constitutionalism and Its Discontents

Thanks to the revolution and the Constitutionalists, the humble and suffering people of Veracruz now are capable of fighting against men whose conservative spirit made them the main enemies of the revolution. Allow us to make a call to all tenants in Veracruz and, in particular, all those affiliated with organized labor; together we shall form the Great Tenant Union of Veracruz to defend our sacred rights, which are being disregarded by a majority of property owners in this heroic city.

—Unidentified Veracruz tenant leaders quoted
in *El Dictamen*, December 19, 1916

While the occupying force imposed its will on the city residents, events taking place elsewhere in Mexico and the United States gradually paved the way for a North American evacuation of Veracruz in November 1914.[1] In the wake of the invasion, revolutionary leaders fanned the fires of Mexican nationalism as they sought to legitimize the emerging revolutionary regime. Yet as their discourse gradually began to reshape the way Mexicans made sense of the world around them, it also gave rise to a number of popular political responses that would prove difficult for state agents to control fully. As the subject of this chapter, grassroots organizing by tenants in several cities beginning in late 1915 was one such "response."

As the Constitutionalists oversaw a gradual transition from military to civilian rule in the tumultuous years following the North American invasion, both central and state governments remained weak and largely incapable of addressing urban problems. Nevertheless, late in 1914, acting Veracruz governor Cándido Aguilar ordered the temporary closing of *cantinas* throughout the city and announced severe penalties for anyone engaging in so-called criminal behavior.[2] Three days later, Carranza, having recently fled from the armies of Villa and Zapata in Mexico City, arrived in the port. Residents throwing flowers and confetti and cheering from their balconies provided an exuberant welcome to the patriarch of the revolution as he and other Constitutionalists paraded through the city.[3] In a speech to the residents of the port, Carranza thanked porteños for their hospitality and told them of his plans to draft a new national constitution: "I came to this hospitable land which once served as a bastion for Juárez to find a secure place to formulate ideas that will serve as the fundamental principles by which Mexico will become a great, powerful, and happy nation. I ask for nothing more than the dignity needed to save our oppressed nation, love to end the disagreements that divide and degrade us, and patience and faith to cure those things that make us poor miserable outcasts in our own land."[4]

Certainly those hearing the optimistic words of Carranza that day must have felt a sense of relief in having their city returned to them after months of occupation by a foreign army. Yet, despite the First Chief's hopeful tone, residents soon entered a new period of instability fraught with rampant inflation, food shortages, the resurgence of epidemic disease, and, finally, a housing crisis.

State Interventions

The arrival and temporary establishment of the Constitutionalist government in Veracruz brought a new wave of migrants to the port. With hotels, guesthouses, and rental housing completely full, some resorted to setting up temporary accommodations near the waterfront.[5] Property owners responded to the increase in demand for rental housing by raising rents, and, at the same time, hotel owners also increased their rates.[6]

Rising prices in late 1914 only compounded financial woes that had been brewing for some time. The cost of living had nearly doubled between 1901 and 1911. Destruction of agricultural lands and transport during the first years of the revolution contributed to significant increases in the cost of basic necessities.[7] Mexicans nearly everywhere faced extremely difficult conditions; food shortages, inflation, and unemployment had created an economic crisis in many cities. Countless small businesses across the nation were forced to shut down while managers at larger industrial sites reduced production and cut jobs. As a result, thousands turned to charity, counterfeiting, or simply begging in the streets.[8]

Further complicating this bleak economic picture, the value of the peso as measured against the U.S. dollar began a steady decline after January 1915.[9] As Mexico's economic future grew more uncertain, residents in the port of Veracruz took action by holding a demonstration on May 9, 1915, protesting the rising cost of living. In response, Governor Aguilar and other state officials promised to do something.[10] Two months later, the Aguilar administration imposed a limit on house rents, declaring that landlords could not raise rates more than 10 percent per year. Officials also required hotels to post their prices in clear view of prospective customers. At the same time, the state government ordered the closing of cantinas at ten o'clock and worked to regulate prostitution, bullfighting, gambling, and the sale of pulque. Then, to help lower the cost of living, Aguilar's government contracted the services of local businessmen such as Angel J. Lagarda, owner of the Agencia Comercial Exportadora, to deliver sugar, coffee, beans, lard, and other items to the city.[11] National officials supplemented these efforts by approving grain shipments to the port. Nonetheless, prices for such staples as corn nearly doubled between March and September 1915.[12]

The new wave of economic hardship that gripped the port in 1915 inspired some groups to increase their philanthropic relief efforts. The Junta Filantrópica de Socorros, for example, purchased foodstuffs and resold them at cost. The Junta de Beneficencia Pública expanded its services during this time by establishing programs to aid widows and orphans. Willing to accept the help of other Mexicans but not of the United States, porteños defiantly turned away assistance offered by the American Red Cross. At a public demonstration organized by labor unions in the city during July 1915, signs and banners exhibited messages that expressed a strong sense of national pride: "There is no hunger here, only a Social Revolution that demands justice! We know how to work, and will never beg for anything!"[13]

Porteños' refusal to accept assistance reflected their identification with the goals of the revolution and determination to rebuild their city. By the time Carranza and his administration left the port on October 11, Constitutionalists had helped establish new supplies of water that more than doubled the amount available to city residents while also adding new public gardens, markets, and parks.[14] Their presence encouraged veracruzanos to look to the government for solutions to many of the problems they faced, and petitions for food, clothing, shelter, and other basic necessities multiplied. Increasingly, porteños organized marches, demonstrations, and other forms of popular protest to assert their renewed status as citizens and demand that the government protect their interests.

Responding to complaints from different sectors of civil society, Veracruz politicians searched for a solution to the economic crisis beginning in winter 1916.[15] On March 1, 1916, for example, revolutionary general Heriberto Jara, the new Veracruz governor, announced the formation of what he termed a commission to regulate trade. Explaining the need for state mediation, Jara reasoned the government should act because "the insufficiency of the measures employed by municipal or political authorities showed that a regulating [state] intervention is necessary under existing economic and social conditions."[16] Jara's proposal set up special committees that attempted to monitor mercantile and industrial establishments as well as transportation firms, commission houses, pharmacies, hotels, and "peddlers of all kinds" to prevent speculation and price gouging.[17] Persons in violation of the regulatory code would be assessed stiff fines, arrested, and possibly denied the right to conduct business. Preoccupied with military matters, Jara found that his urban reform efforts proved largely ineffective.

In October 1916 several cases of malaria in the state prompted the Veracruz sanitation chief, Agustín González, to renew public health efforts in the city. Deploring the "abandoned state of many of the city's tenements" where infection spread easily, he urged property owners and administrators to disinfect and repair their patios. Shortly after issuing this statement, González called for a public meeting to address the situation.

A few days later, city officials called for the organization of neighborhood sanitation committees, and various businesses contributed funds and lent their support.[18] In the process, sanitation agents made over fifteen thousand inspections of houses, rooms, and businesses. Shortly thereafter, officials issued citations to several patio administrators of deteriorating tenements in the city for violating sanitary codes.[19] In effect, these actions legitimated local demands by tenants for better housing conditions and put property owners and administrators on the defensive.

The Property Owners

While public health agents worked to improve the condition of the patios, many owners of urban properties grew increasingly concerned about the economic crisis. On October 19, 1916, nearly one hundred Veracruz landlords had sent a petition to the governor asking that utility rates be reduced. [20] They argued that the circulation of paper money had reduced the value of rental payments, which, in turn, endangered their business. Property-owner frustration was soon increased by the fact that several local labor organizations, including the stevedores, restaurant employees, and graphic artists, had asked that employers pay their workers in the new gold and silver reserve-based currency (*metálico*) rather than in paper money.[21] Then, on November 28, over seventy landlords gathered in the Chamber of Commerce. Discussing the local economic situation, they decided to establish an organization dedicated to protecting their interests and elected Leopoldo H. Palazuelos as their president.[22]

One of the organization's first actions was to express their opposition to the proposal by the new acting governor of Veracruz, Miguel Aguilar, to require that urban and rural rents be paid in metálico and at rates calculated at one-half of 1912 levels.[23] Responding quickly to the idea, landlords again met in Veracruz to decide upon a strategy. Then, in a bold move, they informed city officials that payment of all local taxes would be suspended until "the special situation created by recent decrees and the devaluing of paper money is resolved."[24] At the same time, property owners also sent a telegram to President Carranza objecting to the measure. In particular, their communication found the ruling that city and state taxes be paid in metálico while tenants continued to pay in paper money particularly unfair. To illustrate their point, they claimed that taxes would amount to "three times what they received in rent." The telegram also suggested that earlier legislation be modified to stipulate that rents, along with city, state, and federal taxes, all be paid in metálico. "If the economy, including the payment of salaries, taxes, and rents, could not be fully converted to a stable currency," they asked, "how are we to comply with the law?"[25] Despite their complaints, Aguilar signed the legislation on December 2.

By mid-December 1916, however, many in the port could see that tensions between landlords and tenants had become quite heated. An editorial in *El Dictamen* at the time attempted to consider both sides of the conflict by complaining of a growing shortage of housing in the city while also recognizing that the economic crisis had hurt landlords.[26] According to the author, the urban poor now faced conditions that made it "virtually impossible [for them] to survive."[27] Meantime, a report from the neighboring city of Orizaba stated that the housing situation had reached the point of near desperation. The main source of the problem, according to the report, came from the fact that employers continued to pay their workers in depreciated paper money.[28]

Hoping to remedy the situation, President Carranza issued a decree on December 15 declaring that because of the confusion resulting from the circulation of both paper- and metal-standard currencies, the federal government now strongly encouraged citizens to do all business in metal-based currency.[29] Furthermore, 1 peso in paper money would be worth 20 centavos in metal money. Specifically addressing the housing crisis, Carranza announced that renters owing money to

their landlords should adjust their payment according to the new con-
version rate. Additionally, he mandated reductions in rents, determining that agricultural properties as well as commercial and industrial
businesses whose rents amounted to 50 pesos per month or less should
be reduced by 50 percent.[30] For residential properties, he declared that
landlords charging 30 pesos or less should reduce their rate by 40 percent. Rents between 30 and 50 pesos would be cut in half and those
above 50 but less than 100 pesos would be reduced by 75 percent.
Veracruz landlords saw the measure as a direct threat to their economic
well-being, while tenants, increasingly aware of efforts by citizens in
other cities such as Mexico City, Puebla, and Mérida, began pressuring
state authorities to do more.[31]

The Legalistic Phase of Tenant Organizing

The first stirring of tenant organizing in Veracruz came only a few days
after Carranza's decree when tension between renters and property
owners moved residents to issue a call to "defend the interests of the
public" against local landlords.[32] In an effort to effect local action, a
group that identified itself as "various tenants" published an article in
El Dictamen proposing the formation of a tenant organization to be
called the Great Tenant Union of Veracruz. Readers received notice that
"all tenants in Veracruz" should be made aware of their rights, which
have helped to "lessen the crushing weight of past injustices."[33] Representing the first rallying cry to city tenants, the statement concluded
with the phrase "union, equality, and justice." A subsequent letter to
the paper claimed that tenants were committed to paying in metálico
but at rents based at 1912 levels.[34]

The next day, the landlords issued a communication of their own.
Responding to the tenants' charge, they complained, "How many times
have landlords been required to make unnecessary repairs under the
pretext of improving public health conditions?" They added that the
editors of *El Dictamen* had drummed up xenophobic sentiment among
tenants by suggesting that many local property owners "were foreigners." Defending themselves, the property owners argued: "We can demonstrate that there is a significant number of foreigners among us, but
don't these foreigners have reason to defend their legitimate rights just
as Mexican citizens do? Don't we live in a civilized country where there
are laws to which everyone complies? Are all the tenants citizens?"
Furthermore, the landlords asserted, "anti-foreign sentiment has never
become us. We are more patriotic, more Mexican than that and the law
should be applied equally to everyone, without distinction by nation-

ality."[35] Failing to be mollified by the property owners' response, renters in Veracruz soon decided the time had come for more definite action.

On December 25, 1916, tenants in the port, under the auspices of the Mexican Workers' Union (Sindicato de Obreros de la República Mexicana), officially founded a tenant union to organize for lower rents and improved housing conditions and to lobby the state government for housing reform legislation. During their first meeting, a local organizer, C. Agustín Arrázola, encouraged tenants to organize immediately, given what he saw as the critical housing situation in the port. A few minutes later, tenants went forward with the official incorporation of a renters union in which those present designated Angel F. Baturoni as secretary general and named Manuel Valle, Eracleo Ramírez, Daniel Mota, and Julian González to administrative posts.[36] Then, on the night of December 28, over two hundred residents, many of them women according to the report in *El Dictamen*, met in the Apollo Theater to join the new organization.[37] In their deliberations, renters quickly developed a program of action including an intensive campaign to petition the governor for housing reform.

Negotiating with the State

Late in December 1916, organized tenants sent their first message to the governor asking for housing reform. The document stated, "[Given the housing shortage in the port,] some landlords have committed abuses and launched a series of strategies that have no objective other than to avoid the last decree issued by the federal government regarding the payment of rents. They never tire of finding ways to raise rents, which now far exceed what we paid in 1912."[38] Further, they argued that because of sharp increases in rents and deteriorating housing conditions, the governor should immediately dispatch a commission to investigate the housing situation in the port.[39]

Tenant meetings continued in early 1917. On January 17, for example, an article in *El Dictamen* titled "The Tenant Syndicate Continues to Work to Defend Their Rights" reported that renters had singled out the owners of patio San Carlos as particularly egregious violators of health codes.[40] Expanding their campaign, renters met in the city's local union hall (Cámara de Trabajo) on January 23 to draft a message to President Carranza. In the message they complained that, since October or earlier, landlords had demanded that rents be paid in metálico. If renters did not cooperate, they testified, landlords showed no mercy and immediately served eviction papers. They then suggested that given landlord intransigence, "many more timid residents would be found with their belongings in the middle of the street." Framing their grievances as an affront to their sense of justice as well as local pride, the tenants predicted: "In this city, cradle of the laws of the Reform, impregnable bastion where democracy rose again like a phoenix, police will receive hundreds of eviction notices, residents will see furniture thrown out into the street, and whole families, between tears and lamentations, will become part of a victimized underclass who unhappily are made to atone for the [excesses of] the strong."[41]

In support of their claims, tenants told Carranza that they possessed "a multitude of written complaints" that they planned to present to him. They described the miserable condition of popular housing in the port and suggested that the government name a commission to review rent contracts. This process, they confidently asserted, would reveal that "the strong [landlords] had indeed abused the weak [renters], denying them their rights and leaving them with no one to help them defend themselves." Finally, the tenants' petition closed with a personal appeal to Carranza: "Knowing your commitment to the weak, to the people who have helped achieve the triumph of the noble and sublime Constitutionalist cause, all we ask is that a legal negotiation be reached between both sides in this conflict. We wish only that the magnificent work of the President, work which seeks to revindicate the sacrosanct ideals of the popular masses, be realized."[42]

Clear about their rights as citizens, the new renters organization soon dispatched Diego Caballero and Ricardo Bata to the Veracruz city of Córdoba to meet with the governor. Then they sent union representatives to Querétaro to talk with the First Chief in person. Fortifying their call for public support, they published a petition in *El Dictamen* that made another strong appeal for social justice:

> If we strictly comply with the laws and punctually pay our rents it is unfair that we still stand to lose our houses because the landlord believes that he can evict us on account of back rents not being paid in metallic currency. We have never tried to live rent free or obstruct in any manner the progress of the government. We demand only justice, not favoritism. At the same time, we demand an end to local mafia control so that we no longer have to suffer the impositions of foreigners or be treated in a condescending manner. At present the new government should attend with justice and benevolence to the needs of the proletariat who have given more blood in the service of consolidating the Constitutionalist revolution that we believe will become the fundamental base for progress, prosperity, and enrichment of the Mexican people.[43]

The statement indicated that the tenant commission would present the renters' grievances regarding what they saw as "indiscriminate and arbitrary evictions" being carried out by Veracruz landlords. Here they referred to the fact that property owners expected tenants to pay rents amounting to "triple or four times" what they had paid before the currency crisis. And, if renters did not cooperate, they faced eviction proceedings. Braced to do battle with landlords while hoping state agents would intervene in their favor, tenants declared:

> We will not grow tired of our effort to expose this situation because we have the security of knowing that we represent the people's interests. We know that this will help to influence your decision to close the door on the infinite number of abuses committed by the strong against the weak. Few words are necessary in understanding and remedying this problem. We are fully convinced that the commission will return with a favorable, just, and fair response [to our requests]. We are convinced that the promulgation of the new Constitution will illuminate the nation with the brilliant light of democracy in all its splendor.[44]

Shortly thereafter, tenants in Veracruz learned that the new Constitution had been officially approved.

Article 123 of the document provided the legal basis for an eight-hour day, restricted child and female labor practices, and limited employers' ability to dismiss workers. It established the legal basis for a minimum wage, profit sharing, and compensation for accidents. It banned company stores and debt peonage and decreed that workers have the right to organize and, if necessary, strike. To oversee conflict between capital and labor, the Constitution stipulated that an arbitration board would be established.

In providing the legal pretext for workers' rights, framers of the Constitution also made decent and inexpensive housing for workers a priority. Article 123, Section 12, for example, obligated employers to provide economical and clean housing for employees located outside population centers or businesses in which the number of workers exceeded one hundred. Section 30 considered the construction of cheap and hygienic housing a matter of public utility. Although left somewhat vague, this provision would soon become an important tool for tenant organizers as well as the legal foundation for later housing reform legislation.

Encouraged by the new legal discourse embodied in the Constitution, tenants continued to organize during February 1917. On February 10 at a meeting at the Apollo Theater, renters in attendance under labor leaders Cayetano Fernández de Lara, Agustín Arrázola, Agustín Fernández, Sabino Ganiza, and the Spanish radical Pedro Junco formulated new guidelines for landlord-tenant relations.[45] Grassroots organizing emerged also in other Veracruz cities. Tenants in Orizaba, for example, met on March 21 to form a renters union. The new association stated their mission: to ensure compliance with Carranza's December 14, 1916, decree and to protect tenants "against landlord abuses." They made plans to contact organizers in the port of Veracruz in order to work together in common cause.[46]

Back in Veracruz, Mayor Domingo Ramos initiated a new round of public debates on the housing question in March 1917. An article in *El Dictamen* informed residents of the city council's intention to provide incentives for new construction. Municipal officials were quoted as saying: "Considering that the number of houses in the city is insufficient, it is necessary for authorities to take measures to remedy this shortage. The city council [therefore] declares that all property owners in the city will be exempted from city taxes if they undertake new construction between May 1, 1917, and April 30, 1918."[47]

While the proposal detailed certain restrictions for property owners, the city council's message remained clear: Veracruz desperately needed new and improved housing. By offering incentives to city residents, Mayor Ramos hoped private interests would respond to their offer. The following day, *El Dictamen* took a firm stand in an editorial titled "The Housing Problem in the City of Veracruz":

> The housing problem in the city is one of the most distressing problems we face. Yesterday, the city council announced its plan to suspend taxes for those willing to construct new housing. To us, this initiative appears very acceptable, but alone it is not enough to resolve the problem. The tax incentive cannot produce the kind of miracle that the city needs to realize new, hygienic suburbs. What businessmen looking to invest in urban property want is a secure economic environment. Therefore, we need to encourage a spirit of growth with favorable conditions that help facilitate new projects of value to the city and its inhabitants. What the city should do in dealing with certain structures that remain in a state of complete abandonment is levy a stiff tax on the owners and force them to take action. Authorities should also conduct an inspection of all city housing and require property owners to make immediate repairs. If we hope to make any significant progress in dealing with the housing problem, these and other similar measures need to be acted upon.[48]

In addition to calling for more extensive street paving and other projects and proposing that city lands be immediately made available for individual purchase, editors stressed that city officials needed to take a more assertive role in rectifying the housing situation.

Municipal leaders were successful in encouraging residents to purchase city lots, many of which sold for approximately 300 pesos in 1917.[49] Yet despite the fact that lot sales increased substantially in 1918 and 1919, this option seemed to offer little relief for the majority of residents in the city who remained without property. Three days after publishing the 1917 editorial outlining actions city officials might take to improve the housing situation, the editors of *El Dictamen* suggested that battle lines were being drawn between two clear factions in Veracruz. On one side were landlords "who consider it perfectly within their right to charge as much rent as possible given the increase in the cost of living and the city's shortage of rental housing." On the other side were tenants "who are unable to withstand an increase in their rents. As it stands now, time is on the side of the property owner who can afford to charge high rents because of the tremendous demand for housing. Yet, even if these two groups resolve their current stand-off, the city's housing problem will not have changed fundamentally."[50] While *El Dictamen* made it clear that tenants had gained public sympathy, it was also clear that landlords, without more forceful state intervention, could go on charging as much as they wanted. Facing difficult odds, tenants continued to pressure government officials.

The First Demonstration

On March 30, 1917, members of the tenant union met in the Veracruz Cámara de Trabajo. After a period of discussion, they elected a local tailor, Herón Proal, as moderator (*director de debates*) and decided to send a list of all tenant grievances to the Secretary of the Treasury in Mexico City.[51] Following the meeting they also announced that a major public demonstration would be held in Veracruz on April 1 to protest recent evictions.[52]

That day, a group of tenants gathered outside the offices of the Cámara de Trabajo before circulating through the central district of the city. As they marched through the streets, the procession passed by the homes of some of the city's better-known landlords and administrators. Taunting property owners, the protesters shouted, "Down with the evictions! Down with the exploiters of the tenants!" while encouraging other residents to join them.[53] A report in *El Dictamen* the following day claimed that "in recent memory few protests had created such a stir as the one that took place last night."[54] Additionally, the newspaper noted that the tenant union's leadership had sent yet another

Several months between writing letters + public demonstrations.

petition to President Carranza informing him of their activities and asking for his support.

After this first public display of tenant collective action, many others in the port began to speak out more regularly about the condition of housing. Renters in patio San Gregorio, for example, were reported to have complained to their landlord about "the almost total lack of hygiene" in the tenement, where "the interior of the patio and the central rooms reveal[ed] a detestable filth, not to mention the bathroom, which [was] always a scandalous disaster."[55] Soon, similar complaints prompted public health officials to visit other patios in the city. When the Veracruz Health Department informed thirty-five landlords in early May that their properties stood in violation of city health codes, they started a new round of actions designed to clean up the city's popular housing. Then, over the next few weeks, sanitation agents visited 3,740 houses, 11,915 accesorías, 19,833 rooms, 2,411 second storeys, 2,145 businesses, and 13,490 water tanks. They also handed out 262 notifications to landlords and administrators as well as 320 second notices.[56]

As the sanitation campaign progressed through the summer and fall of 1917, officials occasionally required that tenants be temporarily evicted from deteriorating patios. At one point in early October, sanitation head Agustín González and police chief Carlos Palacios ordered two landlords to repair their properties on Arista Street.[57] The owners took the order as an opportunity to evict their renters permanently. In response, tenants resisted and presented their case to city officials, who issued a statement the next day sympathetic to the rights of tenants: "We require that the properties be vacated for a few days to make repairs, but this does not forfeit the right of the tenant to continue living there, especially when he has a contract and a job and must face the fact that today it is impossible to find housing in Veracruz."[58] The statement went on to suggest that a temporary shelter be provided for renters until they could reoccupy the property. Hearing of similar incidents, the mayor and city council members soon realized that the Arista Street situation was part of a growing pattern of evictions citywide that called for a general review of sanitation procedures. They did not want municipal authorities operating as "unconscionable instruments of landlords and administrators who extort their tenants."[59]

Meanwhile, Veracruz governor Cándido Aguilar sent a message to Mayor Domingo Ramos and tenant organizers regarding a proposed new rent law.[60] According to an article in *El Dictamen*, "the measure was introduced by the governor to the state legislature with the hope of preventing further abuses [by landlords] while also promoting the interests of the poorer classes and workers who have suffered the most significant losses."[61] A month later, Cándido Aguilar decreed that rents in the state were to be kept affordable and that certain articles of the state civil code would be revised to help improve housing conditions.[62] Apparently, the move temporarily satisfied at least a few of the tenants' demands, because little about the cost of rental housing in Veracruz appeared in newspaper accounts for the next five years. The governor's action did not mean, however, that the housing problem had been resolved. Still, following the legislature's review of the situation in late 1917, public discussion concerning popular housing turned more to related matters of sanitation.

Alongside the legislative reforms at this time, private initiatives were undertaken to increase the amount of housing stock in the port of Veracruz. In an attempt to stimulate new construction, for example, a businessman named Ricardo Luna Morales proposed a new initiative to the minister of communications and public works on November 13, 1917, that would be "dedicated for use by employees and workers." To "help resolve the housing problem, which is very serious in Veracruz," Luna Morales called for the founding of a construction company that would specialize in the building of rental housing. Plans stipulated that new housing stock would be built on former grazing lands near the ocean. Most of the structures would be made of wood with prices kept reasonable.[63]

A majority of property owners felt, however, that city taxes stood in the way of their making a profit from new construction. Landlords had met earlier, in January 1917, and complained about the cost of repairs mandated by sanitation officials. The owner of patio El Centro Obrero, for example, suggested that it was impossible to comply with the demands of the local sanitation commission (Junta de Sanidad) because "tenants abuse the property and don't pay their rents."[64] Judging from the tone of his and other communications, an end to hostilities between the two groups appeared to be no more than a distant possibility. Property owners, attempting to defend themselves against challenges by renters, the press, and city officials, thus strengthened their resolve and initiated various retaliatory efforts. In February 1920, for example, *El Dictamen* reported that landlords had recently evicted female tenants living in the city's red light district who paid landlords the excessive rate of 3 pesos per day for a tiny room (about eight square feet) and 6 pesos for a somewhat larger room with a makeshift bed and a few pieces of used furniture.[65] Meanwhile, residents braced themselves for another bout with one of the port's legendary public health epidemics.

The City Infected

In May 1920, Dr. Mauro Loyo claimed he had discovered what he thought to be bubonic plague in Veracruz after a nearly seventeen-year absence. By the end of the month, *El Dictamen* had reported several cases. Once notified of the outbreak, authorities from the Public Health Department in Mexico City dispatched Dr. Octaviano González Fabela to combat the disease. Quickly, officials suspended traffic in and out of the port and created a cordon sanitaire around the city.[66] Although no one knew the original source of the disease, reports suggested that several rats had been spotted on Francisco Canal Street and in other popular districts of the city. Soon, public health agents toured neighborhoods in order to make an assessment of local conditions. For those in violation of sanitary codes, they warned, severe fines would be imposed.[67]

With the cooperation of Mayor Salvador Campa, members of the National Chamber of Commerce (Cámara Nacional de Comercio), and porteños associated with a neighborhood organization called the Junta Vecinal, residents formed an organization to raise funds to defeat the disease. Calling themselves the Committee against the Plague, they began a vaccination campaign on June 11 after receiving supplies brought by a U.S. destroyer from New Orleans.[68] Then, as public health workers endeavored to track down the source of the epidemic, *El Dictamen* printed an article on June 21 that asked, "Where are the centers of infection?" The answer, not surprisingly, was the tenements located on the periphery of the city.

Because of limited access to health and urban services, residents in many of the city's popular neighborhoods suffered most during the epidemic. Officials who inspected patio El 20 de Noviembre on July 3, for example, found the tenement in such a state of disrepair that they commented that "it was impossible to imagine living in this area."[69] Two days later, the paper reported three cases of the plague next door. On July 8, officials decided that patio El Cocal had to be destroyed after new victims of the epidemic were discovered.[70] The following week, sanitation workers determined that two entire city blocks between Prim, Abasolo, 20 de Noviembre, Alambique, and Escobedo Streets needed to be sealed off. Then, beginning in June, inspectors initiated a dramatic program of burning garbage, furniture, and household items as well as destroying merchandise in local stores thought to be contaminated. In the process they targeted certain patios for destruction. If residents resisted, sanitation workers called on the police to intervene.

Soon, other residents found themselves facing what some called the "sanitation dictatorship" as owners of hotels, boardinghouses, and several other establishments fell under the scrutinizing eye of public health inspectors. Guest houses such as Palais Royal and Paraíso saw many of their mattresses, along with heaps of dirty clothes, dragged out into the middle of the street and torched by the sanitation police. Agents inspected and subsequently fumigated countless houses and patios. Probably one of the most dramatic events in the sanitation campaign occurred when officials, after declaring the Mercado Nuevo and one of the public piers two of the most infectious sites in the city, ordered them demolished. Watching this, many people, especially vendors who had worked in these areas, sought ways to express their anger. On June 4 a few outraged citizens organized a public protest in the city center.

Fighting the plague in Veracruz. *Courtesy of AGEV, José Pérez de León Collection*

As the campaign progressed, residents' resentment toward sanitation and public officials grew. Many felt that health workers had exaggerated the danger most porteños faced, and *El Dictamen* began reporting an increasing number of episodes in which residents had prevented public health inspectors from entering their homes. In mid-July, for example, a group of women organized a street protest that criticized the mayor and various sanitation officials. At the same time, residents of the working-class suburb of Los Cocos tried unsuccessfully to appeal a decision ordering the incineration of their homes. A letter to new Veracruz governor Antonio Nava signed by approximately eighty-five residents pleaded that the neighborhood not be razed: "[The

Why the belief that the governor and/or president could or would help them?

burning of] our humble homes is an inhumane act because all who live here are workers who cannot afford to purchase a house. Many of us used to make a humble living selling things at the Mercado Nuevo and now we are being kicked out of our homes too! While authorities believe that the inside of our homes are completely filthy, they are wrong! Destroying them will only leave more than TWO HUNDRED FAMI-LIES homeless."[71] In addition to those complaining from Los Cocos, other dissident voices could be heard elsewhere in the city.

Nevertheless, as the campaign wound down, reports by sanitation officials left little doubt about the sorry state of the city's tenements. In mid-July, members of the Committee against the Plague described conditions in patio San Antonio Marchena as "particularly horrendous." "There is no hygiene," their communication declared, and "there are rats and other animals, [while] the bathrooms remind one of something out of Dante's fifteenth circle of Hell."[72] Then, on July 22, *El Dictamen* printed an article that described the inspection of patio San Antonio de Marchena by sanitation authorities: "In a visit requested by tenants the commission entered the patio and quickly found it to be a disaster. [They saw] rooms in ruins [and] water service and bathrooms in a frightening state of disrepair. [After reviewing the situation] the commissioners determined that San Antonio was a true center of infection." The report added to complaints of deteriorated facilities and foul smells emanating from houses on Avenue 20 de Noviembre as well as certain lots on La Palma and Doblado Streets.[73] Many in the city decided that the entire La Huaca neighborhood required "urgent vigilance" to prevent the spread of disease.[74] As the month progressed, other patios gained the dubious honor of being deemed "uninhabitable."[75] Soon, authorities dispatched sanitary brigades to disinfect other "suspect" areas.

Then, in late July 1920, members of the Committee against the Plague made a report of their inspection tour, noting that 99 percent of the rooms and patios visited were in a nearly complete state of disrepair: "[The condition of] these pigsties that landlords pompously call accesorías is truly scandalous and those who reside in these shacks live in horrible circumstances. In Veracruz the majority of houses are dirty and uninhabitable and have escaped the efforts of sanitation workers to improve their condition. Now is the time for decisive action to be taken on behalf of the city and its residents."[76] As part of their report, public health officials informed residents that they intended to take additional measures to help prevent the spread of disease by further studying housing conditions in the city. Despite their good intentions, however, such a study was never made.

After the first week in August 1920 public health officials reported no new cases of the plague.[77] By the end of the epidemic, thirty-six people had died—suggesting that while significant, the city's brush with the bubonic plague had proved less catastrophic than initially feared. Ultimately, this information seemed to confirm many residents' suspicions that health officials had exaggerated the seriousness of the campaign and, on more than one occasion, initiated unnecessary actions. Added to their resentment was the fact that for all the trouble residents had endured, health workers had failed to improve conditions in the city. The fact was made clear with the return of yellow fever to the port that summer.

The first case in the port surfaced on June 8, 1920. By July the city had witnessed the reappearance of the dreaded disease that had haunted Veracruz for nearly four hundred years. Quickly, the fever spread through the city while also traveling to Papantla and Tuxpan in the north and south down the Gulf Coast. In September 1920 an official campaign began. Soon, health workers busied themselves inspecting the city's water supply and many storage containers. Sanitation agents sprayed hundreds of gallons of petroleum on stagnant pools in an effort to prevent the breeding of mosquitos. By December their efforts had paid off, but not before nearly 150 porteños had died. The following year, an international team headed by the Mexican Department of Health in conjunction with doctors from the Rockefeller Foundation's International Health Board continued the sanitation program and eventually eradicated yellow fever in Mexico.[78] Yet while the campaign against yellow fever proved a success, the sanitation reforms undertaken to prevent its spread, like those against the plague, did little to address housing conditions in Veracruz.

On November 4, 1920, *El Dictamen* printed an editorial that again offered an intimate portrait of living conditions in the city's popular neighborhoods with the observation, "The patios primarily found in the neighborhoods outside the city center leave much to be desired in terms of public health." An editorial the following day asserted that "the sanitation of the tenements is the most important issue of public health in the city" and that responsibility for the problem lay with landlords who "charge inflated rents and do little to maintain their properties while tenants seem only to make deplorable conditions worse."

The High Price of Housing

Not only did renters in Veracruz feel a sense of moral outrage about the condition of the tenements but they also believed that rates charged by landlords represented a real injustice. Rough comparisons with worker housing in North America and Europe, however, suggest that while Mexicans sustained sizable increases, their situation was not exceptional. A report by the Mexican Department of Labor issued in December 1922 rated average rental housing increases between 1914 and 1921 for ten different North American and European nations (Austria, Canada, Denmark, England, France, Germany, Italy, Norway, Switzerland, and the United States). Rent increases for the period ranged from 33 percent in France to 500 percent in Austria.[79] The study did not calculate a national average for Mexico but instead provided data on accesorías and rented rooms for eight districts within Mexico City. There, rent increases for the period 1919–1921 ranged from approximately 17 percent to 40 percent for accesorías and from 21 percent to 83 percent for rented rooms.[80] Although housing rates in the port of Veracruz were not available in the Labor Department figures, some commentators asserted that they exceeded those recorded in Mexico City.[81]

Indeed, between 1910 and 1920 the cost of housing in the port of Veracruz had jumped considerably. According to a report by the governor's office, rents in local patios rose 50 percent in that period.[82] Other sources report increases of up to 500 percent between 1910 and 1922.[83] In 1920 one Mexico City newspaper described rents in the port as "simply out of control."[84] Generally, the percentages workers paid for housing—in renting either an accessoría or a room—ranged from approximately 20 percent to 50 percent of their monthly income.[85] According to Department of Labor sources, housing prices in Veracruz for January 1922 ranked fourth in the nation after Nuevo León, Tamaulipas, and Yucatán.[86] With government reports confirming their complaints, tenants became more aggressive in their protests. And, in line with the resurgence of nationalism brought by the revolution, they began to target foreign landlords. Local Spanish and Cuban landlords especially came under fire.

Framing Tenant Grievances

While U.S., British, French, and German interests did exert a powerful influence in the Veracruz region, many in the port believed that Spaniards (*gachupines*), not gringos, represented the most "pernicious foreigners" when it came to popular housing.[87] A U.S. diplomat observed "a marked difference" during the revolution "between the antagonism directed against the American and the hostility shown toward the Spaniard." Hostility toward Spaniards, he noticed, was not "expressed in newspapers, public writings, clubs nor in public places"; it was "unwritten," because the classes that harbored it had "no medium of public expression."[88] During the housing crisis after the revolution, however, these feelings were openly expressed by Veracruz tenants.

In June 1921, for example, tenants of patio San Ulpiano complained to the governor that the administrator José García Suero managed a "hateful monopoly."[89] They asked that "the unpopular Spaniard be expelled from the country before any further harm could be done." Tenants believed that Spaniards, often labeled "bourgeois" and *gachupín*, represented what one petition described as a "ruthless oligarchy [who] never think twice about improving their own fortunes at the expense of the people of Veracruz."[90] Although foreign influence in the housing market did not constitute a monopoly, residents were keenly aware of the high percentage of Spaniards in the port, and that awareness combined with the discourse of revolutionary nationalism fueled their antagonism.[91]

The state of Veracruz was the nation's third leading area of Spanish residency after the Federal District and Puebla.[92] Taking into consideration not only the distribution of Spaniards throughout the republic but also the ratio of Spaniards to Mexicans in each of these states, the percentage of Spaniards in Veracruz came second only to the Federal District.[93] In addition to the sheer number of Spaniards living in Veracruz, their position in the various local economies may also have contributed to local resentments.[94]

Unlike North American residents, Spaniards often worked as landlords, shopkeepers, pawnbrokers, wholesalers, retailers, moneylenders, and restaurant and bar owners, putting them in regular contact with the port's popular classes. As times got tough during the revolution, Mexicans increasingly saw Spanish merchants as "price-gouging retailers and usurers."[95] Along these same lines, those who dealt with Spanish landlords and property administrators also tended to view these individuals as "exploiters of the people." A closer look at the Veracruz housing market helps one understand resentment toward Spanish (and, to an extent, Cuban) landlords and property administrators.

Profile of Urban Property Investors, 1902–1930

Local notarial records (Registro Público de la Propiedad de Veracruz) for the years 1902 through 1930 reveal that while Mexicans were involved in the largest number of property transactions, Spaniards nevertheless appear to have invested a serious amount of time, energy, and money in the Veracruz housing market. Spanish activity, in other words, constituted a disproportionate influence when figured against their numerical standing in the city population. This disproportionality no doubt helped to provide legitimacy for rent protesters' claims that Spaniards "basically monopolized everything."

In addition to noting the overall Spanish presence in the housing market, it is also important to consider who owned the various tenements where tenants went on strike. A breakdown of patio ownership suggests that Mexican owners were largely responsible for the poor housing conditions and high rents that inspired tenant complaints. The most interesting evidence that corroborates local rhetoric, however, is the degree to which non-Mexicans were involved in local patio administration.

In this category, presumed "foreign" managers who collected rents, arranged for evictions, and oversaw all other housing affairs apparently did corner the market and thus provided reasonable evidence from which tenants could make their claims. Moreover, the prominence of a few individuals (both resident non-Mexican and a recently nationalized Spaniard) gave residents the impression that a small, alien elite truly controlled rental housing. More precise than generalized claims made about the city's economy, documentary source material suggests that it was more the practices of a handful of tenement managers than an imagined "foreign elite" that provided strikers with the real evidence they needed to mobilize renters. Three men can be singled out as the most egregious "enemies" of the Veracruz renting public.

Of the tenement administrators listed in the Registro Público de la Propiedad de Veracruz, the manager José García Suero, a Spaniard who had become a Mexican citizen in 1921, accounted for nearly 32 percent of the sample. Two Cubans, Manuel Cangas and his brother Antonio, were the next most active managers of properties, while other important administrators included Francisco Rúiz Murillo, a Spaniard, and two Mexicans, Ramón B. Marquez and José Antonio Cano. Yet aside from the degree to which each of these men was active in patio management in Veracruz, the compilation of complaints against them helps to explain how rent strikers developed their passionate dislike for these middlemen—particularly García Suero and the Cangas brothers.

Problems with García Suero's allegedly abrasive style and domination of tenement management show up in the historical record about the same time he decided to become a Mexican citizen. In June 1921, for example, renters at the patio San Ulpiano complained that García Suero "managed a large number of dilapidated properties." "This Spaniard," tenants charged, "has already caused great pain to many here in the port."[96] The fact that García Suero had become or was in the process of becoming a citizen in 1921 apparently did little to improve his reputation among local residents. Still, to them he was a "gachupín."

On July 2, 1921, Veracruz mayor Salvador Campa received complaints about García Suero as well as two other men who owned a number of run-down tenements and managed several others, Manuel and Antonio Cangas. Campa in turn informed the governor that many of the patios overseen by the Cangas brothers "were in deplorable condition" and added: "When these individuals make even the slightest repair they feel justified to raise the rent each time."[97] Hoping state officials would intervene, the mayor indicated that he had issued several warnings but the abuses continued.

An examination of the ownership of popular housing in Veracruz suggests that Mexicans accounted for the largest percentages of property ownership and management. Foreigners, however, did enjoy a disproportionate degree of influence over rental properties when compared to their numerical standing in the city population. Spaniards were involved in about 35 percent of all transactions, although they constituted no more that 10 percent of the city population at any given time. Cubans, who represented only a small percentage of the Veracruz population (less than 1 percent), managed, however, to accumulate and supervise sizable holdings.[98] Given the considerable amount of property that these foreign landlords and administrators controlled throughout the first three decades of the century, it is little wonder that tenants angrily portrayed alien elites as "oligarchic tyrants."

Growing popular resentment over housing alone, however, did not lead to the reemergence of tenant protest in summer 1920. At that time, provisional Veracruz governor Antonio Nava reversed rent control laws put into effect during the term of Constitutionalist governor Cándido Aguilar. Nava defended his action by asserting that the "causes that had previously motivated" housing reform now had "disappeared."[99] Contrary to Nava's claim, many felt the condition of housing in Veracruz had gone from bad to worse. Soon, however, the inauguration of former Veracruz senator Adalberto Tejeda as governor in December 1920 offered a glimmer of hope for porteños.

Notes

1. For a discussion concerning the buildup of war materials and support for the Constitutionalists, see John Hart, *Revolutionary Mexico: The Coming and Process of the Mexican Revolution* (Berkeley: University of California Press, 1987), 298–302. For an account of the evacuation, see Robert E. Quirk, *An Affair of*

Honor: Woodrow Wilson and the Occupation of Veracruz (New York: Norton, 1962), 156–71, and Berta Ulloa, *Veracruz: Capital de la nación, 1914–15* (Mexico City: Colegio de México, 1986), 38–45. For city government expenses during 1915 and related business matters, see AMV, Ayuntamiento, box 368, vol. 501.

2. Materials relating to city government during the North American and Constitutionalist occupations can be found in AMV, boxes 356, 357, 358, 407, and 408. City council records for the period beginning November 9, 1915, are located in AMV, Veracruz Actas de Cabildo, book no. 93. A list of businesses in the port in 1913–14 is compiled in E. M. Brime, *Directorio comercial de "Veracruz" para los años de 1913–1914* (Veracruz: Author's edition, 1913). On this period in Veracruz state history, see Ricardo Corzo Ramírez, José G. González Sierra, and David A. Skerritt, *Nunca un desleal: Cándido Aguilar, 1889–1960* (Mexico City: Colegio de México/Gobierno del Estado de Veracruz, 1986), chapters 3 and 4. On Aguilar and early attempts at agrarian reform, see Heather Fowler-Salamini, *Agrarian Radicalism in Veracruz, 1920–38* (Lincoln: University of Nebraska Press, 1971), 17–24.

3. Ulloa, *Veracruz*, 38–45. Carranza first established his administration in Orizaba before moving on to the port. For accounts of this period, see also John Womack, "The Mexican Revolution, 1910–1920," in *Mexico since Independence*, ed. Leslie Bethell, 158–59 (Cambridge: Cambridge University Press, 1991), and Quirk, *Affair of Honor*, 156–71.

4. Quoted in Ulloa, *Veracruz*, 44.

5. Ibid., 96.

6. Ibid., 93–94, and Hart, *Revolutionary Mexico*, 168. See *El Dictamen*, April 10, 1915, for information on the cost of accommodations in the port.

7. See Ulloa, *Veracruz*, 96–97, for a sampling of prices paid for basic goods in Veracruz at this time.

8. Hart, *Revolutionary Mexico*, 313. See also Alan Knight, *The Mexican Revolution* (Lincoln: University of Nebraska Press, 1986), 2:408–9.

9. For exchange rates in Mexico City during this time, see John Lear, "Workers, *Vecinos*, and Citizens: The Revolution in Mexico City, 1909–1917" (Ph.D. diss., University of California, Berkeley, 1993), 407.

10. *El Dictamen*, May 10, 1915. During this period, Veracruz saw a rapid succession of men serve as governor. For a listing of governors, see Corzo Ramírez et al., *Nunca un desleal*, 225–26; and Carmen Blázquez Domínguez, ed., *Estado de Veracruz: Informes de sus gobernadores, 1826–1986* (Jalapa: Gobierno del Estado de Veracruz), 22:12,386–87.

11. Ulloa, *Veracruz*, 97.

12. Ibid., 98.

13. Ibid., 99.

14. See ibid., 99–100, for a listing of other improvements rendered during the Constitutionalist occupation.

15. On March 6, 1916, federal authorities issued a new declaration limiting noncitizens' access to property. For a transcription of the new property laws, see *El Dictamen*, March 7, 1916, as well as May 9, 12, 17, 1916, for discussion about the different currencies circulating at the time and the introduction of new paper money that month. See also Knight, *Mexican Revolution*, 2:409.

16. *El Dictamen*, March 1, 1916, translated by State Department Officials, RDS, reel 161. Carranza had appointed Jara governor on January 27, 1916.

17. Ibid.

18. Ibid., October 18, 19, 1916. The same day, the paper printed the political manifesto of the Partido Obrero Veracruzana, which supported the candi-

dacy of Cándido Aguilar. Future tenant leader Herón Proal signed the document as vice president.

19. Ibid., October 24, 1916.

20. Ibid., October 20, 1916.

21. Ibid., October 24, 1916.

22. Ibid., November 29, 1916.

23. On the new currency, see Berta Ulloa, "Moneda, Bancos y Deuda," in Berta Ulloa, *Historia de la revolución mexicana, 1914–1917: La constitución de 1917* (Mexico City: Colegio de México, 1983), 165–71; and Knight, *Mexican Revolution*, 2:409.

24. *El Dictamen*, November 29, 1916.

25. Ibid.

26. Ibid., December 16, 1916.

27. For commentary on the continued problem with paper money in the fall of 1916, see ibid., October 22, 1916.

28. Ibid., November 6, 1916.

29. Octavio García Mundo, *El movimiento inquilinario de Veracruz, 1922* (Mexico City: Sep–Setentas, 1976), 45.

30. Erica Berra-Stoppa, "Estoy en huelga y no pago renta," *Habitación* 1, no. 1 (1981): 35.

31. This section follows Moisés González Navarro, *Población y sociedad en México, 1900–1970* (Mexico City: UNAM, 1974), 1:179–81, and Manuel Perlo Cohen, "Política y vivienda en México, 1910–1952," *Revista Mexicana de Sociología* 41, no. 3 (July–September 1979): 774–77.

32. *El Dictamen*, December 19, 1916.

33. Ibid.

34. Ibid., December 20, 1916.

35. Ibid.

36. Ibid., December 26, 1916.

37. Ibid., December 29, 1916.

38. Ibid.

39. Ibid., December 30, 1916.

40. For example, see reports in ibid., January 3, 5, 17, 1917.

41. Ibid., January 26, 1917.

42. Ibid.

43. Ibid., January 29, 1917.

44. Ibid.

45. *El Dictamen*, February 9 and 11, 1917. For complaints about the unsanitary conditions of various patios at this time, see reports on February 11, March 6 and 19, 1917. Junco had been one of the founders of the Veracruz Confederación de Sindicatos Obreros in 1912. See Leafar Agetro (Rafael Ortega), *Las luchas proletarias en Veracruz* (Jalapa: Editorial "Barricada," 1942), 154.

46. Ibid., March 21, 1917.

47. Ibid., March 26, 1917.

48. Ibid., March 27, 1917.

49. Veracruz Registro Público de la Propiedad, 1917, AGEV.

50. *El Dictamen*, March 30, 1917.

51. Ibid., March 31, 1917.

52. Ibid., April 1, 1917.

53. Ibid.

54. Ibid., April 2, 1917.

55. Ibid., April 3. 1917.

56. Ibid., May 12, June 7, 1917. City council records beginning in March 1917 suggest that several patios had undergone repairs. See minutes from March 28, April 2, May 9, June 8, August 28, September 29, November 10, 19, and December 29, 1917, meetings. AMV, Ayuntamiento, 1917.

57. Ibid., October 7, 1917.

58. Ibid., October 10, 1917.

59. Ibid.

60. Ibid., October 27, 1917.

61. Ibid., October 28, 1917.

62. Ibid., December 1, 1917. See also García Mundo, *El movimiento inquilinario*, 46.

63. *El Dictamen*, November 14, 1917.

64. Ibid., May 17, 1918.

65. Ibid., February 2, 1920.

66. Ibid., June 2, 1920.

67. Ibid., June 17, 1920.

68. AGEV, gobernación, ramo Salubridad, box 495, "vacunas-1920." Additional documentation on the epidemic can be found in box 497, "peste bubónica," and box 497, "telegramas." Related materials are in boxes 509, 516, 524, and 538, Dirección General de Salubridad.

69. *El Dictamen*, July 4, 1920.

70. Ibid., July 9, 1920.

71. AGEV, gobernación, box 541, "Veracruz Ayuntamiento."

72. *El Dictamen*, July 20, 1920.

73. Ibid., July 3 and 23, 1920.

74. Ibid., July 25, 1920.

75. Ibid., July 22, 1920.

76. Ibid., July 27, 1920.

77. Ibid., August 10, 1920.

78. Details of the yellow fever campaign can be found at Archivo Histórico de la Secretaría de Salubridad in Mexico City; see Fondo de salubridad III, boxes 15–35, for materials relating to Veracruz. See also "Fallecimientos por fiebre amarilla en la ciudad de Veracruz en los años de 1901–1923," Rockefeller Foundation Archive, Records of the International Health Board, RG 5, Series 3, Box 148, Folder 323.

79. Mexican Department of Labor, December 1922, AGN, trabajo, box 503 (1922).

80. Ibid.

81. Berra-Stoppa, "Estoy en huelga," 37. For reports on worker housing in Mexico City, see "El trabajo de sastrería y sus asimilares en México D.F.: Labor a domicilio," *Boletín Mensual del Departamento de Trabajo*, January 1922; "Higiene de la habitación: La habitación obrera en México, D.F.," *Boletín Mensual*, February 1922; and "Las ultimas huelgas en el puerto de Veracruz," *Boletín Mensual*, June 1922. For information on the cost of living in Mexico for 1920–21, see monthly reports conducted by the Department of Labor housed at the AGN, ramo trabajo, boxes 184–89 (1920) and 245–47, 252–55 (1921).

82. Letter from Veracruz Department of Labor to Governor Tejeda, May 12, 1922, AGEV, gobernación, 1922.

83. Berra-Stoppa, "Estoy en huelga," 37; González Navarro, *Población y sociedad*, 181. On rent disputes in Veracruz during the North American occupation, see Quirk, *Affair of Honor*, 142.

84. *El Universal*, August 1, 1920.

85. Hart, *Revolutionary Mexico*, 167–68; Berra-Stoppa, "Estoy en huelga," 37; González Navarro, *Población y sociedad*, 181.

86. Mexican Department of Labor, *Boletín de Trabajo*, April 1922.

87. On the question of an emerging economic nationalism, see Alan Knight, "The Political Economy of Revolutionary Mexico," in *Latin American Economic Imperialism and the State: The Political Economy of the External Connection from Independence to the Present*, ed. Christopher Abel and Colin M. Lewis (London: The Athlone Press, 1985), 290, 310.

88. Consul Bonney to U.S. State Department, San Luis Potosí, May 28, 1913. Quoted in Alan Knight, *U.S.-Mexican Relations, 1910–1940: An Interpretation* (San Diego: Center for U.S.-Mexican Studies, 1987), 62.

89. Vecinos of patio San Ulpiano to Governor Adalberto Tejeda, June 18, 1921, AGEV, gobernación, uncataloged box.

90. Ibid.

91. For earlier perspectives on this situation, see Manuel Castells, *The City and the Grassroots: A Cross-Cultural Theory of Urban Social Movements* (Berkeley: University of California Press, 1983), 38, 44; Olivia Domínguez Pérez, *Política y movimientos sociales en el tejedismo* (Jalapa: Universidad Veracruzana, 1986), 57; and Hart, *Revolutionary Mexico*, 299. Related work on elites in the port during the late nineteenth century includes Julio Contreras Utrera, "Los comerciantes del porfiriato: El puerto de Veracruz, 1880–1890" (bachelor's thesis, Universidad Veracruzana, 1989), and Carmen Blázquez Domínguez, "Empresarios y financieros en el puerto de Veracruz y Jalapa," in *Una inmigración privilegiada: Comerciantes, empresarios y profesionales españoles en México en los siglos XIX y XX*, ed. Clara E. Lida (Madrid: Alianza América, 1994), 121–41.

92. Clara E. Lida, "El perfil de una inmigración, 1821–1939," in Lida, *Una inmigración privilegiada*, 37.

93. *Censo general de población, 1921*, 1:17–18; Bernardo García Díaz, *Puerto de Veracruz* (Jalapa: Archivo General del Estado de Veracruz, 1992), 103; Octavio Ochoa Contreras and Flora Velásquez Ortíz, *Volumen, dinámica y estructura de la población total del estado de Veracruz, 1793–1980* (Jalapa: Universidad Veracruzana, 1986), 7. For Puebla, see Leticia Gamboa Ojeda, "Los españoles en la ciudad de Puebla hacia 1930," in Lida, *Una inmigración privilegiada*, 193.

94. Commentary on anti-Spanish attitudes can be found in Alan Knight, "Peasants into Patriots: Thoughts on the Making of the Mexican Nation," *Estudios Mexicanos/Mexican Studies* 10, no. 1 (Winter 1994): 142.

95. See also Knight, *U.S.-Mexican Relations*, 63.

96. Residents of patio San Ulpiano to Governor Tejeda, June 18, 1921, AGEV, gobernación, 1921.

97. Ibid.

98. *Quinto censo general de la república mexicana, 1921, 1930* (Mexico City, 1938).

99. Quoted in García Mundo, *El movimiento inquilinario*, 46.

3

Divided Elites
Political Process and the Rise of Adalberto Tejeda

> Veracruz, one of the richest and most cultured states, and until recently the most prosperous in the republic, has been becoming for some time the most unquiet, the most irregular region of the country and the place where interests and rights are less guaranteed than anywhere one may live.
> —"The Cancer of Veracruz," *El Universal*, July 23, 1923

The transformation of tenant protest into a social movement required a capacity to mobilize and the political opportunity to do so.[1] In Veracruz, collective action took shape through the conjoining of three important factors. First, the drafting of the 1917 Constitution infused local popular culture with new ideological elements that helped urban renters frame grievances and channel moral outrage. Second, connections forged by the labor movement and social networks established in porteño neighborhoods helped mobilize urban renters. And third, divisions between national and regional elites as well as greater toleration for popular organizing helped shape a political "opening" for grassroots activists. Considering this last point to be the most significant, this chapter briefly focuses on elite conflict at the national level before discussing how the rise of Veracruz governor Adalberto Tejeda helped polarize state politics and thus create increased opportunity for popular protest.

Divided National Elites

Just when it seemed that Mexico had entered a period of relative stability after nearly a decade of civil war, revolutionary elites again engaged in fraticidal conflict. On April 23, 1920, Sonoran general Alvaro Obregón announced the Plan de Agua Prieta, which denounced the government of Venustiano Carranza and declared an open revolt against him. Essentially, the document stated that Carranza's presidency violated constitutional principles and that the sovereignty of the nation rested "in the people."[2] Carranza responded with orders for Obregón's arrest, charging him with "plotting sedition."

Soon, however, with hostile troops advancing on the capital, Carranza made a hasty retreat toward Veracruz. His entourage included some eight thousand people, various family possessions, government documents, treasury funds, and some military equipment as well as a modest amount of water and medical provisions.[3] En route, the First Chief revealed his plans to one of his favorite generals, Guadalupe Sánchez of Veracruz, who replied, "President and father, though everyone else betrays you, I shall not, for if but one man remains loyal to you, I am that man."[4] Despite his words, Sánchez never intended to defend Carranza. In Alijibes, Puebla, the First Chief received news of his general's defection. Shortly thereafter, in mid-May, troops under Sánchez's command intercepted the president's train. During the fighting that followed, Carranza managed to escape on horseback into the mountains of northern Puebla. A week later, however, a group of about thirty men attacked the presidential encampment at Tlaxcalantongo. In the confusion that followed, assassins shot and killed Carranza.

Hearing of the president's death, Sonoran Adolfo de la Huerta called a special session of Congress to name a provisional president. After a quick vote on May 24, lawmakers decided de la Huerta would serve until an elected president could take over. Elections took place that fall, and Alvaro Obregón became the new president on December 1, 1920. Yet despite the rise of the "Sonoran Dynasty," as Obregón, de la Huerta, and Obregón's right-hand man, Plutarco Elías Calles, soon came to be known, the national government remained relatively weak. Their vulnerability became evident in winter and spring 1921 as growing distance from the dominant Liberal Party, the mysterious death of General Benjamin Hill, and criticism of the new administration by members of the Chamber of Deputies suggested considerable disagreement within the ranks of the ruling elite.

Outside the halls of government, popular demonstrations challenging Obregón's regime erupted in the streets. On the night of May 13, 1921, for example, an assemblage of about 150 people gathered outside the legislative chamber and then stormed the hall chanting, "Long live the Russian Revolution, long live Bolshevism!" Once inside, the crowd decked the room with red-and-black flags and planted themselves near the speaker's platform. This event caused many legislators to lash out at cabinet ministers de la Huerta and Calles, claiming that they had somehow encouraged radical movements and antipatriotic socialist propaganda. Not only did Obregón and his circle face internal criticism but, to make matters worse, Mexico's troubled diplomatic relations with the United States complicated elite plans for national reconstruction.[5]

The Quest for Diplomatic Recognition

The Obregón government had taken power at a time when members of the U.S. Department of State were turning a deaf ear to Mexican diplomats. Reestablishment of official recognition hinged significantly, as it had in preceding years under Carranza, on the issue of oil rights. Specifically, many in the United States wondered how Article 27 of the 1917 Constitution, which declared Mexico's right to subsoil resources, would be applied by the new president. Since Carranza's administration, powerful elements in Washington had been working behind the scenes to monitor and, if necessary, to influence the course of Mexican affairs.

Throughout the first part of 1921, State Department officials in the newly elected Harding administration maintained that Mexico would be required to meet what they saw as "its obligations." The U.S. press speculated that if Obregón did not abolish Article 27, Harding's attitude toward his neighbor to the south would be tough or "exactly the opposite of the policy pursued by President Wilson."[6] On June 7, Secretary of State Charles Evans Hughes held a press conference and indicated the terms under which U.S. diplomatic recognition of Mexico could be achieved. For the United States, the main issue had to do with property rights. Here, Hughes claimed that the Mexican Constitution challenged "the foundations of international intercourse."[7] To remedy this, the secretary proposed a "Treaty of Amity and Commerce" intended to secure the protection of U.S. investments. In his offer, Hughes indicated that if Mexicans agreed to the terms, official recognition would subsequently take place.[8] Although he did not reveal the full conditions of the treaty, the Mexican press soon responded with harsh criticism.

Eventually, Obregón rejected the advance on the grounds that his administration had indicated that they would not agree, under any circumstances, to a treaty before the new government had been officially recognized.[9] On this point he had written to President Warren Harding early in May 1921 saying, "When diplomatic relations have been completely restored it will be timely and appropriate to enter into an agreement with the United States."[10] For Obregón, any discussion

DQ: What impact has U.S. foreign policy / intervention had on Mexico?

[handwritten annotation: With such political turmoil/turnover, why do tenants believe that presidents can/will listen to their pleas? The people are not the ones overthrowing their gov't.]

regarding property rights, claims commissions, and the settlement of debt would be considered only after the United States granted recognition. In August, Obregón again wrote to Harding suggesting that a meeting could be held between the two sides and an agreement made without a treaty.[11] For the United States, however, the treaty had to come first. At this point, the dialogue stalled. Meanwhile, Obregón's attention to oil diplomacy had neglected various political issues at home.

"Experimental Laboratories"

Shortly after the Sonorans' triumph in spring 1920, Francisco Múgica, Lucio Blanco, Marciano González, Miguel Alemán, Alberto Salinas, Cándido Aguilar, and other generals—many of them formerly loyal to Carranza—began a conspiracy to overthrow Obregón. Declaring, in his Plan de Saltillo, a desire to "restore constitutional order," Múgica called Obregón a "usurper" and set out to overthrow the president. After a brief offensive against federal forces, however, Múgica's rebellion crumbled and the upstart general fled to Texas. Meantime, other rebel groups also sought to challenge Obregón's rule. From a base in northern Guatemala, Cándido Aguilar led a force that launched a series of attacks in the state of Tabasco.[12] Obregón usually responded to these acts with quick, often brutal repression, but the outbreak of minor rebellions made it clear that the government in Mexico City faced growing opposition. Thus, to strengthen his control over the country, Obregón looked to the states.

Whereas Carranza had resorted to bribing regional leaders to keep them loyal, Obregón assumed "an uneasy truce" with those men who had been working to build their own political bases.[13] Given the relatively high degree of political autonomy in the provinces, Obregón was required to negotiate. Describing the political situation that this accommodation produced, Thomas Benjamin writes:

> Within this political framework, the reformers and radicals used the power of state government to patronize (and in some cases, to arm) labor and campesino organizations; employed reform to mobilize popular support; established mass-based political parties; and attempted to redress the social and economic injustices that persisted after ten years of intermittent social revolution and civil war.[14]

In effect, Mexico's regions in the 1920s became, as radical journalist Carleton Beals called them, "experimental laboratories [where,] for the first time in history, a fundamentally new method of social control" had evolved.[15] During Obregón's administration this new atmosphere encouraged the rise of several populist governors who, while often loyal to the president, also pursued independent political goals. At the grassroots level, the relationship between the central government and state reformist regimes helped create important political opportunities for local organizers. In Veracruz, this situation was aided by the populist politics of Governor Adalberto Tejeda.

Prominent Reformist Regimes during the Obregón-Calles Presidencies, 1920–1928

State	Governor	Period
Chiapas	Carlos Vidal	1925–1927
Jalisco	José Guadalupe Zuno	1922–1926
Michoacán	Francisco I. Múgica	1920–1922
San Luis Potosí	Aurelio Manrique	1920–1922
Tabasco	Tomás Garrido Canabal	1922–1926
Tamaulipas	Emilio Portes Gil	1925–1928
Veracruz	Adalberto Tejeda	1920–1924
Yucatán	Felipe Carrillo Puerto	1922–1924

Source: Thomas Benjamin, "Laboratories of the New State, 1920–29," in Thomas Benjamin and Mark Wasserman, eds., *Provinces of the Revolution: Essays on Regional Mexican History, 1910–1929* (Albuquerque: University of New Mexico Press, 1990), 74.

The Rise of Adalberto Tejeda

The inauguration of Colonel Adalberto Tejeda as governor of Veracruz in December 1920 brought a new type of actor to the state political stage. Although largely beholden to Obregón, Tejeda wasted no time in setting an independent agenda, forging alliances with popular groups while establishing a system of patronage articulated through the state bureaucracy.[16] Like other revolutionary caudillos at the time, including José María Sánchez in Puebla, Saturnillo Cedillo in San Luis Potosí, and Felipe Carrillo Puerto in Yucatán, Tejeda developed techniques and programs in the early 1920s that the official national party would also eventually employ in their quest to reconsolidate federal power.

Soon after taking office, the new Veracruz governor began building a broad political base by courting labor, peasant, and tenant groups. The new politics employed by the Tejeda administration showed greater tolerance of popular organizing and mutually empowered the governor and grassroots associations. This political arrangement helped prepare the way for unprecedented social ferment in the state.[17] As Mexican historian Mario Gill comments, "The arrival of Tejeda began an era of dramatic and desperate popular struggles . . . unique in the history of Mexico."[18]

Early in Tejeda's career, many in the state had seen him as an ally of the working classes. As an enthusiastic participant in the revolution, he had envisioned a gradual transition to socialism while still respecting the traditions, customs, and values of working people. With his first legislative efforts as governor, Tejeda attracted popular support as well as sharp criticism from political and commercial elites. The subsequent dividing of the Veracruz political scene provided a critical opening for grassroots organizers.

Adalberto Tejeda had not participated in the various political battles in the state before 1913, but Victoriano Huerta's coup d'état in February and the subsequent assassination of President Francisco Madero pushed him into the conflict. His first action was to form a volunteer corps in his native Chicontepec in February 1913. The following December, he enlisted in the Constitutionalist army and established close connections with revolutionary generals Cándido Aguilar and Heriberto Jara.[19] With their support, Tejeda quickly became a rising star on the Veracruz political scene. Together, the three men would dominate the state for years to come.

In early 1916, Tejeda's political idealism and desire for national self-determination reached new heights when the fear of a North American invasion spread throughout Mexico. A few months earlier, Pancho Villa's attack on Columbus, New Mexico, had caused President Wilson to send U.S. forces into northern Mexico.[20] Responding to Villa's action, many in Washington, including Senator Albert Fall, lobbied for a full-scale invasion to protect U.S. investments.[21]

To Tejeda and other revolutionary leaders, the two countries appeared close to war during spring and summer 1916. If armed conflict broke out, it seemed logical that his home turf—the northern Veracruz oil region—would be one of the first areas targeted for North American occupation. Responding to the perceived threat of "Yankee imperialism," Tejeda had written to President Carranza: "Careful, Citizen Carranza! From today and for always the fate of the nation . . . requires us to think carefully about the meaning of patriotism [and the] pain brought by the invincible and immortal revolution. Citizen Carranza, we [stand to] suffer more from what has followed [the years of fighting]. We salute you and ask you to think about this."[22]

Tejeda, in fact, had sent those under his command to prepare against a possible North American invasion in communities throughout northern Veracruz. Additionally, he gathered a force of approximately thirteen hundred men to protect and, if necessary, destroy the oil wells in the region.[23] A communication with one of his commanders during this time reflects his sense of urgency: "A war with the United States has been declared and in these moments all Mexicans should take up arms in defense against the unjust Yankee aggression. . . . A large number of citizens in this area have been called and are prepared to burn all the oil wells in Tuxpan."[24]

Maintaining a high political profile during summer and fall 1916, Tejeda was elected as a delegate to the Constitutionalist convention in Querétaro for the district of Chicontepec along with the Porfirian intellectual Justo Sierra. The death of his mother, however, prevented him from attending. Not long out of the political spotlight, he reentered the scene in March 1917 to serve as state senator in the National Congress. There, he would continue to distinguish himself as a staunch defender of Mexico's oil reserves as he spoke out against granting concessions to foreigners. While serving his legislative term, he took an active part in debates regarding the application of Article 27. And as a member of the National Petroleum Commission, he engaged in heated discussions over the issue of U.S. and English oil company influence. Tejeda's position on the oil question impressed those who felt that foreign businesses in the past had exploited Mexican oil. Years later, one of Tejeda's biographers idealized his patriotic stance: "Oil exploitation in Mexico by foreign companies, as everywhere, represents a particularly bleak episode in the nation's history. The abuses by these companies, the threats, the rip-offs, the crimes, and the lack of respect for authority and national sovereignty are well known. Adalberto Tejeda, with patriotism and dignity, naturally confronted the thieves of our subsoil. With this, the foreigners had no doubt about his love for Mexico."[25]

While many throughout the country acknowledged that foreigners earned large profits from Mexican oil, only a handful of revolutionary elites, including Tejeda, considered the issue in terms so decidedly nationalistic.[26] In particular, the Veracruz senator, along with several other lawyers and engineers who took a radical stand against foreign oil, claimed they opposed the companies because their managers appeared unconcerned about the long-range environmental and economic interests of the nation.[27] On this score, Tejeda argued passionately in favor of restricting U.S. and English oil company control in Mexico.

In fact, when the Congress passed legislation on the oil issue in late 1919, many felt that the National Petroleum Commission had failed to address the matter adequately. Some even accused certain senators of working on behalf of the foreign oil companies. Others, including Tejeda, distanced themselves from Carranza's moderate position and appealed to the Senate for tight controls. Tejeda made the following appeal:

In Romania, Russia, and other petroleum-rich countries, oil has been the object of national dominion. In the United States the same has also been true. Proof of this can be found in the fact that in the United States there are laws and taxes imposed on the oil industry that are much more significant than what is being proposed here with the Executive Project. Let me remind you of the urgent necessity that the nation and industry have in these [proposed] regulations, . . . which will define once and for all, reasonably and fairly, the rights of [the nation over these resources]. With this initiative, we will, in the eyes of the world, maintain our moral and economic control.[28]

Adalberto Tejeda (*center*). *Courtesy of AGEV*

Yet despite Tejeda's passionate rhetoric, a renewed threat of military conflict with the United States forced him to back off in late 1919.[29] Nevertheless, he remained committed to the idea of full national control over oil resources. This stand would soon gain him the reputation among foreign diplomats and businessmen of being a troublemaker. One letter, written by the British consul in Tuxpan, described Tejeda as "the aggressive and rude type of Mexican [who] possesse[s] a strong character [and seems] extremely anti-foreign."[30]

To many, however, he was a hero. The following year, Tejeda made use of his recent notoriety in his campaign for governor. When former governor and loyal *carrancista* Cándido Aguilar fled the country in June

1920, General Guadalupe Sánchez took it upon himself to propose three candidates for provisional governor of Veracruz to Obregón. These included Adalberto Palacios, Tomás Barragán, and Antonio Nava.[31] Obregón soon chose Nava for the temporary job, but exactly who would become governor on December 1, 1920, remained undecided.

By July 1920, Adalberto Tejeda and rival state *políticos* Gabriel Gavira and Jacobo Rincón had emerged as the three official candidates for governor. For his part, Tejeda's passionate stance against the foreign oil companies had made him one of the most promising young politicians in the state. Sixteen years older than the Veracruz senator, Gavira, a well-known *maderista*, enjoyed greater prestige and political connections and had campaigned for the governorship in both 1911 and 1917.[32] Like Gavira, Jacobo Rincón hailed from Orizaba but differed in that his support came largely from the old Porfirian elites: large landowners, businessmen, foreigners, and the clergy.[33]

Considering the field, Guadalupe Sánchez soon lent his support to Tejeda as the Veracruz Liberal Party candidate for governor. Some believed that Gavira should have been selected by the party, but the expectation that the new governor would remain loyal to Obregón favored Tejeda.[34] Yet despite the backing of Sánchez, Tejeda also needed the help of other important figures in the state. Winning this support meant courting influential veracruzanos living in Mexico City as well as long-time associates Heriberto Jara and porteño congressman Enrique Meza—each of whom commanded important constituencies.

Setting out on the campaign trail that summer, Tejeda thus faced several major obstacles. One important matter had to do with the fact that regional caudillo Manuel Peláez enjoyed a tremendous influence over the Huasteca region. Lack of campaign funds constituted another problem. Attending to this matter, Tejeda quickly solicited contributions from businessmen in the region in return for assurances that they would be compensated with positions in his administration. Meanwhile, the thorny issue of Paláez would have to wait.

At the request of Antonio Nava, state congressmen set state elections for August 8, 1920. Trouble soon began, however, as supporters of Gavira called for the dissolution of the Veracruz legislature as well as Nava's provisional governorship. Both, they claimed, had essentially become promotional tools for Tejeda. In the wake of these complaints, acting president Adolfo de la Huerta requested that Nava travel to Mexico City in early August. Quickly, de la Huerta replaced Nava with the president of the state legislature, Gabriel Garzón Cossa, as provisional governor one day before the state election was to be held.[35] The following day, a judge in Mexico City determined that the Veracruz contest be called off altogether. At first, federal intervention appeared to work against Tejeda. Soon, however, it became clear that, with Garzón Cossa's support, the former senator's campaign would proceed as planned. Shortly thereafter, state officials rescheduled the election for September 5.

When the election results finally appeared in October, a sharp division in the state legislature between *tejedistas* and followers of Rincón and Gavira (who had since formed an alliance) emerged with the former enjoying only a slight advantage. Divided into rival factions, the legislature soon split. On October 12 the Veracruz newspaper *El Dictamen* reported that there were "definitely two legislatures operating in Jalapa: the tejedistas in the legislative chamber and the *rincón-gaviristas* in the main auditorium of City Hall." Each side turned to Mexico City for help as politicians from the state swarmed into the nation's capital with the hope of gaining formal recognition from federal officials. On October 9 a group of Tejeda supporters talked with Subsecretary of Government José Inocente Lugo, who apparently reassured them that "there was no conflict."[36] Then, a few days later, Obregón surprised everyone by getting involved.

Hoping to neutralize the influence of Rincón and the more conservative elements in the state, Obregón called for the installation of a new state congress without the rincónistas. This move gave Tejeda the necessary leverage to force an agreement with the gaviristas by offering them control of the Orizaba district while at the same time gaining a slight majority in the legislature. Initially, Gavira protested vehemently but eventually gave in. Shortly thereafter, the state electoral commission verified the victory by announcing that Tejeda had defeated Gavira by over ten thousand votes.[37]

It soon became clear, however, that Tejeda had entered the governor's office "despite the profound doubt of the military commander [in the region] as well as the Sonoran caudillo" and only because countless friends, loyal officials, and powerful politicians had rallied to his defense.[38] Historians Romana Falcón and Soledad García Morales note that Tejeda's "candidacy had been reduced to a personalistic platform sustained by those professional politicians, countrymen, friends, and certain leaders who were disposed to be loyal, for a time." Furthermore, "neither Tejeda nor any of the other contenders [had] made their political program or any other ideological ideas the heart of their campaign. These factors were relegated to a secondary level in spite of the marked ideological differences between some of the rivals."[39] While minor conflicts had broken out in Orizaba and the port over the decision, many in Veracruz remained unconcerned with the election results.[40] Soon, however, new populist policies initiated by Tejeda would turn the state political scene upside down.

Divided Regional Elites

With the help of federal troops ordered by Adolfo de la Huerta, the new governor assumed power on December 1, 1920. Yet while officials in Mexico City helped secure Tejeda's position in Jalapa, the larger situation in Veracruz required that he co-exist peacefully with regional caudillos Guadalupe Sánchez and Manuel Peláez. Realizing this kind of near-impossible balance, however, would prove difficult. Soon after Tejeda took office he replaced Enrique Soto as state treasurer and the tension between Tejeda and Sánchez began to grow. Recommended by Sánchez, Soto had been appointed provisionally to the state government while officials settled the election controversy. But Tejeda chose three other candidates for the job. He defended his choices by suggesting that Soto had acted in an "inappropriate manner" that favored the "excesses of past regimes."[41] Careful not to offend the general, Tejeda wrote an appeasing letter to Sánchez on December 29 in which he tried to make clear that the rejection of Soto represented, in no way, a criticism of him: "I profoundly regret this incident [especially after] I have tried time and again to maintain harmony between all the elements of the administration, to realize all the responsibilities of my office charged as a trusted servant of the state. After [reading] these words, you will surely understand [my] good intention[s]."[42] Yet while this communication gave the impression of a tenuous peace between the two men, friction would continue to build in the coming months. Working to keep Sánchez in his favor was only one part of Tejeda's approach to consolidating power in the Huasteca. He also had to manage *peláecista* control in the area. At the federal level, Obregón and de la Huerta treated Peláez with a certain degree of respect. This situation created a dilemma for Tejeda.

To challenge Peláez, the governor gathered support from other powerful individuals in Mexico City. He began by trying to win the confidence of Veracruz senator Heriberto Jara. Tejeda wrote to Jara criticizing the poor conditions in which Peláez had left oil workers' camps in the Huasteca. He pointed out that many of these areas had become "true centers of vice where alcohol and prostitution abound. Municipal officials have not been able to enforce their authority to bring an end to this disorder. [Instead] the petroleum companies have paid peláecistas [to patrol] the mining camps, enforcing the will of the companies by threat rather than safeguarding the interests of the workers."[43]

Curiously, Tejeda's complaint fell on deaf ears. The new governor then attempted to persuade the minister of war, General Enrique Estrada, to send a military force into the region with the goal of installing loyal municipal officials and removing several generals from their posts. Yet without the support of de la Huerta and Obregón, who both refused to confront Peláez, Tejeda's proposal went nowhere.

Eventually, tension between Tejeda and Peláez escalated to the point where, in June 1921, a group of peláecistas took up arms against the governor. Peláez, who at that point was living in the United States, justified these actions to President Obregón by claiming that Tejeda represented a threat to "peace in the region" as well as the central government.[44] While the governor's forces eventually succeeded in neutralizing the peláecista uprising, the conflict gave a clear indication of the political battle lines being drawn throughout Veracruz early in the governor's term.[45]

In addition to these caudillo politics, landowners and other disgruntled local elites made their dissatisfaction with Tejeda known. Shortly after his taking office, forces hostile to the governor in the Huasteca harassed state authorities and renewed efforts to regain control over territory that they believed had once been theirs before the revolution.[46] Complicating matters was the fact that Tejeda faced continuing challenges from former gubernatorial candidates Gabriel Gavira and Jacobo Rincón as well as Veracruz senator Manlio Fabio Altamirano. At the same time, Tejeda was forced to confront challenges posed by a nationwide economic recession.[47] His response to a difficult situation was to look for new ways to secure his position, and he began by establishing his own state security force to collect information on "suspects," municipal governments, and political rivals.

From the beginning, Tejeda set out to increase his autonomy by solidifying political ties throughout the state at the local level. Specifically, he concentrated on city and town councils (*ayuntamientos*), where he did not hesitate to use his personal influence and, if necessary, employ a "creative" tallying of votes to secure his preferred candidate. Here, Tejeda used this technique to such a degree that by the end of the first six months of his term, over half of the state's mayors and town councils had been replaced with individuals loyal to the new administration in Jalapa.[48]

Not surprisingly, many local officials resisted these impositions by the governor. Protests on the part of politicians ousted by Tejeda in the towns of Puerto México, Huatusco, Tuxpan, San Juan Evangelista, and the port of Veracruz demonstrated the highly contested political climate in Veracruz. Many in the Orizaba area, for example, professed their loyalty to Cándido Aguilar while others supported Gavira and Rincón. In the port, businessmen, local officials, and other influential elites expressed a clear dislike for Tejeda's politics.

Early in 1921, members of the Chamber of Commerce (Cámara de Comercio) and the Property Owners' Association (Unión de Propietarios), as well as the editors of *El Dictamen*, found themselves in common cause against the governor. As the year progressed, the paper increasingly voiced strong criticisms of Tejeda. On various occasions they attacked the governor by calling him an "agitator," a "cannibal," a "man without culture," and "incompetent," all the while deriding him in their editorials. To counter opposition from the editors at *El Dictamen* as well as other hostile elites in Veracruz, Tejeda soon launched a major campaign to appeal to the state's popular classes.

Building a Political Base

Tejeda set out to win the support of popular groups, supplementing the kind of patriotic pronouncements he had become known for during his career as a senator with the establishment of new social policies. In the countryside, he began to work closely with peasant organizers. Responding to requests from rural organizers (*agraristas*), he bolstered the state's civil guard and quickly made it his own protective force independent of Guadalupe Sánchez. But first he had to remove Abraham Sánchez, the older brother of Guadalupe, who remained in command of the guard. When Tejeda proposed the appointment of two of his longtime associates, Enrique Hernández and J. Araiza, Sánchez stepped down from his post and Tejeda's men took charge.

Then, working to harness the power of organized labor in Veracruz, Tejeda made strong overtures to win their backing through legislative action. Only five days after taking office, Tejeda sent a profit-sharing bill (Ley de Utilidades) to the Veracruz legislature. The measure, a revision of a 1918 state labor law initially drafted by former governor Cándido Aguilar, stipulated that, after working for one year, each laborer would receive approximately one month's additional salary from his employer.[49] Supervision of this process would be entrusted to local commissions under the guidance of the state labor relations board (Junta Central de Conciliación y Arbitraje). Yet, although Tejeda provided additional details that sought to guard against excessive action being taken by either "Capital or Labor," many opposed him passionately on the initiative.

Some legislators denounced the bill as "Bolshevik Communism" while *El Dictamen* quickly dubbed the measure the "Hunger Law," which, they argued, "would bring the ruin of industry and commerce."[50] An editorial noting the governor's presence at a workers meeting in Jalapa in March sarcastically asked whether Tejeda wanted to turn Veracruz into "another soviet."[51] Opposing voices were heard continually while the governor and legislature debated the proposed law during spring 1921.[52]

In June and early July, public debate grew more intense both inside and outside of Veracruz. A representative of a Mexico City law firm, for example, argued against the measure in a letter to Obregón, stating that it "created a grave situation [especially since] no other state has proposed such a law."[53] The writer went on to suggest that "a solution to labor's problems should be sought without injuring the interests of capital."[54] Other businessmen wrote to the president, suggesting that Tejeda's proposal be withdrawn from consideration.[55] Two representatives in the state legislature published a letter in *El Dictamen* that argued that the proposed law "would encourage capital flight to other states thereby endangering the needed economic growth in Veracruz."[56] Thus, while lawmakers continued to discuss the matter, any sort of compromise agreement appeared out of reach.[57] Then, in a surprise move, the legislature approved the bill on July 6, 1921. In response, business interests moved quickly to block its implementation.

Employers in Veracruz filed *amparos*, legal actions comparable to "writs of relief" in other countries and guaranteed under Articles 14 and 16 of the Constitution.[58] Many argued that Tejeda's profit-sharing law violated their right to private property. More specifically, they objected strongly to a section that required them to compensate their workers retroactively from 1917. After considering arguments against the Veracruz Ley de Utilidades, the Supreme Court granted a temporary restraining order that blocked application of the law. Even President Obregón defended the court's actions by declaring in a communication to Tejeda that "the sovereignty of the Court and the Constitution must be respected."[59] He suggested the law favored only a "small minority" and proposed instead the addition of a moderate worker-security measure to existing labor legislation.[60] *El Dictamen* added fuel to the fire a few weeks later by claiming, "It is certain that the application of this law will leave the state without industry and commerce or at the very least a reduction in these areas to the most rudimentary level. These losses will affect all the inhabitants of the state."[61] At the same time, several national elite groups added their voices. Members of the Industrialists Association (Cámara de Indus-triales) and the National Chamber of Commerce met with Alvaro Obregón to discuss the matter. They told the president that if an imme-diate resolution in their favor could not be negotiated, they would move their factories and businesses out of Veracruz. In response, Obregón insisted that Tejeda reach a settlement with business owners. Strongly disagreeing, the governor told Obregón that he saw insufficient rea-son to revise the law. Representatives from the textile industry in Orizaba, Tejeda pointed out, had failed to appear at the negotiating table.

Employers in Veracruz successfully circumvented the governor's program by creating various ad hoc committees in the port, Orizaba, Córdoba, and Jalapa. Hundreds of others throughout the state, includ-ing many hotel, restaurant, and small-business owners, also rallied against the law. Further complicating matters for Tejeda, opposition in the press continued unabated during summer 1921 and support in the legislature dwindled. By late 1921, nearly 130 amparos had been granted by the Supreme Court. In the end, Tejeda's first major piece of legisla-tion, and his first significant populist appeal in Veracruz, had been successfully frustrated through the combined efforts of industrial and commercial elites. Soon, the governor would take on the problem of popular housing in the hope of solidifying his base of political support.

Tejeda and the Housing Situation

After Governor Antonio Nava's reversal of 1917 housing reform legis-lation that limited rent increases, popular concern regarding housing issues grew. Porteño Juan Sánchez and several other citizens, for ex-ample, had written Nava in protest. In his letter, Sánchez complained that the burning of tenements during the city's bout with the bubonic plague in summer 1920 had compounded the housing problem. Given these difficult circumstances, he argued, Nava's changes to the rent law constituted "unjustified and shameful" acts.[62] In August 1920 the Mexico City newspaper *El Universal* noted that rents after Nava's de-cree in the port "exceeded those in the interior of the country."[63] Soon, in considering what appeared to be a growing problem with popular housing in several Veracruz cities, Tejeda began to deal with some of these grievances.

One letter to Tejeda, signed by over one hundred residents of Veracruz, complained that the city's streets, sewers, jails, cemeteries,

Patio scene, early 1920s. *Courtesy of Rocke-*
feller Archive Center

hospitals, markets, and slaughter-house lay "in a shameful state of disrepair" and represented "a public disgrace."[64] At the same time, Tejeda learned that the Veracruz City Council had also heard many complaints from the public as well as sanitation officials regarding the "bad state" of tenements in the port.[65]

Tejeda also received complaints about landlords. Citizens asked that the governor take action against certain individuals who, tenants felt, mercilessly charged them exorbitant rents.[66] During July, Veracruz mayor Salvador Campa forwarded complaints to Tejeda about the Cuban brothers Manuel and Antonio Cangas and indicated that the city had previously issued warnings to several landlords and administrators but their abuses continued.[67] In response, Tejeda helped to coordinate legal action against the Cangas brothers.

By the beginning of 1922 not only the governor but also many throughout the state knew of the substandard housing conditions that

Laundry drying on patio, early 1920s. *Courtesy of Rockefeller Archive Center*

existed in urban Veracruz. Soon, residents in the port would engage in a more militant wave of collective action as a way to do something about the situation. Their protest began shortly after the inauguration of Worker Party mayor Rafael "El Negro" García in January 1922.

Notes

1. This point follows Doug McAdam's definition of social movements as "rational attempts by excluded groups to mobilize sufficient political leverage to advance collective interests through noninstitutional means." McAdam, *Political Process and the Development of Black Insurgency, 1930–1970* (Chicago: University of Chicago Press), 37.

2. John F. Dulles, *Yesterday in Mexico: A Chronicle of the Revolution, 1919–1936* (Austin: University of Texas Press, 1961), 33.

3. Ibid., 36.

4. Quoted in Anita Brenner, *The Wind That Swept Mexico: The History of the Mexican Revolution of 1910–1942* (1943; reprint, Austin: University of Texas Press, 1993), 60.

5. Dulles, *Yesterday in Mexico*, 127–28, 132.

6. *Washington Post*, March 8, 1921. Quoted in Donald C. Baldridge, *Mexican Petroleum and United States-Mexican Relations, 1919–1923* (New York: Garland, 1987), 170. On Obregón's response, see Narcisco Bassols Batalla, *El pensamiento político de Alvaro Obregón* (Mexico City: Editorial Nuestro Tiempo, 1967).

7. Baldridge, *Mexican Petroleum*, 174.

8. Ibid.

9. Ibid., 175.

10. Ibid., 176.

11. Obregón to Harding, August 18, 1921. Quoted in ibid., 179.

12. On Aguilar during this period, see Ricardo Corzo Ramírez et al., *Nunca un desleal: Cándido Aguilar, 1889–1960* (Mexico City: Colegio de México/Gobierno del Estado de Veracruz, 1986), 245–51.

13. Ibid., 74.

14. Thomas Benjamin, "Regional Social Reform and Mass Politics," in *Provinces of the Revolution: Essays on Regional Mexican History, 1910–1929*, ed. Thomas Benjamin and Mark Wasserman (Albuquerque: University of New Mexico Press, 1990), 73.

15. Ibid. On the relationship between Obregón and the states, see Randall G. Hansis, "Alvaro Obregón: The Mexican Revolution and the Politics of Consolidation, 1920–1924" (Ph.D. diss., University of New Mexico, 1971), 54–56.

16. Heather-Fowler Salamini, "Revolutionary Caudillos in the 1920s: Francisco Múgica and Adalberto Tejeda," in *Caudillo and Peasant in the Mexican Revolution*, ed. David Brading (Cambridge: Cambridge University Press, 1980), 190–91.

17. This section draws on Romana Falcón and Soledad García Morales, *La semilla en el surco: Adalberto Tejeda y el radicalismo en Veracruz, 1883–1960* (Mexico City: Colegio de México, 1986).

18. Mario Gill, "Veracruz: Revolución y extremismo," *Historia Mexicana* 2, no. 4 (April–July 1953): 618.

19. On the political career of Jara, see Silvia González Marín, *Heriberto Jara: Un luchador obrero en la revolución mexicana, 1879–1917* (Mexico City: Sociedad Cooperativa Publicaciones, 1984).

20. On the attack and U.S. dealings with Villa, see Friedrich Katz, "Pancho Villa and the Attack on Columbus, New Mexico," *American Historical Review* 83, no. 1 (February 1978): 101–30.

21. Lorenzo Meyer, *Mexico and the United States, 1917–1942* (Austin: University of Texas Press, 1977), 53.

22. Quoted in Falcón and García Morales, *La semilla*, 98.

23. The fact that independent caudillo Manuel Peláez controlled much of the oil zone complicated things, however. On his role in the region, see Soledad García Morales, "Manuel Peláez y Guadalupe Sánchez: Dos caciques regionales," *La Palabra y El Hombre* 67, no. 1 (January–March 1989): 126.

24. Adalberto Tejeda to Higinio Melgoza, June 18, 1916. Quoted in Falcón and García Morales, *La semilla*, 99.

25. Angel J. Hermida Rúiz in *Adalberto Tejeda Olivares: Dimensión del hombre*, ed. Miguel Bustos Cerecedo (Jalapa: Author's edition, 1983), 90.

26. On nationalist ferment related to the oil question, see Alan Knight, *U.S.-Mexican Relations, 1910–1940: An Interpretation* (San Diego: Center of U.S.-Mexican Studies, 1987), 203–4.

27. On economic nationalism and the oil question, see Jonathan Brown, *Oil and Revolution in Mexico* (Berkeley: University of California Press, 1993).

28. "Discusión en la H. Cámara de Senadores del proyecto de ley del petroleo presentado por el C. Senador Tejeda, Sesión del día 10 de octubre 1919," in Secretaría de Industria, Comercio y Trabajo, *Documentos relacionados con la legislación petrolera mexicana* (Mexico City: Talleres Gráficos de la Nación, 1922), 655–66.

29. On the 1919 intervention crisis, see Manuel A. Machado and James T. Judge, "Tempest in a Teapot? The Mexican-U.S. Intervention Crisis of 1919," *Southwestern Historical Quarterly* 74 (July 1970): 1–23.

30. British Viceconsul in Tuxpan to Hohler, April 26, 1916. Quoted in Falcón and García Morales, *La semilla*, 97–98.

31. Ibid., 110.

32. Ibid., 112.

33. Ibid.

34. Ibid.

35. *El Dictamen*, August 9, 1920.

36. Falcón and García Morales, *La semilla*, 118.

37. *El Dictamen*, October 17 and 27, 1920.

38. Falcón and García Morales, *La semilla*, 119.

39. Ibid.

40. Ibid., 120.

41. Tejeda to Guadalupe Sánchez, December 22, 1920. Quoted in ibid., 122.

42. Ibid.

43. Adalberto Tejeda to Heriberto Jara, December 13, 1920. Quoted in García Morales, "Manuel Peláez y Guadalupe Sánchez," 130.

44. Peláez to Obregón, June 29, 1921. Quoted in Falcón and García Morales, *La semilla*, 131.

45. A telegram from Calles to Obregón on June 25, 1921, reassured the president that rumors of continued rebellion in the Huasteca were inaccurate and that things "were under control." Calles to Obregón, June 25, 1921, AGN, Obregón-Calles, 101-RI-H.

46. Ibid.

47. Tejeda's first address to the legislature on May 5, 1920, clearly indicated a strong desire to stabilize the economic condition of Veracruz. See Adal-

berto Tejeda, "Informe que rinde el ejecutivo del estado libre y soberano de Veracruz-Llave ante La H. Legislatura del mismo por el período comprendido del 16 del octubre de 1920 al 5 de mayo de 1921," in *Estado de Veracruz: Informes de sus gobernadores, 1826–1986*, ed. Carmen Blázquez Domínguez (Jalapa: Gobierno del Estado de Veracruz, 1986), 10:5423.

48. Falcón and García Morales, *La semilla*, 124–25.

49. The 1918 Veracruz Labor Law provided the most immediate legal precedents to Tejeda's bill but did not provide for their implementation and enforcement. My discussion of the Ley de Utilidades controversy follows Olivia Domínguez Pérez, *Política y movimientos sociales en el tejedismo* (Jalapa: Universidad Veracruzana, 1986), 40–45.

50. *El Dictamen*, December 26, March 9, 1921.

51. Ibid., March 11, 1920.

52. On May 11 legislation requiring the observance of an eight-hour day went into effect throughout the state. Ibid., May 10, 1920.

53. AGN, Obregón-Calles, 243-VI-L-2. July 25, 1921.

54. Ibid.

55. See, for example, Cámara Industriales de los Estados Unidos Mexicanos, Mexico City, to Obregón, July 7, 1921, and Cámara Nacional de Comercio de La Comarca Lagunera, Torreón, Coahuila, to Obregón, August 5, 1921, AGN, Obregón-Calles, 243-V-L-2. At the same time, several labor groups encouraged Obregón to support the law. A sampling includes Pedro Ipiña and Florencio Chávez, secretaries of the Sindicato de Obreros y Campesinos, Santo Nino, Coahuila, to Obregón and Dionisio Montelongo, Confederación Regional Obrera Mexicana, Santa Ana del Pilar, Coahuila, September 21, 1921, AGN, Obregón-Calles, 243-V-L-2. Some, observing Tejeda's obvious move to court labor, reported back to Obregón on the governor's attendance at worker gatherings. General Fortunato Mailotte, Head of Military Operations in Puebla, to Obregón, August 31, 1921, AGN, Obregón-Calles, 243-V-L-2.

56. *El Dictamen*, July 2, 1920.

57. Ibid., June 18, July 1, 1921.

58. The identity and number of several businesses who joined in this effort are revealed in the records of the Junta Central de Concilación y Arbitraje de Veracruz at the AGEV.

59. Quoted in Domínguez Pérez, *Política*, 45.

60. Later, the Court decided that the issue would be better resolved by somehow adding the workable aspects of Tejeda's proposals to existing labor legislation.

61. *El Dictamen*, July 21, 1921.

62. Juan L. Sánchez to Antonio Nava, August 2, 1920, AGEV, gobernación, 1920. As part of an effort to eliminate the epidemic, officials had also closed the port in late May 1920 and required residents to be vaccinated. *El Dictamen*, May 31, 1920. Armando Solorzano notes that in 1920, U.S. President Woodrow Wilson had offered to contribute $50,000 "to improve the city's sanitary conditions and combat bubonic plague," which officials rejected. Armando Solorzano, "The Rockefeller Foundation in Revolutionary Mexico: Yellow Fever in Yucatán and Veracruz," in *Missionaries of Science: The Rockefeller Foundation in Latin America*, ed. Marcos Cueto (Bloomington: Indiana University Press, 1994), 54.

63. *El Universal*, August 1, 1920.

64. Petition from residents in the port to Adalberto Tejeda, December 12, 1920, AGEV, gobernación, box 504.

65. See Veracruz City Council records of August 26, 1921, where a representative of the Dirección General de Salubridad registered complaints about patios San Carlos and Castilla, and on September 2, where a similar official discussed public health code violations at patios La Geralda, La Ciudad de Roma, La Gloria, and La Pastora.

66. Residents of patio San Ulpiano to Governor Tejeda, June 18, 1921, AGEV, gobernación, 1921.

67. Ibid.

4

"¡Denle caballo!"
The Emergence of Tenant Protest

I am on strike and am not paying rent.
This is the law of Herón Proal:
To whoever pays rent I will "give the horse"
So that they won't pay rent again.
—Protest song of Veracruz tenants

In late 1921 porteños elected the well-known labor organizer and stevedore Rafael García as mayor of Veracruz. Under the banner of the Veracruz Worker's Party (Partido de Trabajo), the victorious García took the stage in the city's Principal Theater for the inauguration ceremony. As hundreds packed inside the building to watch, they saw the new mayor accept the national flag and the keys to the city and proclaim the "victory of the working people of Veracruz." In his address, he called on porteños to join together and stand up for their rights as patriotic citizens: "We are charged with the spirit of the revolution to combat the problems the city has struggled with for so long. The people, too many times deceived by those who claim to represent them, have now demonstrated their power with incomparable force. The working people of Veracruz have won and, if we continue to be well organized, we will never lose power. Veracruzanos are not a conquered people."[1]

García's address had a powerful appeal. His promise to work as a loyal and patriotic servant of the people under the law inspired many in the city to view their local government in a new light. For the first time in Veracruz, ordinary men and women were being heralded as true patriots.[2] This chapter discusses the rise of a new popular politics in Veracruz and the founding of the Revolutionary Syndicate of Tenants under the leadership of Herón Proal.

The Labor Movement and Tenant Organizing

The outbreak of revolution gave rise to a dynamic wave of labor organizing. In 1912 various anarchists, libertarians, and socialists founded Mexico's first national worker organization, the House of the World Worker (Casa de Obrero Mundial). Shortly thereafter, Casa-supported anarchists in Veracruz, led by Spaniards Pedro Junco and Narciso Faixat, established the anticapitalist, anti-Catholic Mexican Confederation of Labor Unions (Confederación de Sindicatos Obreros de la República Mexicana) in Veracruz.[3] Caught up in the excitement of the time, a number of young porteños including Manuel Almanza, Agustín Arrazola, Ursulo Galván, Rafael García, and Herón Proal joined. Less than two years later, however, Carranza's recruitment of urban workers into military brigades (known as the Red Battalions) to fight against the armies of Villa and Zapata in 1915 and subsequent repression of the House of the World Worker significantly weakened organizing efforts.[4]

Soon, however, militants in Mexico City affiliated with the Federation of Federal District Syndicates (Federación de Sindicatos Obreros del Distrito Federal) chose Veracruz as the site of their national conference in late 1916. The meeting—dubbed the Preliminary Workers' Congress (Congreso Preliminar Obrero)—represented a significant attempt to build the labor movement at the national level. Acting as president of the meeting's Executive Committee was Herón Proal.

In spring 1918 labor organizers met at a national convention in Saltillo and founded the Regional Confederation of Mexican Workers (Confederación Regional Obrera Mexicana or CROM), an association that combined two diverse strains within the overall labor movement. On one side were anarcho-syndicalists who adhered to the practice of direct action, while on the other were those who believed that effective use of political association would best strengthen labor's cause. For a time, the CROM was the most important state-sponsored organization for labor. Under the leadership of Luis M. Morones, however, the CROM took a decidedly reformist approach, so that by spring 1919 a group of dissatisfied members had left to form other associations.[5]

In the following year, Obregón signed a secret pact with Morones. Fulfilling his part of the deal, Morones founded the Mexican Labor Party and shortly thereafter came out in support of Obregón for president. To counter what some viewed as a dubious remarriage of state and organized labor, a diverse group of militants inspired by the ideals of international socialism moved quickly to create a radical alternative to the CROM.[6]

Out of this heady period of social and cultural change came a new national labor organization, the General Confederation of Workers (Confederación General de Trabajadores or CGT), which was founded in February 1921 by delegates assembled at the Radical Red Convention in Mexico City.[7] Of the seventy representatives who attended the conference sponsored by the Communist Federation of the Mexican Proletariat, twenty came from areas outside of the Federal District. They pledged themselves to an ideology they called "libertarian communism," which endorsed the ideas of class struggle, direct action, and the emancipation of workers and peasants.[8] One of the local organizations that pledged their support was the Veracruz Local Federation of Workers (Federación Local de Trabajadores del Puerto de Veracruz or FLTV), which had formed a year earlier in 1920.[9]

Meantime, communist delegates to the Mexico City Socialist Congress in August and September 1919 founded the Mexican Communist Party (Partido Comunista Mexicano or PCM) on November 28, 1919.[10] Two years later, the party held their first official national gathering in Mexico City between Christmas and New Year's 1921. At the meeting, militants agreed to form a "united front" to intervene in labor politics. A small group of nonparty members, including a handful of radicals from Veracruz headed by Herón Proal, took up agitation on behalf of urban renters. After reports from local delegates, the fiery anarchist spoke to the convention delegates and argued that the urban housing problem represented one of the most urgent issues to be addressed in the nation. If communists wanted to unite the Mexican proletariat, Proal suggested, then dealing with the problems of urban tenants would surely be the place to start.[11] While this strategy probably made sense to some delegates, others must have wondered who the charismatic speaker from Veracruz was.

The Making of a Local Leader

Herón Proal, son of Víctor Proal and Amada Islas, was born in Tulancingo, Hidalgo, on October 17, 1881. Proal's father had emigrated from France; his mother came from Mexico City. During his youth, Proal lost his right eye in an accident while living with his family in Mexico City. At age thirteen, he took a job working in a money exchange and then spent time employed in a small shop, where he read books and various publications of the day. In 1897 he enlisted in the navy and served as an artillery foreman until 1903 when he began a career as a tailor in Veracruz, producing uniforms.[12]

Proal first took an interest in labor organizing in 1906 when he shared a room with a Peruvian exile named Montoya and the two men worked together on a small newspaper that circulated in the port.[13] During the next ten years, Proal developed a reputation in Veracruz, especially among the port's maritime workers.[14] On January 7, 1916, he spoke at a meeting commemorating the ninth anniversary of the Río Blanco strike in the Olimpia Theater.[15] In February that same year,

the thirty-four-year-old Proal attended the Preliminary Workers' Congress in the port, where delegates selected him to serve on the executive committee. After marrying Hermina Cortez, he then began attending labor meetings held under the auspices of the House of the World Worker-sponsored Mexican Confederation of Labor Unions. At these gatherings, participants regularly discussed important issues, including land reform, the eight-hour day, class consciousness, the World War, and a topic moderated by Proal himself titled "The Truth about Religion."[16]

As the Veracruz militant gained access to labor organizing circles, he also began to mature as a political thinker. Al-

Herón Proal, circa 1922. *Courtesy of* El Dictamen

though it is uncertain to what degree he endorsed anarchist thinking at this time, there is little doubt that Proal, along with several of his colleagues, had been attracted by radical social thought brought to Mexico by immigrants over the past few decades, such as Spaniards José Fernández Oca and Pedro Junco.[17] Proal then began to associate with a small group of other radical porteños in a reading club known as Antorcha Libertaria founded by communist Manuel Díaz Ramírez in 1921.[18] Many men affiliated with Antorcha Libertaria, including Rafael García, Manuel Almanza, Sóstenes Blanco, and Ursulo Galván, would go on to shape the course of Veracruz history in the 1920s. In their discussions members forged a hybrid ideology that combined the ideas of Pierre-Joseph Proudhon, Mikhail Bakunin, Peter Kropotkin, and the Israeli radical Max Nordan. Additionally, one can imagine that these men also talked about the housing situation in the port when militants in the neighboring states of Campeche and Yucatán began agitating for reform.

Housing Reforms in Campeche and Yucatán

As in Veracruz, dockworkers in Tabasco, Campeche, and Yucatán had organized labor unions that formed a powerful network of affiliates, such as the Gulf Union of Sailors and Stokers (Unión de Marineros y Fogoneros del Golfo).[19] Subsequently, news reached Veracruz of housing reform legislation in Campeche decreed by Governor Enrique Gómez Briceno and approved in April 1921 as well as similar action instituted early the following year by Felipe Carrillo Puerto's government in Yucatán.[20]

In fact, revolutionary elites in Campeche and Yucatán had actively promoted socialist ideas. Among the radical governors of the time, Felipe Carrillo Puerto came to be known as Yucatán's "Red Caesar" because of his support for the state's agrarian leagues (*ligas de resistencia*), which had been established between 1915 and 1919. Additionally, Carrillo Puerto's government formed the Socialist Party of the Southeast, which extended its influence to neighboring Campeche, where organizers established an Agrarian Socialist Party. As Gilbert Joseph writes, "Yucatán came to be regarded by the rest of the republic as a social laboratory for the Revolution, where exciting experiments in labor and educational reform and women's rights were carried out."[21] Not surprisingly, housing reform imposed by the governors of Yucatán and Campeche elicited a strong reaction from property owners, a number of whom also wrote to Obregón and declared the reforms there unconstitutional. Also, U.S. chargé d'affaires George Summerlin sent a letter to the secretary of state describing the Campeche housing reform as "extremely radical."[22] Thus, as debate over elite-led housing reforms continued in Campeche and Yucatán, local organizers and state officials watched in Veracruz.

The Strike Begins

Despite considerable labor unrest in Veracruz, tenant organizing and the possibility of housing reform remained on the margins of the public discourse between 1920 and early 1922. Then, in mid-January 1922 representatives of the dockworkers union helped to return these

DQ: How does Wood's analysis/use of local newspapers
compare to Sabato? Work in Habermas.

issues to the public spotlight. In a letter to City Hall that council members discussed at their January 16 meeting, local laborers urged Mayor García to do something about the "truly disagreeable condition of the patios," insisting that "abuses of patio administrators [could] no longer be tolerated."[23] Following this discussion, concern over popular housing grew as tenants and health officials registered a number of complaints regarding various tenements in late January.[24]

Articles began appearing in the port's conservative daily newspaper that suggested the beginnings of a tenant rebellion. An article published in El Dictamen on January 29, for example, reported that women living in the red light district had confronted Mayor García at a meeting held two days earlier, complaining that landlords and their administrators charged between 4 and 6 pesos per day and sometimes used extortion to collect payments. In response, the mayor declared that property owners should be advised to lower their rents as soon as possible and warned that strict measures would soon be taken by the city government if they failed to act.[25]

Then, on February 2, El Dictamen announced that "efforts to do something about the problem of high rents and poor housing conditions are being undertaken today with a general meeting of tenants in the People's Library [Biblioteca del Pueblo]." The paper reprinted a handbill circulating throughout the city that stated that "tenants in the port have long been victimized by innumerable abuses committed by usurious landlords who have increased—to a shocking degree—rents for the pigsties we occupy." Organizers encouraged tenants to attend the meeting to be held that night. "All Veracruz," the text read, "can testify to the fact that it is impossible to pay rents so high!" With such a clear case of social injustice, the stage was set for dramatic action.

That evening, a crowd of approximately six hundred porteños gathered at the library.[26] Nicolás Sandoval, a member of the Sailors and Stokers Union, spoke first. Sensing that the time had come for housing reform, he mentioned the legislation recently enacted in Yucatán and Campeche and suggested that Veracruz adopt similar laws. Next, Roberto Reyes Barreiro, a doctor and noted reformer in the port, declared:

> In Yucatán there has been socialist legislation to protect workers. An energetic campaign needs to be started here in the press and everywhere against the excessive prices for these uninhabitable pigsties. We renters, who make up approximately 90 percent of the city's residents, must defend ourselves against the fierce cruelty of the landlords. We must organize a tenant union to fight their abuses. It is not fair that they, who live more than comfortably on what we are forced

to give them, gather in their offices to pass off another increase in the rent for the deteriorated tenements we live in.[27]

With a chorus of voices encouraging him, Reyes Barreiro went on to testify that in his work he had seen many people die as the result of poor sanitation. Improved health conditions in the poor districts of the city have never been realized, he charged, "because of the selfishness of the rich." The doctor's speech provoked a tumultuous response from the audience. Building on this enthusiasm, Cayetano Huerta then challenged the assembly, accusing the meeting's organizers of too much talk and too little action. "We don't want sermons," he said. "The organizers here have paraded speaker after speaker and offered us empty promises and flashy phrases. Even the mayor has spoken but suggested nothing practical for us to follow. Besides, he already lives in a comfortable room and earns a fabulous salary of 800 pesos. With that kind of money, he could live in an even better house if he wanted!"[28]

Huerta's words provoked an immediate response from the audience. People began shouting for action. Eventually, the room grew quiet and someone proposed that Reyes Barreiro be appointed president of a new renters organization. The doctor accepted and moved toward the podium. Before he could retake the stand, Herón Proal dashed up to the speakers' table holding a stack of newspapers under his arm. But some members of the audience wanted to block his intervention. Hearing them yell "Sit down! Sit down!" Proal stormed out of the room, drawing a good portion of the crowd with him. Outside, the anarchist railed against Veracruz landlords as well as local politicians who, he suggested, had convened the meeting with the goal of manipulating the frustrations of tenants for their own ends. "Things don't have to be this way," Proal argued. "Open your eyes and see who is trying to use you."[29] Proal then called for the creation of an alternative, "red" union. The first meeting of this group, he declared, would be held "in the shadow of the statue of don Benito" in Juárez Park the following evening at eight o'clock.

On February 3, 1922, a crowd of approximately six hundred people assembled in the park for the first of what would soon become daily, open-air meetings. Proal and about twenty other speakers exhorted them to go on strike until "the bourgeois dogs" lowered local rents to 1910 levels.[30] According to the report the following day in *El Dictamen*, Proal electrified his audience with charges against local landlords and arguments in favor of a rent boycott: "Let us protest and reclaim our rights. The time has come for us to throw off the infernal yoke of these bourgeois dogs because some of them are pigs, vipers, and scorpions and should be destroyed! Now, what all the city's poor should do is agree not to pay their rents." Proal then launched into a rambling commentary, suggesting that politicians concerned themselves only with the people's vote, not their social condition. "The legislature and city council," Proal charged, were only "a useless bunch of cream puffs!" Passionately, he told the crowd that direct action was the "only way to achieve revolutionary change." Sensing that the time had come for a full-scale confrontation with city elites, Proal then left the meeting to begin planning for the next day.

That morning, Proal's supporters (soon to be dubbed *proalistas*) gathered for a rally at Ferrer Guardia Park and then a march to the Principal Theater. After parading through the streets for a time, demonstrators soon were surprised to discover that police had sealed off the entrance to the theater. Shocked by this significant show of force on the part of the police, some who had joined the march quickly left the area while Proal redirected the remainder of the group toward Juárez Park. Once assembled, the anarchist angrily complained: "They make me out to be crazy, a public disgrace. What's a shame is that there should be four, maybe five thousand people here. Didn't we make a commitment to work toward our goal, to establish the tenant union? And why did so many run away like a bunch of scared old women? Was it because the reactionaries sent the police to guard the theater?"[31] Continuing with his impassioned rhetoric, Proal then encouraged his audience to fortify their commitment to a full-scale protest in the city: "Let us go to the theater and take it by force if we need to. If, when we arrive, the police try to stop us, we will, with stones, sticks, pistols, and whatever else is available, take it, because the theater is ours, it is the people's! There we will hold our meeting, no matter what intrigue and controversy the bourgeoisie may stir up. There we will form our tenant union!"

Inspired by Proal's call to arms but unwilling to initiate another confrontation with the police, fellow organizer Oscar Robert immediately outlined a careful plan to begin the strike. Each patio in the city, he suggested, should organize itself and immediately stop paying rent. Then, he added, "Let's see what the landlords will do if the authorities [dare to] throw us out. If they do, they will have committed a great injustice." Robert then echoed Proal's determination to bring the housing issue to the public's attention through the use of direct action. If a strike drew criticism from city residents, he promised that tenant protesters would take to the streets, blocking traffic and interrupting business operations until officials took action. As the meeting progressed, all agreed that rents would not be paid until authorities recognized the new union as representative of the city's tenants. They drew up a list of demands that included the requirement that landlords annul individual contracts with tenants and write new agreements mediated by the renters union. Owners were to reduce rates to 1910 levels or 2 percent of the current property value. Those in attendance also agreed that landlords must undertake a complete cleaning of all patios. Finally, they elected a provisional directorship for the union with Herón Proal, José Olmos, Porfirio Sosa, and several other men affiliated with the Mexican Communist Party named to leadership posts. By the end of the meeting, participants declared that the Veracruz Revolutionary Syndicate of Tenants had officially been founded.[32] Wasting no time, syndicate members began coordinating the establishment of strike committees in patios throughout the city.

Tenant syndicate handbill, 1922. *Courtesy of AGN*

Thus, with militants of various stripes busily preparing renters for grassroots protest during February, many residents in Veracruz eagerly anticipated the next move by strike organizers. To the surprise of some, however, it was not Proal and his associates or local union men who initiated what would eventually prove to be several years of wild demonstrations, marches, and direct actions in the city. Instead, it was a handful of prostitutes who rented rooms in the Veracruz red light district who took the first steps to escalate the protest.

"Do Not Stand for This Exploitation!"

Although the prostitutes' civil disobedience was one of the first acts of collective resistance to local landlords, public discourse regarding the interrelated issues of female prostitution, housing, and sanitation had a long history in Veracruz.[33] Efforts to control and regulate the sex trade had begun during the first decade of the century. At that time, measures undertaken by municipal authorities to combat problems of disease, crime, and other urban pathologies in Veracruz included contracting the local entrepreneur José González Bueno to develop a designated area for sexual commerce in the southeast corner of the city.[34] Yet despite elaborate plans made for such an endeavor, civil war prevented the project from being realized.

Then, during the North American and Constitutionalist occupations, prostitution flourished. The women conducted their business in several of the city's popular neighborhoods, including the La Huaca barrio located on the southeast side. Because of its reputation as one of the city's vice districts, this area represented fertile soil for urban reformers who associated immorality, uncleanness, and criminality with the urban poor.[35]

Following local battles with bubonic plague and yellow fever, the Veracruz City Council on February 4, 1922, again put the question of prostitution and public health in the spotlight by reporting that certain residents had violated sanitation codes meant to regulate the sex trade. Curiously, the report declared that immediate measures needed to be taken in order to prevent the "degeneration of the races" and spread of "exotic diseases in the country."[36] Expressing her own frustration about the situation, María González, a resident of the red light district, sent a telegram to President Obregón on March 1 complaining that renters paid 5 to 8 pesos per day for rooms that she believed should be renting for no more than 30 pesos per month. She pointed out that efforts by municipal officials had failed to counter the exploitation of renters by a group of "pernicious foreigners."[37]

While resentment had been brewing for some time, grassroots political action linking prostitution and popular housing began on the afternoon of February 27, 1922, when Herón Proal visited a cantina called El Bosque. With a number of prostitutes present, he proposed that a meeting be held in a nearby tenement. Soon, almost eighty women gathered in patio de la Vega to hear Proal. "Dearest *compañeras*," he began, "the hour of social vindication is here and for you it is the time of liberation. You are great citizens and I am here, sisters, to tell you to burn these filthy hovels where you are being miserably exploited by the bourgeoisie. You need to burn these houses and destroy them [because] all of you are dignified people who do not have to stand for this exploitation!" When they returned to the street after hearing the tenant leader, the women encountered their rent collector, José "El Chato" Montero. Inspired by Proal's incendiary discourse, they pelted the administrator with stones.[38]

On the night of March 6, women from the patio San Salvador took their anger over housing to the streets of Veracruz.[39] Two days later, *El*

Dictamen wrote that "many of the prostitutes [had dragged] their rented mattresses, chairs, and other furniture into the street with the idea of starting a giant bonfire." While police, having received a tip about the women's plans, managed to intervene at the last minute to prevent a fire, they could not keep the prostitutes from announcing their decision to quit paying rent. Inspired by the dramatic actions of these women, porteños in several other patios throughout the city soon declared themselves on strike. In the next few days, *El Dictamen* registered the protest of renters from patios El Perfume, La Hortaliza, El Aserradero, Vallejo, La Providencia, La Josefina, San Bruno, Ni Me Olvides, Paraíso, Liébano, La Conchita, and 21 de Abril. According to the paper, representatives of the tenant syndicate had established themselves in each of these patios to coordinate the action.

Hotel Diligencias. *Courtesy of AGEV, Bernardo García Díaz Collection*

As renters came together to make their grievances known, patio residents and union propagandists hung hundreds of red banners outside their homes. Posters declaring, "I am on strike and not paying rent!" (*¡Estoy en huelga y no pago renta!*) could be seen tacked on doors, fences, and the outside walls of the tenements. Then, on the evening of March 12, an open-air meeting and march revealing the growing magnitude of the strike took place.

After gathering in Juárez Park, the assembled crowd took their red flags and banners and marched to the offices of the Cangas brothers. At the corner of La Palma and 1 de Mayo, protesters shouted, "Death to the Cangas, down with the bourgeoisie!" and "Death to the exploiters of the people!" All along the way, they shot off firecrackers before moving to the city's central square. Once there, militants Proal, Sosa, and Olmos gained access to a balcony room in the Hotel Diligencias facing the plaza. Standing above the crowd, Sosa encouraged his audience to unite in the renters' struggle. Proal specifically took the opportunity to honor the women of patio San Salvador: "Dear compañeras, you deserve a vote of confidence from the strike committee and all the residents of Veracruz because you were the first to declare yourselves part of a strike that today has taken on gigantic proportions. You are true heroines for having placed the first stone in the edifice that we are now building. You were the first, and the Red Syndicate opens its arms and welcomes its dear sisters."[40]

Tenant rally. *Courtesy of AGEV, Alejandra Islas Collection*

When some of the men in the crowd scoffed at Proal's use of the term "sisters," he quickly responded to them by saying, "Don't laugh, these poor and despised women not only are our compañeras but also are our sisters. They are flesh and blood just like us." He continued, "There is no reason to exclude them from our struggle, especially when you consider that they are the exploited flesh of the bourgeoisie."[41] With this phrase, Proal openly acknowledged the importance of the women's contribution to the movement while connecting their efforts to his larger vision of international class struggle. In the years to come, many of these women would constitute the majority of rank-and-file participants in the tenant protest.

Syndicate women, 1923. *Courtesy of AGN*

Syndicate men, 1923. *Courtesy of AGN*

Women's use of the anarchist practice of direct action proved especially important to the movement. Early on, militant women banded together to form an action committee known as the Libertarian Women (Mujeres Libertarias). They united under a creed stipulating that if a renter stood in danger of being evicted, a general alarm (usually a loud whistle) would be sounded and those in the vicinity would gather in defense. Patrolling the city, these women regularly challenged housing administrators, police, and other tenants unfriendly to the union. One of their favorite tactics was what they called "giving the horse" (*denle caballo*). Like the practice of "donkeying" or "charivari" in Europe, it was a form of public humiliation in which a group of people would grab an individual and violently shake him by each limb. Their direct actions included installing homeless people in vacant buildings and openly scorning landlords and rent collectors while generally enforcing the terms of the strike. As the protest progressed, tenant women turned their attention to local markets, where they encouraged female servants working for middle-class and elite households to organize and strike for higher wages.

El Dictamen cartoon, July 2, 1922. *Courtesy of* El Dictamen

The strong presence of women in the Veracruz protest during these years sometimes encouraged observers, including the editors of *El Dictamen*, to imagine that Proal had cast some kind of seductive spell, "conquering [them] with his strange theories."[42] Others, including the activist Arturo Bolio Trejo, simply referred to the strike as "the women's rebellion" (*rebelión de mujeres*), thus confirming the central role female residents played in the movement.[43]

Wood focuses on leaders of movements, specific names. Subaltern issues here?

Troubled Relations with Mayor García

With growing numbers of women and men joining the Veracruz protest each day, the strike escalated during the second half of March 1922. Adding to the list of grievances, Proal made it clear that tenants aimed to lower not only the high cost of housing but also the high cost of food in the city. At the same time, he expressed a determination to attack what he saw as various "centers of vice," such as cantinas and bars. In their place, Proal declared that schools would be established. Soon, however, the tenant syndicate faced its first major challenge as Mayor Rafael García, realizing the need to maintain his authority independent of either conservative or radical forces in the city, criticized Proal and his organization. García, long associated with the CROM, constantly faced pressure from some of the port's labor leaders who identified Proal as an uncooperative and unpredictable "agitator." Nevertheless, up to this point García had worked to keep lines of communication open with Proal and his followers. Soon frustrated with what he saw as the increasingly "subversive" character of the protest, however, García ordered a ban on tenant gatherings on March 20. In a telegram explaining his actions to Secretary of Government Calles, the Veracruz mayor stated that Proal's organization had publicly insulted both President Obregón and city government officials.[44] Hearing of rising tensions between belligerent renters and landlords, he also announced that evictions of "troublesome tenants" would go forward.[45] Outraged, Proal denounced García as a "betrayer of the working class."[46] Openly defying the mayor's command, the syndicate continued its meetings in Juárez Park.

García, determined to enforce his will, countered with orders for Proal's arrest on the morning of March 22. In a short time, police found Proal near the flower market on the corner of Vicaro and Zaragoza Streets and around nine o'clock began apprehending the tenant leader. A crowd quickly assembled to take a closer look. When police took Proal away, several residents sympathetic to the anarchist followed close behind.

Once inside the police station, García charged Proal with sedition. The accused defended himself by saying that it was "the people" who made up the tenant syndicate, not simply "a handful of scheming militants," as the mayor had suggested. By the time García had finished interrogating Proal, nearly one thousand supporters had assembled outside. Shortly thereafter, a commission from the tenant union met with the mayor to negotiate for Proal's release, while outside some tried to break into the jail.[47] In the midst of this commotion, García ordered Proal to be taken from the jail in a car. When a vehicle did not arrive, police took the anarchist to a nearby corner, where they waited for a trolley. Soon, however, members of the crowd spotted Proal and rushed to his aid. They tore him away from the police and hoisted him onto a horse. With one arm triumphantly waving the union's red flag, he rode to Juárez Park. Later that night, as Rafael García left the Salón Variedades Theater after a show, a group of protesters assaulted him with derogatory slogans and a handful of stones.[48] After this incident, city officials began to take more seriously the idea that they would have to negotiate with striking tenants rather than simply outlaw their activities.[49]

García proposed another meeting with Proal, who at first refused, suggesting that the mayor had tried to destroy the renters union, but eventually agreed to talk. When they sat down to discuss their differences, García told Proal that he did not want to be considered an enemy of the tenants. "My working-class origins are well known here in Veracruz," he asserted and gave permission for tenant gatherings to resume in Juárez Park. [50] The very next day, however, the death of a woman outside the syndicate headquarters again put the reputation of proalistas in jeopardy.

The First Casualty

On the afternoon of March 23, after small groups of tenants had organized to block evictions ordered for that day, a crowd began to gather in the street near the syndicate's offices on Landero y Cos. A young man carrying a red banner to place on the top of the building climbed the drainpipe outside Proal's office window to the balcony above, where two Spaniards, Micaela García de Torres and her husband, José, lived. Seeing a stranger nearing her window, García de Torres ordered him to get down immediately. When he ignored her, she tried physically to prevent the young man from climbing onto her balcony. In the exchange of blows that ensued, García de Torres was left bleeding and unconscious. In the next few minutes her brother Maríano pulled her back inside the apartment and closed the balcony door.

When the Red Cross arrived on the scene, a few individuals tried to prevent the rescue team from recovering the injured woman. Finally, amidst a hail of sticks and stones, Red Cross workers loaded García de Torres into the ambulance. While some in the crowd were aggressively attacking the vehicle, General Guadalupe Sánchez arrived to help disperse the gathering. He and Proal, who appeared horrified by the violence, ordered a path to be cleared for the ambulance. But before it could drive away, one of the attendants inside informed Sánchez that García de Torres had died.

No one knew who would be held responsible for the death of García de Torres. Many in the city believed, however, that blame lay ultimately with Proal. A letter in *El Dictamen* from a Veracruz resident, Guillermo Andrade, articulated this point of view:

> As your newspaper is of good quality and of high morality, I surely hope that you will take the following seriously. I, Mexican by birth, honorably and conscientiously object to the brutal violence caused by the followers of Proal yesterday afternoon. This unlucky woman, brutally assassinated by the crowd in her own house, has become the victim of a crime that violates the very principles of our society. As the head of household and a father I am obliged to raise my voice in protest. I only hope that the authorities will not leave this crime unpunished. If they do, our own security and public order will be at stake.[51]

Thus, while Proal appeared to have been riding a wave of public acceptance the previous day, the mob outside his office on the afternoon of March 23 had now caused a reversal of fortune for the tenant syndicate. By association, Proal and his union had become implicated in the death of an innocent woman.

A March 25 *El Dictamen* editorial titled "The Red Danger" asserted that Proal represented "the first appearance of dangerous communist influence in the port." With an "agitator" like him "declaring the illegality of property and the need to abolish government, borders, and nationalities in favor of establishing World Communism," the newspaper charged, "we need to better educate the popular masses in order to safeguard our threatened society." For his part, Mayor García told Obregón that the activities of the tenant syndicate had indeed reached "scandalous proportions." Worried that the incident might leave the impression of total lawlessness in the city, García informed the president, "We now are ready to adopt whatever measures are necessary to protect the rights of Veracruz residents and restore order."[52]

Proal would have to weather a second storm of public criticism when porteños learned of yet another incident, which occurred on March 28. That afternoon, Emilio Herrera, a dockworker and syndicate supporter, was accidentally shot in the tenant leader's workshop. Apparently, a loaded gun that Proal stored in a cabinet went off in the direction of Herrera after he had casually placed some materials on a table. When the pistol discharged it hit Herrera in the head. Quickly, members of the union called the Red Cross for assistance. An ambulance arrived and rushed him to the Aquiles Serdán Hospital. With Herrera in serious condition, the event became a matter of immediate public concern. Not surprisingly, police took Proal into custody.[53] Then, on the night of April 2, tenants gathered in Juárez Park and demanded that he be freed. After a brief rally, the group marched around parts of the city, shooting off fireworks and, at one point, interrupting the showing of a film in a local theater. They then proceeded to the offices of the Cangas brothers. There, several speakers denounced the Cuban landlords while the crowd set off firecrackers and shouted proalista slogans until around eleven o'clock.

Meantime, the official investigation of the shooting continued. *El Dictamen* reported that detectives had revisited the tenant headquarters with Proal, inspected the place, and figured the path that the bullet had taken when the gun discharged. After studying the scene, investigators ordered Proal to remain in jail.[54] Gradually, however, officials somehow became convinced of Proal's innocence. On Sunday, April 9, they cleared him of all criminal charges and permitted him to walk free. Yet despite his release, criticism of the tenant leader persisted, especially from property owners who had again organized their own association.

Counter-Movements: The Landlords Association

The specter of a powerful, independent tenant union headed by Herón Proal deeply concerned many property owners in the port and put them on the defensive. The idea for a property owners association grew out of what they saw as the need to defend society against "the threats, brutality, demagoguery, bolshevism, and shame" currently threatening Veracruz society. Assuming a conservative posture, owners saw themselves as working for the restoration of law and order.[55] Behind this defense of "fundamental principles" lay a growing fear of popular protest felt not only by landlords but also by many other members of the Veracruz elite.[56]

Most of the city's powerful landlords saw private investment and free market exchange rather than intervention by the state as the solution.[57] In agreement with this approach, the editors of *El Dictamen* mildly proposed: "There can be additional incentives to investing in [housing] construction because state and municipal government can suggest measures that would facilitate the building of houses [and would] invest the highest sums possible in drainage and colonization of the southern part of the city. In this manner, measures that increase the number of houses will automatically lower rents."[58] Veracruz, according to property owners, could remedy the housing problem itself without the intervention of state and local governments.

Fearing the direction organized tenant protest was taking, landlords in the port began presenting belligerent tenants with eviction notices. Confrontations between the two groups became so common that rarely a day went by without at least one judgment against a renter being decided in the courts.[59] When landlords sent a letter to President Obregón in mid-March, offering to reduce rents if the government would simultaneously lower property taxes, the president responded by stating his refusal to become directly involved in the conflict.[60] Negotiations, many figured subsequently, would have to take place at the local level.

At a March 23 city council meeting, property owners Alejandro Sánchez and Francisco Suárez threw down a challenge to other landlords by asking how many new housing units could be constructed during the remainder of 1922. Other property owners at the meeting effectively ignored the challenge and declared that the idea "needed to be studied more carefully."[61] These men as well as other powerful individuals in the city feared what they saw as a growing "lack of respect for law and order" and made clear to García that they had no intention of compromising with striking tenants.[62]

A few days later, Manuel Díaz Cueto, on behalf of landlords, suggested in a letter printed in *El Dictamen* that the protest was "a joke" to most residents and that the majority of tenants and landlords "would like to see reasonable concessions without necessarily having to advocate utopian radicalism." If the strike continued, he asked, "who will benefit?" His response was, "only the marginals who try to live rent free for a month or so while honorable tenants who pay their rents are the ones being hurt." Property owners throughout the city seemed to find Díaz Cueto's proposal quite reasonable and hoped that a solution to the conflict would be realized as soon as possible.[63] In the meantime, city officials continued to pursue their own ideas about a solution.

An inspection team sent by Mayor García visited a sampling of patios to gain a better sense of what tenants paid for rental housing. Discussing the rent protest among themselves, members of the city council determined that the governor should be informed of recent events in the port. Taking action, Rafael García proposed that a commission be sent to Jalapa as soon as possible.[64] On March 30 the city council issued citations to property owners whose tenements remained

in violation of sanitation codes. Among those ticketed for noncompliance were patios La Industria, San Antonio, and La Angelita, all owned
by the Cangas brothers.[65]

While many wondered what the council planned to do about the
housing crisis, García stated that the city government would not necessarily intervene to end the strike but rather would endeavor to "alleviate the situation of those living in filthy shacks—especially those
patios owned by the Cangas."[66] In the meantime, members of the tenant syndicate pursued their own agenda.

When Proal proposed in a letter published in *El Dictamen* that tenants would end the strike if landlords met their demand that rents be
based at 2 percent of property values, his initiative failed to break the
resolve of the city's more powerful landlords.[67] Nevertheless, other
property owners continued to look for ways to end the strike. One
action they took was to form a new negotiating committee, the Property Owners Steering Committee (Mesa Directiva de la Agrupación de
Propietarios). The purpose was "to defend the interests of landlords
against the threat posed by the tenant strike." As one of the leaders of
the group, Díaz Cueto argued the need for strengthened landlord defense coupled with a willingness by the landlords to take responsibility for their part in the housing crisis: "It matters little to these tenants
if the doors [to their houses] are wet and fall off because the roof is
leaky or the wood is rotten. They live in houses without stoves, without floors, without baths and now today, if we see the dynamite in
their hands, it is because it is our fault. We now have the obligation to
put out the fire because we have made mistakes that we should now
correct. Our attitude should be one of cooperation, of honest and sin-
cere fraternity."[68] Although their intent was to communicate a desire
to resolve the housing conflict, landlords nevertheless remained suspicious of Proal.

The editors of *El Dictamen* criticized property owners for forming
the new organization. In an editorial printed on April 1, the newspaper argued that deliberations by local landlords were a waste of time.
With what they figured was 99 percent of the city's working population in support of the tenant strike, editors reasoned that further intransigence on the part of property owners only put the possibility of a
speedy solution in greater danger. That is, "When the situation is allowed to continue, it will become more dangerous. The example is contagious; the necessity is great and it could very well happen that the
tenement strike will spread. The Property Owners Association is ab-
surd and only an obstacle in this situation. If each followed [his] con-
science, without looking to see what his neighbor was doing, the conflict

could be easily resolved." Yet despite criticism from the press, property holders maintained their largely defensive approach to the housing crisis.[69]

On April 18, three hundred members of the Property Owners Association and residents of the port wrote to President Obregón complaining of "abuses" committed by the tenant syndicate. In addition to numerous threats to individual property, owners claimed, there had been many instances of "tenant violence." Calling the protest a "disreputable" movement headed by "outsiders," they wrote that the "syndicate was led by a longtime agitator and three or four foreigners who commit reprehensible excesses and violate all notions of order, morality, and respect for the law and human life."[70] Furthermore, the demand that rents be fixed at 2 percent of property values would forever be "impossible to realize." If action was not taken by authorities soon, their petition concluded, "anarchy would surely result."[71]

Obregón also received a letter from a representative of the Veracruz Power Company complaining that members of the tenant syndicate had demanded rate reductions. Strikers, the letter stated, had also encouraged market vendors to quit making payments. These actions, according to company officials, were a serious threat to the utility's financial standing.[72] Indeed, in their efforts to increase pressure on uncooperative tenants, landlords, and public officials, protesters had increased the number of direct actions during April and May 1922.

On April 4, for example, in response to orders from syndicate leaders, more than one thousand tenants came together on Guerrero Street to block the eviction of a tenant named Juan Caballero. In small groups, tenants crowded around the door of the shelter, successfully barring police entry. A small delegation then went to ask the judge to cancel the eviction notice. In another confrontation, approximately fifty men and women carrying red banners went after a rent collector known as María "La Chiquirriosa" Huerta because they believed she had verbally abused several tenant women in the La Huaca neighborhood. Finding Huerta at home, members of the renters "commission" grabbed her by her four limbs, shook her violently—"giving her the horse"— and then paraded her down Independencia Avenue toward the syndicate headquarters. The next day, agents of the tenant union clashed with an administrator named Jose "El Chato" Montero, enacting what they liked to call "citizens' justice" as they harassed and taunted him.[73] Yet despite the enthusiastic reception that tenant organizers had enjoyed during the first few months of the protest, realizing significant housing reform would not prove to be an easy task. In the weeks to come, Proal and his followers prepared to do battle on a number of fronts.

Notes

1. *El Dictamen*, January 2, 1922.

2. For elaboration, see Rafael García Auli, *La unión de estibadores y jornaleros del puerto de Veracruz: Ante el movimiento obrero nacional e internacional de 1909 a 1977* (Veracruz: Author's edition, 1977), esp. 44–45.

3. Manuel Almanza García, "Historia del agrarismo en el estado de Veracruz," Manuscript, Jalapa, 1952 (no page numbers); John Hart, *Anarchism and the Mexican Working Class, 1860–1931* (Austin: University of Texas Press, 1978), 167; Leafar Agetro (Rafael Ortega), *Las luchas proletarias en Veracruz: Historia y autocrítica* (Jalapa: Editorial "Barricada," 1942), 154–56.

4. On working-class groups in Mexico at the time of the Red Battalions, see Barry Carr, "The Casa del Obrero Mundial, Constitutionalism, and the Pact of February 1915," in *Labor and Laborers through Mexican History*, ed. Elsa Cecilia Frost, Michael C. Meyer, and Josefina Zoraida Vázquez (Mexico City and Tucson: Colegio de México and University of Arizona Press, 1979), 603–32; Jean Meyer, "Los obreros en la revolución mexicana: Los 'bataliones rojos,' " *Historia Mexicana* 21, no. 1 (July–September 1971): 1–37; and John Hart, *Revolutionary Mexico: The Coming and Process of the Mexican Revolution* (Berkeley: University of California Press, 1987), 302–19.

5. Hart, *Revolutionary Mexico*, 158–59. On the history of Mexican labor during the early 1920s, see Agetro (Ortega), *Las luchas proletarias*; Luis Araiza, *Historia del movimiento obrero mexicano* (Mexico City: Editorial Cuauhtémoc, 1964–66); Jorge Basurto, *El proletariado industrial en México* (Mexico City: Instituto de Investigaciones Sociales, UNAM, 1975); Barry Carr, *El movimiento obrero y la política en México, 1910–1929*, 2 vols. (Mexico City: Sep-Setentas, 1976); James Cockcroft, *Intellectual Precursors of the Mexican Revolution* (Austin: University of Texas Press, 1968); Ricardo Corzo et al., "Balance sobre la investigación de la formación de la clase obrera veracruzana, 1850–1932," in *75 años de sindicalismo*, ed. Alejandra Moreno Toscano and Samuel León González (Mexico City: Instituto Nacional de Estudios Históricos de la Revolución Mexicana, 1986), 189–221; Jacinto Huitrón, *Orígenes e historia del movimiento obrero en México* (Mexico City: Editores Mexicanos Unidos, 1975); Jaime Tamayo, *La clase obrera en la historia de México*, vol. 7, *En el interinato de Adolfo de la Huerta y el gobierno de Alvaro Obregón, 1920–24* (Mexico City: UNAM/Siglo Veintiuno Editores, 1987); Marjorie Ruth Clark, *Organized Labor in Mexico* (Chapel Hill: University of North Carolina Press, 1973); and Rosendo Salazar, *La casa del obrero mundial* (Mexico City: Costa-Amic, 1962).

6. The circulation of ideas regarding the Russian Revolution came, in part, through the Spanish radical press, such as the anarchist paper from Barcelona *Tierra y Libertad*. For a discussion of radicalism in Mexico, see Barry Carr, "Marxism and Anarchism in the Formation of the Mexican Communist Party, 1910–1919," *Hispanic American Historical Review* 63, no. 2 (February 1983): 290. Indian socialist M. N. Roy also comments on the situation in Mexico during this time in M. N. Roy, *Memoirs* (Bombay: Allied Publishers, 1964), 65–80.

7. Roy, *Memoirs*, 289. See also Hart, *Revolutionary Mexico*, 159–60, and Paco Ignacio Taibo II, *Bolshevikis: Historia narrativa de los orígenes del comunismo en México, 1919–1925* (Mexico City: Editorial Joaquín Mortiz, 1986), 113–18.

8. Hart, *Revolutionary Mexico*, 160.

9. Octavio García Mundo, *El movimiento inquilinario de Veracruz, 1922* (Mexico City: Sep-Setentas, 1976), 61.

10. On the founding of the PCM, see Barry Carr, *Marxism and Communism in Twentieth-Century Mexico* (Lincoln: University of Nebraska Press, 1992), 16–27.

11. García Mundo, *El movimiento inquilinario*, 15. In this view, Proal eventually would not stand alone. During the 1920s, CROM organizers played an important role in forming renter organizations in Puebla, San Luis Potosí, Ciudad Juárez, and Córdoba, Veracruz. The CGT supported tenants in Guadalajara, Tampico, Aguascalientes, and Monterrey. For their part, members of the Mexican Communist Party soon would take a leading role in Mexico City.

12. Arturo Bolio Trejo, *Rebelión de mujeres: Versión histórica de la revolución inquilinaria de Veracruz* (Veracruz: Editorial "Kada," 1959), 26; García Mundo, *El movimiento inquilinario*, 51.

13. Interview with Porfirio Sosa, April 10, 1971. Quoted in García Mundo, *El movimiento inquilinario*, 53.

14. Ibid., 54.

15. *El Dictamen*, January 8, 1916.

16. See, for example, reports in *El Dictamen* on February 13 and 20, 1916.

17. On the history of socialism, communism, and anarchism in Mexico, see also Gastón García Cantú, *El socialismo en México, siglo XIX* (Mexico City: Ediciones Era, 1969); Arnoldo Martínez Verdugo, ed., *Historia del comunismo en México* (Mexico City: Grijalbo, 1985); and Carr, *Marxism and Communism*.

18. Heather Fowler-Salamini, *Agrarian Radicalism in Veracruz, 1920–30* (Lincoln: University of Nebraska Press, 1971), 29, 30.

19. Documents in the AGN, gobernación, 1922, show evidence of radical organizing in Campeche and Ciudad del Carmen.

20. On the connections between workers in the Gulf ports see Gilbert M. Joseph, *Revolution from Without: Yucatán, Mexico, and the United States, 1880–1924* (Durham: Duke University Press, 1988), 225.

21. Gilbert Joseph, quoted in Thomas Benjamin, "Regional Social Reform and Mass Politics," in *Provinces of the Revolution*, ed. Thomas Benjamin and Mark Wasserman (Albuquerque: University of New Mexico Press, 1990), 75. The housing initiative went into effect in April 1922. *Diario oficial del gobierno socialista del estado libre y soberano de Yucatán*, April 12, 1922, AGN, gobernación, vol. 11, exp. 317, 1922. On this period see also Gilbert Joseph, "The Fragile Revolution: Cacique Politics and Revolutionary Process in Yucatán," *Latin American Research Review* 15, no. 1 (Winter 1980): 39–64.

22. Summerlin to Department of State, August 11, 1921, RDS, reel 161. See also Fletcher to Summerlin, October 26, 1921, RDS, reel 161.

23. Veracruz City Council, January 16, 1922. See also *El Dictamen*, January 18, 1922.

24. City officials later sent detailed information to President Obregón concerning sanitation violations at patios San Antonio, Angelita, and Tanitos, owned by Manuel Cangas. Rafael García to Obregón, April 26, 1922, AGN, Obregón-Calles, 243-VI-VI.

25. Meanwhile, pressing financial and labor issues also kept García busy. A lack of funds necessary for improvements to the city's water system, public markets, slaughterhouse, and other projects persisted despite the fact that local officials had written to Obregón in June 1921 asking for assistance. City Commission to Obregón, June 2, 1921, AGN, Obregón-Calles, 816-V-21.

26. Description of this meeting and subsequent founding of the Revolutionary Syndicate of Tenants can be found in Agetro (Ortega), *Las luchas*

proletarias, 70–71, and García Mundo, El movimiento inquilinario, 71–77. This history is also memorialized in chapter 2 of José Mancisidor's novel La ciudad roja: Novela proletaria (Jalapa: Editorial Integrales, 1932), 27–46.

27. El Dictamen, February 3, 1922.

28. Ibid.

29. Ibid.

30. Ibid., February 4, 1922.

31. The description of the open-air meeting and the speakers' words are drawn from ibid., February 6, 1922.

32. See also Bolio Trejo, Rebelión de mujeres, 78; Agetro (Ortega), Las luchas proletarias, 72; and Gill, "Herón Proal," 70. José Mancisidor tells the story of the syndicate's founding in chapters 3 and 4 of La ciudad roja ("La Sesión" and "El Manifesto"). A full listing of the syndicate's organizing principles was printed in El Dictamen on March 12, 1922. See also Agetro (Ortega), La luchas proletarias, 74, and Bolio Trejo, Rebelión de mujeres, 57.

33. For requests to the city council to close houses of prostitution and deal with what they saw as the associated problem of tenement housing, see the minutes from the February 8, 1922, city council meeting. Earlier complaints about prostitution in city cantinas can be seen in AGN, Obregón-Calles, 425-V-6, and in a letter from Rafael García to Tejeda that asks that foreigners José Montero and Enrique Gómez be deported for their dealings in prostitution. García to Tejeda, February 28, 1922, AT, vol. 68.

34. AGEV, gobernación, 1912, various documents dated July–December 1912 in file titled "Barrio para las prostitutas," file 50, letter C.

35. For details on earlier efforts to control prostitution in Veracruz, see El Dictamen June 29, 1917, November 25, 26, 1917, November 26, 1917, June 22, 1918, and March 23, 1920, as well as city council records from April 1919 to January–March 1920. By January 1921, sanitation officials had instituted the use of registration books (libretos) for prostitutes listing their assigned bordello. Records between January and November 1921 appear to reveal close to two hundred women registered. AGEV, gobernación, 1921, box 488.

36. Rafael García to Obregón, February 4, 1922, AGN, Obregón/Calles, vol. 425-V-6.

37. María González to Obregón, March 1, 1922, AGN, Obregón-Calles, 808-V-5.

38. El Dictamen, February 28, 1922.

39. Ibid., March 7, 1922.

40. Ibid., March 13, 1922.

41. Ibid.

42. Ibid. See also Bolio Trejo, Rebelión de mujeres, 90.

43. On the participation of women in the movement, see also Mario Gill, "Veracruz: Revolución y extremismo," Historia Mexicana 2, no. 4 (April–July 1953): 622–24; Manuel Castells, The City and the Grassroots: A Cross-Cultural Theory of Urban Social Movements (Berkeley: University of California Press, 1983), 32; and Antonio García de León, "Los patios danzoneros," La Jornada Seminal 223 (September 19, 1993): 36.

44. García to Calles, March 22, 1922, AGN, gobernación, 24–107. García also elaborated on these and other events in a letter to Governor Tejeda dated March 28, 1922, AGEV, gobernación, 1922.

45. El Dictamen, March 21, 1922. Reports of renters resisting evictions can be seen in El Dictamen throughout March. A letter from Veracruz representa-

tive Primitivo R. Valencia to Governor Tejeda mentions "growing difficulties between Rafael García and the tenant syndicate recently created and headed by Herón Proal." Valencia to Tejeda, March 24, 1922. AGEV, gobernación, 1922. On March 19, porteños read in *El Dictamen* that a merging of the city's "yellow" or CROM-sponsored renter association and Proal's "Red" tenant unions had occurred the night before. While scant evidence of the so-called CROM-backed union could be found, the paper had mentioned briefly the existence of two rival tendencies within the larger tenant movement a month earlier. On a Sunday morning in mid-February, CROM-affiliated workers had gathered in the city's Principal Theater to address the housing issue. Two members of Proal's syndicate asked to join the meeting but organizers denied them entry. *El Dictamen*, February 11.

46. *El Dictamen*, February 11, 1922. A telegram from Syndicate Secretary General Miguel Salinas to Governor Tejeda also objected to actions taken by García. Salinas to Tejeda, March 21, 1922, AGEV, gobernación, box 676, 1922.

47. García to Calles, March 24, 1922, AGN, gobernación, 24–107.

48. Proal to Calles, March 24, 1922, ibid. *El Dictamen*, March 24, 1922.

49. In support of the tenants, Congressman Primitivo R. Valencia wrote to Governor Tejeda attacking García's attempted crackdown on syndicate meetings. Primitivo R. Valencia to Tejeda, March 24, 1922, AGEV, gobernación, 1922.

50. *El Dictamen*, March 24, 1922.

51. Ibid.

52. García to Obregón, March 28, 1922, AGN, gobernación, 24–107. García to Tejeda, March 28, 1922, AGEV, gobernación, 1922.

53. *El Dictamen*, March 29 and 31, 1922.

54. Ibid., April 6, 1922.

55. Ibid., February 4, 1922.

56. Members of the city's Junta de Mejoras Materiales, including General Guadalupe Sánchez and *El Dictamen* owner Juan Malpica Silva, soon wrote to President Obregón indicating their desire "to restore the prestige, health, and comfort of Veracruz." For them, tenant protest represented a "step backwards" for the city. Guadalupe Sánchez to Obregón, February 13, 1922, AGN, Obregón-Calles, 816-V-21.

57. See city council records for February 27, 1922, for discussion concerning a request by Manuel Contreras to form a private construction company to build worker housing on municipal lands. A letter to Tejeda from A. Bulnes Tavaren in Brooklyn, NY, dated June 28, 1922, suggests a number of improvements that would help to "modernize" the city. Among the needed reforms stated in the letter is the elimination of "shacks in the city that act as centers of infectious disease." AT, vol. 75, no. 99.

58. *El Dictamen*, February 7, 1922.

59. Ibid., March 3, 1922.

60. Ibid., March 13, 1922.

61. AMV, Actas de cabildo, March 23, 1922.

62. See, for example, ibid., March 27, 1922.

63. Ibid.

64. Ibid., March 30, 1922.

65. AMV, Actas de cabildo, April 3, 1922.

66. *El Dictamen*, March 27, 1922.

67. Ibid., April 1, 1922.

68. Ibid., March 31, 1922.

69. Ibid., April 14, 1922. Meantime, local officials continued to press the Cangas brothers and other landlords in violation of health codes to clean up their tenements.

70. Union de propietarios de Veracruz to Obregón, April 18, 1922, AGN, Obregón-Calles, 407-V-17.

71. Ibid. At the same time, a number of small property owners wrote to the governor asking for help. See Guadalupe Bustamante Aguilar to Tejeda, April 8, 1922, and C. F. Jiménez González to Tejeda, April 15, 1922, AGEV, gobernación, 1922. Tejeda responded by issuing "guarantees" for "all the residents of the port" on April 24, 1922. Tejeda to Rafael García, April 24, 1922, AGEV, gobernación. Tejeda also received a letter from Manuel Cangas complaining about "unfavorable treatment" from Rafael García. Manuel Cangas to Tejeda, April 14, 1922, AT, vol. 63.

72. M. E. Barrán to Calles, April 22, 1922, AGN, gobernación, 24–107, 1922.

73. *El Dictamen*, April 24–27, 1922.

5

"¡Estoy en huelga y no pago renta!"
Collective Action and State Intervention

There is not a scintilla of doubt in the mind of public opinion that moral justice is on the side of the petitioners. Despite this, the proprietors, chiefly Spaniards, puffed up and intractable, seem to be insensible to the crime against humanity that they have committed.

—Adalberto Tejeda, June 1922

During spring 1922, the protest in the port had grown to include nearly forty thousand residents, more than 75 percent of the total city population. Elsewhere, the activities of the tenant syndicate had become notorious not only in the state of Veracruz but also throughout much of the nation. In mid-March, renters in several northern towns, including Ciudad Juárez, Durango, and Torreón, asked Herón Proal to help establish tenant organizations. Meantime, residents in the neighboring Veracruz cities of Orizaba, Córdoba, and Jalapa requested that the syndicate leader assist them in founding unions. Soon, tenant mobilizations took shape in several other urban areas across Mexico.[1] At the same time, lawmakers in Veracruz responded to grassroots protest and began work on a housing reform bill. After considering the spread of the renters movement to other Veracruz cities as well as continuing activities by the Revolutionary Syndicate of Tenants in the port, this chapter then examines early efforts by state officials to negotiate an end to the housing crisis.

Protests in Veracruz Cities

The Orizaba protest began on April 1, 1922, when renters demanded that landlords repair two deteriorating tenements. In their action, residents presented complaints to the mayor, who suggested they stop

93

paying rent until property owners took appropriate action.[2] The next day, several hundred residents gathered in the city's Llave Theater to form a renters union.[3] Soon, they sent a list of demands to Governor Adalberto Tejeda that included reducing rents by 75 percent, naming a committee to evaluate property values, and establishing propaganda committees in the city's tenements.[4] In support of the new union, the Orizaba paper *Pro-Paria* ran an article on April 9 that decried the deplorable state of rental housing in the city and pointed out that several patio owners were charging high rents for rooms with deteriorating doors and roofs. Furthermore, the article asserted, landlords exploited workers in Orizaba by requiring them to provide proof of employment and rental payment three months in advance. Exasperated with what they saw as "property owners having their way," the paper insisted that tenants' coming together to protest the housing situation in the city was an urgent matter of necessity. [5] Shortly thereafter, the Orizaba syndicate affiliated itself with the Regional Confederation of Workers and Peasants (Confederación de Obreros y Campesinos de la Región de Orizaba), while the local communist Aurelio Medrano— famous for his agitation as a railway worker—emerged as one of the most powerful leaders of the new Orizaba syndicate. By late June, the organization claimed four thousand adherents and had asked Governor Tejeda for official recognition.[6]

- ¡"Estoy en Huelga No Pago Renta"! -

Solo reconozco al SINDICATO REVOLUCIONARIO DE INQUILINOS, y a nuestro representante y apoderado Herón Proal facultado por el Pueblo.

No admito insinuaciones de nadie y menos de los que traten de dividirnos.

Soy sindicalista de convicción, no convenenciero.

Para el Avalúo, solo reconozco la Comisióm del SINDICATO REVOLUCIONARIO DE INQUILINOS.

REVOLUCION PRO-COMUNISMO

Veracruz, Mayo de 1924.

"Estoy en Huelga" handbill. *Courtesy of AGEV*

In neighboring Córdoba, the housing situation resembled that of the other major cities in the state. When complaints about abuses by landlords circulated in early 1922, labor activists began to organize. In April, local leaders visited the port of Veracruz to meet with Proal. In turn, the anarchist introduced them to his colleagues Manuel Almanza, Ursulo Galván, Sóstenes Blanco, Porfirio Sosa, and a handful of other founding members of the Veracruz syndicate. After a hearty exchange, the delegation began work on a manifesto.[7] A few days later, militants sent out a call to the Córdoba renters, imploring them to "break the chains" of landlord oppression and declare themselves on strike. Committee members then divided the city into various districts and initiated a door-to-door recruitment campaign. Then, on the evening of April 21, tenants gathered in the city's Madero Park.

Soon, however, local authorities told organizers that the meeting must be disbanded. Hearing this, Gonzalo Hernández challenged the order, arguing that citizens had the right to assemble under Article 9 of the Constitution. When police pushed him away, he climbed a set of stairs in the park and shouted to the crowd that "from this moment" the Revolutionary Syndicate of Tenants (of Córdoba) was officially founded.[8] Hernández and the others then walked to the Mora Lira brothers' barbershop nearby and designated it the headquarters of the new organization. There, Hernández, Jesús Mendoza, Antonio Rebolledo, Raúl Cárdenas Calderón, and Manuel Mora Lira formed an executive committee. Over the next few days, Córdoba residents hung red-and-black banners on tenement doorways with many containing the same message that had been seen in the port: *"¡Estoy en huelga y no pago renta!"* Responding to the challenge, property owners in Córdoba, like those in Orizaba and the port, moved to establish their own organizations.

With rent protests taking shape in Orizaba and Córdoba, word quickly circulated to smaller cities in Veracruz. Organizers in the Orizaba valley towns of Santa Rosa and Nogales formed unions in spring 1922. On May 4 renters gathered in the Juárez Theater in Santa Rosa and elected the Executive Committee of the Progressive Syndicate of Tenants (Sindicato de Inquilinos Progresistas). Shortly thereafter, members wrote to Governor Tejeda stating that they sought to "defend themselves against the avarice of the landlords who are the exploiters in this city."[9] In the letter, they spelled out their demand for a 75 percent reduction in rents. Residents in neighboring Nogales followed suit and employed the same organizational model set by Proal and his collaborators.

In the weeks that followed, Governor Tejeda received a letter from tenants in the southern oil town of Minatitlán asking him to lend recognition and support for their fledgling renters union. As they saw it, tenant protest represented "a principal factor in the life of the nation" as well as a "valiant" aspect of "class struggle." The group signed the letter, as almost all tenants did at the time, "Revolution and Pro-Communism."[10]

In the coming months, tenants in the state capital of Jalapa also began organizing. Renters in the smaller cities of Río Blanco, Tierra Blanca, Soledad de Doblado, and a few other towns also created tenant organizations. Protest over popular housing was not limited, however, to the state of Veracruz. In several cities across the nation, renters took to the streets to complain of landlord abuses and demand that something be done about the sorry state of urban housing. Further, hearing that hundreds of tenants in the port of Veracruz had declared themselves on strike, renters began organizing in Monterrey, Puebla, San Luis Potosí, Mazatlán, Tampico, and Aguascalientes,[11] while activists in the Federal District and Guadalajara initiated public demonstrations in March 1922. A few weeks later, renters in Veracruz took the protest to a new level when they invaded land outside the city limits. They called their improvised encampment the Colonia Comunista.

The Colonia Comunista, May 1922

Learning of new clashes between tenants, landlords, administrators, and police, Mayor Rafael García called for an emergency session of the Veracruz City Council to be held on April 26. In the meeting, officials decided that "scandals" provoked by renters "would no longer be tolerated." Subsequently, García sent telegrams to Governor Tejeda, President Alvaro Obregón, and Secretary of Government Plutarco Elías Calles informing them of recent incidents involving protesters. In turn, Tejeda's reponse indicated that difficulties with tenants could possibly be resolved with a new rent law.[12]

Meantime, the editors of *El Dictamen* wrote that Mayor García had been "seduced" by "Red" radicalism and viewed the protest with a certain glee.[13] Acting on a suggestion made by Governor Tejeda, García soon contacted Proal to arrange a meeting.[14] On the afternoon of April 28, members of the city council, García, and Proal sat down to discuss how the strike might be ended. Despite good intentions, their exchange produced few positive results. In an interview a few days later, Proal asserted that "the tenant union is thoroughly revolutionary and therefore it refuses to recognize any political authority." An editorial printed later in *El Dictamen* commented that the tenant syndicate and the landlords union appeared to be "two forces engaged in a fight to the death."[15] Thus, while many prepared to celebrate International Workers Day, compromise between tenants and landlords appeared to be only a distant hope.

On May 1 businesses closed and virtually all activity in the port of Veracruz came to a halt in honor of the popular holiday. Throughout the city, red flags flew outside the offices of all the labor unions as workers prepared placards for a march to Juárez Park. Later, renters gathered at a rally where they listened to a series of speeches before marching through the city streets. Meanwhile, Proal led a group of tenants under the burning tropical sun in a march that headed south from the city center to an area known as Pocitos y Rivera, the property of Francisco Portilla. Once they arrived with their banners and flags, tenants took part in a ceremony to dedicate the cornerstone of the new "communist" settlement.[16] Complications regarding the workers' colonia arose a few days later, however, when Proal and members of the tenant syndicate revisited the site.

Proal with female strikers in the Colonia Comunista. *Courtesy of AGEV, Alejandra Islas Collection*

When Proal had asked García to visit the neighborhood with him to endorse a transfer of title for the property to the tenant syndicate, the mayor told him that he did not have the authority to do so. Instead, García informed Proal that Governor Tejeda intended to turn over the ownership of Pocitos y Rivera (and a neighboring area known as Las Bajadas) to residents in a more peaceful and orderly manner. Frustrated by the mayor's hesitation, Proal immediately declared the land the property of the people. "Regardless of who may say they own the land, the area will soon have many different kinds of homes, baths, gardens, electric lights, asphalt roads, and a number of other amenities," he declared.[17] After Proal's announcement, organizers gave instructions for tenants to bring construction materials to the site. Then, a few days later, the tenant leader and several other members of the syndicate returned to the site to install another cornerstone at the newly founded colonia because someone had stolen the first one earlier that week.

After the syndicate members' second visit to the settlement on Sunday, May 7, tenants visited the central square in Veracruz to hold a rally. Speaking across from the Hotel Diligencias, Proal told his audience in a lengthy speech that the new communist neighborhood offered a healthier environment than the city for renters. He concluded, "We must leave this badly smelling port, where the bourgeoisie exploit the people. [While we are making a better life for ourselves,] they are welcome to stay and keep this so-called heroic port, with its cocaine, its heroin, and its marijuana."[18] With no more than a tenuous foothold on the outskirts of town, militants sought to fashion a new society safe from what they saw as the corrupting influence of the city. Yet while members of the syndicate began colonizing the new area, they also continued their direct actions against landlords and housing administrators. In response, property owners pressed municipal authorities for protection,[19] threatening to suspend all local tax and utility payments. Their efforts raised grave concerns for municipal and state authorities. Discussion of the housing issue in Veracruz would soon prompt action by Governor Tejeda and his staff.

The Beginnings of State Intervention

With complaints about tenant protests flooding government offices, the housing conflict worried not only state officials but federal leaders as well. In early May, Mayor García traveled to Mexico City to participate in a conference attended by mayors throughout the country. In special meetings, President Obregón and Secretary of Government Plutarco Elías Calles questioned García about recent events in the port and asked his opinion about how the rent strike could be settled. Obregón and Calles then told García of their desire to have Governor Tejeda take immediate steps to bring the situation under control. If either Tejeda or municipal officials could find no middle ground, Obregón warned, then federal intervention would be necessary. Hearing this, García tried to assure the president that local officials alone could resolve the housing crisis. In support of his claim, the mayor informed Obregón of a plan to bring tenants and landlords together to negotiate an end to the conflict.[20]

Back in Veracruz, García met with small property owners, who told him they would make whatever concessions necessary to end the strike.[21] The mayor then spoke with Proal, informing him that a group of landlords in the city had demanded police protection against possible tenant attacks and asking for Proal's assurance that there would be no need for such protection. Proal eyed his associates while telling the mayor that no one would be harmed.[22] Later that night, city council members read a letter from the property owners union saying several individuals in the guesthouses Paris and La Sirena and the Hotel Arista had announced their participation in the rent strike. In the discussion that followed, many agreed that the most difficult issue concerned the extent to which the city government would intervene in the conflict. While some property owners had requested support from both municipal and federal officials, García preferred to maintain a neutral position. Yet just as he and the city council tried to take the political high road, events in the street dragged them back into the conflict.

On May 9, after a confrontation with members of the tenant syndicate, police successfully evicted a squatter named Luis Campos from a dilapidated house. In the mêlée, Proal had ordered protesters, armed with knives, to defend Campos against the police. While tenants had initially taken an aggressive stance toward authorities, the arrival of fifteen armed soldiers persuaded them to back down. Taking their banners and homemade weapons, they eventually left the scene quietly. The following morning, *El Dictamen* described the confrontation as "the first case of the tenant syndicate's power weakening."

Bracing themselves for another confrontation, female members of the syndicate rallied outside Proal's house the next day. Soon they walked down Vicaro and Independencia Streets to the Hotel Diligencias in the central plaza. Ignoring the owner's insistence that the hotel was full, Proal and his entourage made their way to the first floor, where they entered an occupied room and went out on the balcony to address the crowd that had gathered.

As the tenant leader and his compañeras gave their speeches, military commander Aaron López Manzano, readying his troops for the possibility of civil disorder, called twenty soldiers mounted on horseback from the 56th Regiment as well as a number of infantry to the scene. As soon as Proal and the others saw federal forces surround the plaza, they ended their rally. Given the show of force by local authorities, syndicate members feared that their imprompu rallies would not long be tolerated. Meantime, word of tensions in the port made state officials in Jalapa intensify their efforts to come up with a peaceful solution.[23] In fact, plans for new housing legislation had been in the works for nearly two months.

A Room at the Imperial: Toward State Housing Reform

Earlier in March, Rafael García had drafted a housing reform proposal based, in part, on legislation passed in Yucatán and Campeche. After presenting the document to the city council for review, he sent it to members of the state legislature.[24] A few days later, the governor pointed out to lawmakers that the state needed a new rent law because so many workers were having "to hand over a good portion of their earnings to their landlord" in order to acquire even modest shelter.[25] As a temporary solution to the housing situation, Tejeda proposed that rural residents pay rents based at no more than 6 percent of the value of the land—a formula that was used in Yucatán and that he hoped would also be the basis for the regulation of urban rents.[26] But a report soon reached Tejeda informing him that the 6 percent rule could not be imposed in Veracruz because "no accurate assessment" of urban property holdings had yet been conducted.[27] Furthermore, the report suggested, a reform bill that imposed significant rent and sanitation controls could potentially improve living conditions throughout the state. Also, in Veracruz there remained the problem of "the inquilinos," who paid exceedingly high rents. And although there had been quite a bit of talk in the national press about these high rents, the report said, "nothing up to this point has been done to resolve it."[28]

After circulating García's plan, the governor began drafting a new rent control law that he would present to the legislature in early July. Above all, Tejeda hoped to impose a legal solution to the housing crisis. Following the suggestions of the tenant union, he sent an early offer to property owners stipulating that, in exchange for new contracts drawn up between landlords and tenants that calculated monthly rents at 2 percent of property values, owners would be guaranteed prompt payment from their renters. The proposal also made provisions for basic water, light, and sanitary services in all tenements. Not surprisingly, landlords rejected Tejeda's proposal while at the same time lobbying city officials for additional protection against striking tenants.[29] Seeing that more direct intervention might be necessary, Tejeda then dispatched two staff members, Benigo Mata and Salvador González García, to the port.

With negotiations at a standstill during the first weeks of May 1922, Rafael García called a meeting with Proal in the Hotel Imperial on May 10 that would include Tejeda's commissioners, Mata and González García. At three o'clock, Proal arrived, accompanied by a few of his colleagues, while outside in the plaza, forty members of the tenant syndicate waited patiently. When Mata informed Proal that the governor and federal officials wanted to work toward resolving the housing conflict, the tenant leader responded that landlords and state authorities were the ones who needed to come to an agreement in order to end the strike. The Revolutionary Syndicate, he declared, was ready to enter into negotiations.[30]

Taking Proal's comments into consideration, Mata interviewed property owner representatives Antonio Moreno and Manuel Díaz Cueto the following day. Whereas the landlords had earlier offered to reduce rents in exchange for lower property taxes, Moreno and Díaz Cueto now said they wanted to avoid making any agreement with renters. Stubbornly, they told Mata they now found tenant action to be "utterly contemptible." From now on, they wanted only to negotiate informally with individual renters.[31]

Seeing a difficult road ahead, Mata and González García began collecting information on local housing conditions. On May 13 they visited patios Variedades, San Bernardo, La Vega Grande, Josefita, and Enrique Barrera on the city's west side and then traveled to the La Huaca neighborhood, where they inspected patio San Antonio owned by the Cangas brothers. After walking through these tenements, the commissioners reported to the governor that the port's rental housing indeed "was shockingly overpriced, overcrowded, and in a pitiful state of disrepair." According to *El Dictamen*, they had encountered a variety of social "horrors" in the La Huaca and Guerrero Street neighborhoods. Furthermore, the inspection results told city residents something they already knew: a majority of the patios were "absolutely uninhabitable."[32]

On May 16, Mata and González García again spoke with representatives of both the tenant and landlord unions.[33] This time, property owners presented the two officials with a petition titled "Propositions for the Solution of the Problem Called the Tenants' Strike." The document suggested that rents could be reduced slightly but also stated the landlords' refusal to negotiate with "agitator" Proal or any other members of the syndicate who maintained "communist ideals."[34] Their proposal expressed a fundamental belief in property rights and confidence that the authority of government would help to protect those rights.

Not to be outdone, Proal presented Tejeda's representatives, Mata and González García, with the tenants' strike demands on the night of Wednesday, May 17. Then, after some discussion, Proal and a few of his associates accompanied the state officials on another inspection tour of patios in the city.[35] The next day, *El Dictamen* printed the demands given to Mata and Gonzalez García by both groups. Tenants assured property owners that they would resume rent payments if landlords signed rent agreements drawn up by the union stipulating that rents be lowered to 2 percent of the property value and that properties be repaired and fully sanitized. In contrast, property owners presented a list of expenses to help justify their position that rents be figured at 1910 levels plus 50 percent. Additionally, their proposal included a clause that indicated a provision for tenants to pay back-rents over a certain period.[36] Once each side had made their bargaining position clear, the state commissioners attempted to move the negotiations along by setting the date of Friday, May 19, for the next meeting between property owners and tenants. Sharp differences between the two groups, however, would soon prevent further progress in the negotiations from being realized.

After reading the tenants' proposal, Díaz Cueto and Moreno informed Mata that a number of modifications would need to be made before property owners would seriously consider it. In fact, Díaz Cueto told Mata that rents based at 8 or even 15 percent of the property value would still unfairly favor tenants at the expense of landlords. Yet despite such deep skepticism expressed by Díaz Cueto, Mata managed to arrange another meeting between representatives of the two groups to be held on May 21 in the Hotel Imperial.

That day, Proal and members of the syndicate's central committee arrived first. Soon thereafter, Díaz Cueto, followed by other representatives of the property owners union, made their way to the commissioners' room. When the landlords entered and saw Proal and the other militants talking with Mata, they quickly turned around and left, telling the commissioners that they would return later. Although Mata and even Proal pleaded with the landlords to return, they paid him no heed. Back inside Mata's room, tenants reminded the commissioners of their demand that rents be based at 2 percent of property values and no more. They pointed out, however, that without a standard assessment of property values in the city they would have to continue to strike.[37] Meanwhile, as negotiations mediated by Tejeda's commissioners appeared to come to a standstill, city officials began another effort to resolve the crisis.

On May 25 the city council took up the issue of nonpayment of local taxes by property owners. Landlords present at the meeting passed the blame on to their tenants. Hearing this, several councilmen suggested that if landlords refused to pay taxes, the city could place a lien on their properties. One councilman stated that this action alone might help bring an end to the tenant strike. Mayor García added that the landlords' nonpayment left him worried about city finances. For the time being, he commented, "at least we have the satisfaction of seeing those not paying rent no longer being exploited."[38]

Further city government action took place on May 27. In the council's chambers, the mayor, property owners, administrators, and a group of tenants headed by Proal gathered to exchange views. Proal spoke first. He said he felt pleased to see city officials taking the initiative to deal with the housing problem. Representing property owners, Díaz Cueto and Moreno stated that their group refused to meet directly with leaders of the syndicate. Instead, they suggested that a commission composed of landlords, tenants, and city officials circulate throughout the city to make a full assessment of property values. After such a consultation, rents would be negotiated individually rather than according to a predetermined formula. In front of Proal, Díaz Cueto reiterated forcefully that under no circumstances would landlords agree to cooperate with members of the tenant syndicate.

Hearing this, Proal told Díaz Cueto and the others that tenants had a constitutional right to organize themselves. He strongly reasserted that some renters would be willing to resume payment as long as landlords figured rates based at 2 percent of property values. "In the meantime," Proal informed them, "we are quite content to continue our strike." He concluded with a remark directed at the landlords in the room: "Whereas before, tenants were without money for clothes, hats, and the basic goods they needed, now your loss is our gain."[39]

Editorials printed in *El Dictamen* at the end of May discussed the strike and García's administration in an increasingly critical manner, calling the mayor a "socialist" and "monomaniac capable of any monstrosity in order to win applause and cultivate a populist aura."[40] When a group of small property owners, tenants, and city officials met for the first time to negotiate patio rents, editors, in an opinion piece titled "Is There Hope for an Agreement in the Tenant Conflict?" accused García of ineptitude and dishonesty in dealing with the strike:

> We have been aware, well before the mayor declared his sympathies, of the fact that tenants in Veracruz live in some of the worst [housing] conditions in the world and are terribly exploited by the landlords. While we would like to see a resolution of the conflict, we stand opposed to the manner in which some deluded bon vivants and politicians have pursued the renters' cause without any respect for justice as well as the rights and freedoms of others. The consequences of their actions have been disastrous for society as a whole. As long as the city government continues to deny its responsibility in helping to bring about a peaceful solution to the conflict it will be impossible to reestablish a climate of order and mutual respect in the city.[41]

Refusing to be intimidated by the press, local government officials redoubled their efforts in early June.

On June 1 a committee composed of landlords, city councilmen, and members of the tenant syndicate piled into two automobiles and headed out to inspect several nearby patios. Along the way they picked up a local treasury and a public works official—both of whom had been appointed by the mayor to lend technical assistance to the negotiations. Eventually, the group arrived at the entrance to the tenement Los Tres Símbolos and soon began their tour of the surrounding neighborhood. Along the way, they stopped at the nearby patios El Bosque and La Tortuga as well as a few other smaller tenements. Carefully, they took account of the operating costs and other possible expenses for each of the property owners. Once compiled, this information was to be tabulated by city engineers and become the basis for fixing rents. As the entourage went on their rounds, a thaw in relations between property owners and tenants appeared to be in the making.

Then, on June 3, *El Dictamen* reported an important breakthrough in negotiations by claiming that sixty small property owners had shown an interest in negotiating a settlement with the tenant syndicate. In part, the initiative had come as the result of Proal's reassuring landlords that once an evaluation of properties could be undertaken and new rental rates agreed upon, contracts could be drawn up for renters to resume payment. Soon, however, the realization of a settlement between tenants and small property owners would be put on hold.

Difficulties developed, in part, because the property owners present at the inspections owned mostly moderately sized tenements and represented a minority in the city. Some of the larger landlords told reporters that they flatly refused to cooperate with city officials in any evaluation procedure and that they planned to wait for the state government to propose a full legal solution before taking action. At the same time, large landlords continued to insist that they had no intention of dealing with the leaders of the tenant syndicate. Furthermore, they wrote to President Obregón and Governor Tejeda that the situation had only "continued to get worse" and that Mayor García was making "slanderous imputations."[42]

Frustrated with the way negotiations had slowed, members of the Veracruz renters union launched a new offensive. They began by calling a boycott of general stores in the port to protest high prices and demand immediate reductions. In their communication to the Veracruz public, striking tenants argued that owners charged too much for foodstuffs and items "of basic necessity."[43] Soon, members of the National Chamber of Commerce received a petition from the Revolutionary Syndicate of Tenants saying that prices for primary goods well exceeded what most renters could afford to pay. The document presented a list of basic goods and what syndicate members believed would be a fair price for them. At the same time, protesters distributed leaflets to local businesses and threatened to impose a citywide boycott of stores if owners refused to lower prices.

Those businessmen who received the notice expressed serious concern. Some, according to *El Dictamen*, worried that they would have little choice in the matter given the syndicate's propensity for direct action.[44] Militant tenants then gave them further cause to be worried as word of new direct actions targeting landlords, property administrators, and other "uncooperative residents" spread throughout Veracruz. On June 2, for example, tenants attacked the former administrator of patio Los Minerales on Pino Suárez Street. The same day, a group of women "gave the horse" to a female resident of patio La Concepción after she refused to respond to syndicate charges against her husband. Then, less than two weeks later, tenant women launched a drive to organize domestic workers in the city.[45] A telegram from legislators in Jalapa to Obregón described the situation in Veracruz as "chaotic"[46] about the time that police and federal forces again received orders to prevent any public disturbances initiated by tenants. In the next few weeks the situation in Veracruz would become even more heated as workers throughout the city walked off their jobs and launched a general strike. This action, along with continued agitation undertaken by members of the Revolutionary Syndicate of Tenants, would soon lead to a major confrontation between protesters and federal forces.

Notes

1. Files at the AGN on tenant activism outside the state of Veracruz include 428-G-8, 407-G-8, and 407-G-16 for conflict in Guadalajara; 408-Y-4, 407-M-9, and 808-M-13 for Mérida; 407-P-21 for Puebla; 242-D2-I-4, 816-I-16, 805-C-318, 805-C-301, 731-I-5, 423-C-15, 407-S-21, and 407-I-2 for Mexico City; 707-S-26 for San Luis Potosí; and 241-H-M-215 for Mazatlán.

2. *El Dictamen*, April 3, 1922.

3. Tenant Syndicate of Orizaba "Acta Primordial," April 1922, AGEV, gobernación, "Sindicato de Inquilinos, Orizaba," 1922.

4. Ibid.

5. *Pro-Paria*, April 9, 1922.

6. Tenant Syndicate to Tejeda, June 23, 1922, AGEV; Paco Ignacio Taibo II, *Bolshevikis: Historia narrativa de los orígenes del comunismo en México, 1919–1925* (Mexico City: Editorial Joaquín Mortiz, 1986), 176.

7. Beatriz Calvo Cruz, "Historia social de Córdoba, Veracruz, 1915–1932" (bachelor's thesis, Universidad Veracruzana, 1986), 66–67. Early evidence of

deteriorating housing conditions in Córdoba can be found in reports by the Córdoba Junta de Sanidad, AGEV, Dirección General de Salubridad, box 482, no. 3, "D."

8. Calvo Cruz, "Historia social de Córdoba," 69.

9. Progressive Tenant Syndicate of Santa Rosa to Tejeda, May 19, 1922, AGEV, gobernación.

10. López to Tejeda, May 24, 1922, AGEV, gobernación.

11. Taibo II, *Bolshevikis*, 155–97.

12. Tejeda to Calles, April 29, 1922, AGEV, gobernación, 1922.

13. *El Dictamen*, April 25 and 28, 1922.

14. Tejeda to García, April 28, 1922, AGEV, gobernación, 1922. *El Dictamen*, April 30, 1922.

15. *El Dictamen*, April 29, 1922 and May 1, 1922. On May 1 the *Revista de Yucatán* in Mérida began coverage of the strike by describing one of the tenant syndicate's rallies. Two days later the paper reported on Worker Day celebrations in the port, telling readers of street demonstrations where porteños shouted, "¡Abajo los chaquetones, Abajo la burguesía!" *Revista de Yucatán*, May 3, 1922. Descriptions of the conflict in the port as well as protests in Ciudad Juárez, San Antonio Texas, Córdoba, Orizaba, Perote, Pachuca, and Mexico City continued throughout the month.

16. *El Dictamen*, May 2, 1922. Arturo Bolio Trejo sarcastically calls the neighborhood a "paradise of the crazies" (*el paraíso de los locos*). Bolio Trejo, *Rebelión de mujeres: Versión histórica de la revolución inquilinaria de Veracruz* (Veracruz: Editorial "Kada," 1959), 63–67.

17. *El Dictamen*, May 7, 1922.

18. Ibid., May 8, 1922. Also quoted in Manuel Castells, *The City and the Grassroots: A Cross-Cultural Theory of Urban Social Movements* (Berkeley: University of California Press, 1983), 48.

19. *El Dictamen*, May 4 and 7, 1922. Veracruz City Council, May 8, 1922.

20. *El Dictamen*, May 5, 1922.

21. Ibid., May 7, 1922.

22. Ibid., May 9, 1922.

23. Ibid., May 10, 1922.

24. Veracruz City Council, March 9, 1922.

25. Tejeda's proposal soon influenced the repeal of former Governor Antonio Nava's revisions to the 1917 Veracruz rent control law on March 25. Manuel Valdez to Tejeda, March 13, 1922, AGEV, gobernación, 1922.

26. Tejeda to members of Veracruz State Legislature, March 29, 1922, ibid.

27. Barranco to Tejeda, March 31, 1922, AT, vol. 96, no. 72.

28. Report signed by Carlos F. de Castro, March 28, 1922, AGEV, gobernación, 1922.

29. Property Owners Association of Veracruz, Antonio Moreno, and Manuel Díaz Cueto to the State Legislature, April 6, 1922, AGEV, gobernación, 1922. Octavio García Mundo, *El movimiento inquilinario de Veracruz, 1922* (Mexico City: Sep-Setentas, 1976), 117–18.

30. *El Dictamen*, May 11, 1922.

31. Ibid., May 10, 1922.

32. Ibid., May 14, 1922. See also a report sent by Tejeda to Obregón on housing inspections and labor conflicts in the port dated June 7, 1922, AGN, gobernación, vol. 24, file 107.

33. *El Dictamen*, May 16, 1922.

34. Property Owners Association, May 16, 1922, AGEV, gobernación, 1922.

35. While investigations by state officials had begun, *El Dictamen* published an editorial on May 11 suggesting that Proal might be "a foreigner," perhaps from Guatemala. The same week the Mexico City paper *Excélsior* printed a similar editorial. Proal later told Mario Gill that it was about this time that housing administrator José García Suero offered him 500,000 pesos if he would be willing to leave Veracruz for Europe. Mario Gill, "Veracruz: Revolución y extremismo," *Historia Mexicana* 2, no. 4 (April–July 1953): 626.

36. Letter from Union de Propietarios de la ciudad de Veracruz to Secretary of Government Calles, May 22, 1922, AGN, gobernación, 24-107, 1922.

37. *El Dictamen*, May 22, 1922. Responding to the question about the percentage of property values on which rents should be based, *El Dictamen* printed a letter on May 23 that listed the names, properties, value, and rents charged for twenty-seven different tenements whose worth had been evaluated for various legal reasons.

38. Ibid., May 26, 1922.

39. Ibid., May 28, 1922. A fund-raiser fair organized by tenants the following day in Ciriaco Vázquez Park further boosted the protesters' morale. Various booths sold tamales, Coca-Cola, beer, popcorn, flowers, and confetti and others took collections for the tenant union and the Red Cross. *El Dictamen*'s publication of a full description of all the booths and the many women staffing them was the first time that rank-and-file tenant identities had been made public.

40. See, for example, "Como resolver el problema de Veracruz," *El Dictamen*, May 29, and "El socialism de 'el negro,' " ibid., May 30, 1922.

41. Ibid., June 2, 1922.

42. Property owners to Tejeda, June 1, 1922, AGEV, gobernación, 1922.

43. *El Dictamen*, May 25, 1922.

44. Ibid.

45. Ibid., June 14, 1922.

46. AGN, gobernación, 24–107.

6

"A Perfect Dress Rehearsal for Sovietism"
The July Massacre

> Throughout the city circulated a wave of terror so bloody it was as if the sea had instantly turned red.
>
> —José Mancisidor, *La ciudad roja*

> It was the hope of every citizen of Veracruz that the Swedish Consul would consent to overlook and forgive the tragic error [a bomb explosion] since these were stern days with danger lurking everywhere for all. In the meantime, the lamentable incident might even so have its good uses if it should serve as a warning to the heartless, shameless exploiters of honest Veracruz tenants that the revolution had indeed arrived in its power, that the workers were adamant in their determination to put an end to social and economic wrongs as well as to avenge themselves fully for wrongs already done to them.
>
> —Katherine Anne Porter, *Ship of Fools*

On June 10, 1922, dockworkers in Veracruz walked off their jobs and launched a citywide general strike. In accordance with the conditions of the protest, ships in the harbor went unserviced or simply left the port. *El Dictamen* reported that owners of hotels, restaurants, and bars had closed their doors and that city streets were "devoid of trolleys, cars, and much activity of any kind." Labor unrest had brought almost all business in Veracruz, with the exception of emergency medical care, to a halt. Then, less than a month later, a battle between members of Herón Proal's tenant union and federal troops left several dead or disappeared, many more injured, and nearly one hundred members of the Revolutionary Syndicate in jail. The confrontation led to a crackdown on popular organizing and the imposition of martial law in the port.

The General Strike

During the months that preceded the first phase of the rent strike, workers had engaged in an unprecedented wave of labor organizing in the port of Veracruz. A host of unions in the city, ranging from dock workers to bakers, printers, cigar makers, restaurant workers, electricians, streetcar operators, market vendors, and domestic workers, negotiated with their employers for improved working conditions.[1] Some even managed to secure modest gains. Others, however, saw a need for more dramatic action.

Thus, in early June 1922, Veracruz barbers formed their own association, and city sanitation employees protested the firing of thirty of their co-workers by walking off the job.[2] On June 4 they joined with members of the tenant syndicate just outside the streetcleaners' headquarters to prevent temporary laborers hired by the city from taking their place. As strikebreakers tried to drive a vehicle out of a garage, the crowd stopped them and began hounding them until the police arrived to defuse the situation.

In the mood for confrontation, militants began hurling stones. The police fought back and eventually forced the strikers to disperse but not before leaving three of their own as well as seven strikers injured. Outraged, members of the tenant union joined sanitation workers in disrupting traffic and spreading garbage through many of the central streets.[3] The next day, the conflict continued as agitators again dumped waste into the streets while groups of strikers confronted temporary workers. Their action prompted orders from City Hall for mounted police to escort sanitation brigades as they worked to clean up the mess. But while officials tried to calm restless elements in the city, militant workers prepared for further action.

On June 7 the signalmen's union at the railroad terminal declared themselves on strike and vowed that no rail traffic would be allowed to pass in or out of the Veracruz terminal until their demands were met. Bracing themselves for the possibility of conflict, they obtained help from members of the tenant syndicate in forming committees and enforcing the terms of the strike.[4] Yet while residents in the port witnessed bold new initiatives by local unions, the action taking place in Progreso, Yucatán, helped catapult the labor conflict in Veracruz to even greater heights.

During the first week of June, workers in Progreso began informing like-minded organizations in the neighboring Gulf states of Campeche, Tabasco, and Veracruz that company staff had fired workers affiliated with the railroad workers union (Liga Obrera de Ferrocarrileros) without just cause. They told their colleagues that, with the support of Governor Felipe Carrillo Puerto, scabs had been called in to run passenger trains. Hearing this, the radical press in Mexico City sharply criticized Carrillo Puerto while dockworkers in Veracruz walked off their jobs.[5]

On June 10 members of the Veracruz Maritime League (Liga de Trabajadores de la Zona Marítima) officially launched a general strike in solidarity with railroad workers in the Yucatecan cities of Progreso and Mérida, as well as Ciudad del Carmen in the state of Campeche. Quickly, other organized groups affiliated with the local union hall (Cámara de Trabajo) also joined the effort. Related action meant to paralyze business in the city began shortly after labor leaders declared the general strike. [6]

Around two o'clock that afternoon, a delegation of workers visited the central station of the city's streetcar company to interrupt service. At the same time, dockworkers announced that ships entering the Veracruz harbor would not be unloaded. In solidarity, sympathetic residents ordered cantinas and restaurants either to close or to remain open for only a few hours during midday. Bakers promised to work on Saturday but not Sunday. By late afternoon, these and other similar actions had closed almost all businesses in the city.

Dockworkers contacted the heads of several commercial houses in the port to declare that only unionized laborers would be allowed to enter the maritime zone. In protest, representatives of the Terminal Company wrote letters to the National Chamber of Commerce (Cámera Nacional de Comercio) in Mexico City while also complaining to General Guadalupe Sánchez and President Alvaro Obregón. Shortly thereafter, Veracruz Customs House administrator Alejo Bay, Sánchez, and two other businessmen boarded a train for Mexico City to meet with Obregón and Secretary of Government Plutarco Elías Calles.

While business and labor groups prepared to do battle in Veracruz, members of the Revolutionary Syndicate saw the occasion as an opportunity to advance their own cause. On June 10, for example, tenants gathered in Juárez Park and then marched down Independence Avenue to the central square, where Proal, standing above the others, addressed the crowd. He railed against those he termed "bourgeois elites" before turning his attention to the Yucatecan governor: "Down with Carrillo Puerto! Now is the time for tyrants to fall. Now is the time for the people to bring justice to replace [those who have] betrayed them. Down with Carrillo Puerto! Down with government! Now is the time to get rid of government and governors because the people should rule. Down with government! Long live the people!"[7]

Taking advantage of the opportunity to articulate his views, Proal made clear his distrust for all politicians. To officials, however, his ideological fury suggested the need for extra security forces in the port. Having received orders to maintain the peace from the secretary of war in Mexico City, General Sánchez soon told Colonel Aarón López Manzano to put federal forces on alert in order to "prevent any incidents."[8]

As the general strike began its second day on June 11, the city appeared relatively calm. That morning, a worker delegation from Yucatán arrived to announce that, surprisingly, the conflict there largely had been resolved.[9] For a few, this news suggested that the walkout in Veracruz should also come to an end. A majority, however, wanted the protest to continue. Throughout the day "strike police" could be seen monitoring local activity as organizers instructed workers to limit commercial transactions while staying away from their jobs.

One example of strike enforcement involved the cessation of beer and liquor distribution. When representatives of the Moctezuma Brewery attempted to make their rounds that morning, a delegation of workers blocked their way. After some discussion, the group agreed to allow no more than five kilos of ice to be sold to any one establishment. But no beer or liquor, they insisted, could be sold. To this, the distributors objected and called upon federal forces for assistance. When troops arrived, they suggested that the brewery trucks remain out of circulation "to avoid further difficulties" but that the sale of beer to whoever wanted to buy it would be allowed. They then ordered the strikers to disperse.[10]

While the beer blockade proved relatively benign, a skirmish involving members of the tenant syndicate outside the cantina Las Brisas del Malecón that afternoon constituted one of the more dramatic outbreaks of violence to take place during the general strike. Conflict arose when several members of the tenant syndicate insisted that the bar be closed in compliance with the labor stoppage. When the proprietor objected to their demand, Colonel Ezequiel Mateos intervened, telling the group that their request stood in violation of the cantina owners' rights. Tempers flared and Mateos fired two pistol rounds into the air to disperse the militants. Several individuals then rushed toward the colonel and attacked him. After taking a number of blows to the head, he managed to escape. A passing car found him and took him to the hospital.

Not surprisingly, the editors of *El Dictamen* strongly disapproved of the incident and blamed members of the tenant syndicate. They called the labor protest "a perfect dress rehearsal for sovietism" and accused

Rafael García of happily turning over his authority to the strike committee. Under his "soviet rule," one column read, "the dictatorship of Porfirio Díaz seems as a heavenly memory in comparison to the current tyranny of the masses."[11] In part, it was action undertaken by female militants associated with the tenant syndicate that fueled the reaction by the staff at *El Dictamen*.

In the Markets

Early on the morning of Tuesday, June 13, members of the Libertarian Women positioned themselves outside the entrances of the city's Fabela Market. In an effort to block sales while handing out propaganda to domestic workers shopping there, small groups of women prepared to prevent anyone from entering or leaving the building. As shoppers began to gather outside the market, militants eventually could not keep several from breaking through, creating a noisy exchange of insults, yelling, and shoving. Soon, the women walked over to a different market where they encouraged domestic servants there to organize and go on strike.[12]

Upon hearing the commotion, City Councilman Tomás Pérez Morteo accused Proal of being the main instigator behind the confrontations taking place at the markets and advised him that the "scandals" would have to stop. Proal responded by charging that maids and cooks had asked the tenant syndicate for help. To this he added that it remained the constitutional right of every Mexican to organize and strike.

The following day, police received orders to position themselves outside each of the markets. Worried that not only tenant but also other labor organizing activities might result in major civil disorder, federal officials also sent in four hundred soldiers from Jalapa to help maintain the peace. Additionally, Governor Adalberto Tejeda urged Commissioners Benigo Mata and Salvador González García to negotiate a solution. While they met with labor leaders on the afternoon of June 13, Proal and his followers prepared for a demonstration in Juárez Park.

By June 15, federal forces regularly patrolled Veracruz. Feeling increasingly frustrated with events in the city, Colonel López Manzano spoke to a group of workers gathered inside the local union hall: "I am a son of the people and it pains me to see how things are developing here. You have now closed the nixtamal mills, so there will be no tortillas. Good, but to whom are you causing pain? The capitalists? The bourgeoisie? No, you are hurting the poor people, your own people."[13]

The colonel's speech left many in his audience confused. Some suggested that it was the heightened presence of police and federal troops in the city, not grassroots action, that had caused many residents to panic. Responding to growing tension, labor leaders met with López Manzano and Councilman Pérez Morteo in a secret session to discuss the strike situation. City officials also conferred with Mata and González García, who then left the next day to talk over matters with lawmakers in Jalapa. Whatever the character of negotiations going on around the city, opinions differed about the direction the strike would take.

Then, on June 16, *El Dictamen* reported that port workers had decided to return to their jobs. Others, including bakers, restaurant employees, barbers, tailors, and various terminal and dock employees remained on strike. Meantime, residents received word of a telegram from President Obregón that warned workers in the city to "avoid acts of violence." At the same time, however, criticism of the tenant syndicate sharpened. On June 14, *El Dictamen* reported that while "the strike had taken place in a relatively tranquil manner, the militant followers of Proal had required the intervention of federal troops." Officials in Mexico City sent out a call to Veracruz leaders expressing their desire to discuss the local situation.

A Matter of Law and Order

One day after the general strike had begun, Governor Tejeda received word that Obregón and Calles wanted him in Mexico City. He called a special session of the state legislature to appoint an interim governor. After a day of deliberations, lawmakers selected Representative Angel Cesarín to serve. On June 12, Alejo Bay, General Guadalupe Sánchez, and Rafael García also were ordered to confer with the president. At the same time, a group of labor representatives, headed by Anselmo Mancisidor, made their way to the nation's capital.[14]

With the general strike still in full effect, President Obregón met with Bay, Sánchez, and Tejeda on June 13 and 14.[15] Despite a desire not to meddle in the internal affairs of individual states, Obregón charged that Tejeda's politics had encouraged "tumultuous and disorderly" events.[16] Listening to the report of General Sánchez had persuaded the president that the situation in the city was on the verge of chaos. In addition to worries about the labor conflict, Sánchez also encouraged officials to be concerned with recent developments in the tenant protest.[17]

Soon, diplomatic officials also felt the need to express their frustration with the strike.[18] Possibly in response to this and other negative commentary on tenant mobilization, Governor Tejeda received orders to provide additional protections for "foreigners and residents against the aggressive attitude of the [tenant] syndicate."[19] At the same time, the Mexico City paper *El Universal* reported that the Veracruz governor had offered a description of popular housing conditions to public officials in the capital. Tejeda's report strongly supported the striking tenants: "The state of complete abandonment now existing in the *viviendas* in Veracruz demonstrates clearly the want of consideration of the owners for the tenants . . . and they [stubbornly] refuse to satisfy the most rudimentary requirements of the petitioners who aspire to better living conditions because of the nature of the difficulties they seek to overcome and the historic moment through which we are passing."[20]

Despite the criticism directed toward Tejeda by federal officials and foreign diplomats, his sympathy for the fundamental demands of the movement helped maintain public enthusiasm for the renters' protests. In fact, lawmakers in Jalapa had been studying a proposal sent to them by the governor's staff in early June. On the whole, it appeared to respond favorably to many tenant demands. It stipulated that rents be reduced to 1910 levels plus 10 percent or, in cases where significant modifications or new construction had taken place after 1910, 9 percent of the property value. It included measures designed to protect renters against unauthorized evictions and other potential abuses. It also set guidelines for landlords to register their rental contracts with city officials, make repairs, and follow strict procedures regarding evictions while giving tenants a four-month moratorium on back rents, after which they would be expected to resume payment.[21] Yet despite what appeared to be progressive measures being acted upon in Jalapa, events in the port would soon throw state-mediated negotiations off course.

A Contested Ruling on Tenant Propaganda

In mid-June, Herón Proal sent a telegram to President Obregón complaining about the presence of federal forces and asking for the removal of Colonel López Manzano as local commander. Rather than receiving a positive response to his request, Proal learned two days later that a local judge had prohibited all tenant demonstrations after six o'clock in the afternoon. The order also issued a call for the removal of all strike propaganda in the city.[22]

Learning of the ban, Proal decided to call a meeting in Ciriaco Vázquez Park for the night of June 16. Later, as the crowd illuminated the evening with the flash of firecrackers and the waving of red banners,

Councilman Miguel Melche arrived on the scene. Seeing him approach, renters burst into a show of solidarity by singing the "Internationale." Unmoved, Melche began talking with Proal, who, after arguing about the ruling for some time, asked Melche to help him speak directly with Rafael García. To their chagrin, García was nowhere to be found.

Ciriaco Vázquez Park. *Courtesy of AGEV, Bernardo García Díaz Collection*

The next morning, mounted police patrolled the city's popular neighborhoods and tore down tenant banners and syndicate propaganda. Predictably, their actions provoked a strong response from residents. As police enforced the new ruling, men and women poured into the streets to protest. In one patio, two militants, Aurora "La Chata" Ramírez and Dolores Castillo, energetically resisted attempts by authorities to tear down the syndicate's red banners. Overpowered, they and a few of their compañeras ended up at the police station.

Left without strike propaganda, many patio residents took red paint to the outside of their houses and wrote "S. R. D. I. R." (Sindicato Rojo de Inquilinos Revolucionarios) and "We're not paying rent" on patio doors and gateways. Some in the La Huaca neighborhood, frustrated that their banners had been taken, went looking for municipal authorities. Seeing a group of police nearby, they shouted insults and revolutionary slogans. Meanwhile, others busily found other material from which to fashion banners, so that later that morning porteños on their way to work saw several new examples of syndicate propaganda.

As the morning progressed, groups of tenants began gathering in different spots throughout the city. Along 20 de Noviembre, Libertad, González Pages, Ferrocarril, Hidalgo, Bravo, Allende, and Guerrero Streets, renters came together to protest the ban on syndicate propaganda. True to form, many shouted slogans, insults, and obscenities at federal officials, Rafael García, and the police. Then, around noon, a large crowd assembled outside the syndicate's headquarters. Addressing the gathering, Proal advised renters to avoid any more confrontations with police until further notice. Later that day, representatives of the union visited with the mayor. Asked why he had had strike materials removed from the patios, García told the tenants he had issued no such order. He suggested that possibly the command had come instead from military officials in the city. Pressing him further, renters asked García to call off the police and release members of the syndicate who had been taken into custody.[23] Yet while renters fortified their resistance to challenges by public officials, important political and philosophical differences among tenant leaders began to surface.[24]

Internal Combustion: Anarchists versus Communists

Since the founding of the syndicate, militants had supported the need for a rent boycott but at the same time expressed various dissatisfactions with Proal. As the protest developed, several factions within the movement, especially those that included members of the Mexican Communist Party, negotiated with the anarchist for control. Throughout spring 1922, Proal managed to maintain the upper hand despite the fact that Porfirio Sosa, Mateo Luna, José Olmos, Ursulo Galván, Sóstenes Blanco, and Manuel Almanza all filled influential posts within the Revolutionary Syndicate. With the outbreak of the general strike, however, the contrasting views of these Veracruz radicals began to tear at the fragile solidarity they had achieved up to that point.[25]

By early June 1922, communists within the movement had stepped up their campaign in favor of formal political involvement at the local and national levels. Proal, however, would hear nothing of it as he vowed never to allow the syndicate to lend its support to any political party. While Proal tended to view the state in somewhat contradictory terms—as an instrument for social progress as well as an agent of worker repression—he maintained a fierce commitment to independent organization. Direct action rather than electoral politics, Proal believed, would allow the Revolutionary Syndicate to achieve its goals. Yet while his anarchist ideals had initially helped fan the fires of local radicalism, Proal's unwillingness to negotiate with those in his own camp with whom he shared a difference of tactical opinion distanced some from the tenant movement while others openly criticized Proal.

The division was heralded by the announcement in *El Dictamen*, "The tenant syndicate has experienced a tumultuous split."[26] The paper explained that thirty members of the syndicate and residents of five patios had broken with Proal. Denouncing the tenant leader for mismanaging union funds, several dissidents had affiliated themselves with a new organization led by the local communist José Olmos. Working to drum up support for an anti-Proal faction, they initiated an intense propaganda war throughout the city. When Olmos addressed a crowd assembled in Juárez Park on the night of June 29, he explained his reasons for breaking with the syndicate: "Not everyone agrees with achieving one's goals through blind and violent means."[27]

He went on to explain that his group appealed to communist principles and that in doing so, they denounced what they essentially saw as the "demagoguery" of Proal. Furthermore, Olmos declared, "communism has been a noble and sublime goal that the world's proletariat has aspired to. Precisely because of this ideal we should be suspicious of those men who preach the 'new value of communism' to the multitudes."[28] Yet despite Olmos's strong accusations against Proal, other notable communists in the port, including Miguel Salinas, Mateo Luna, Porfirio Sosa, and Manuel Almanza, criticized Olmos while reaffirming their support for Proal. Not surprisingly, the syndicate's central committee announced on July 1 that Olmos had been relieved of his union duties.[29] Carefully monitoring the situation, Proal instructed sympathizers to be on the watch for "dissidents," telling proalistas to apply direct-action techniques if necessary.

As tensions mounted between factions within the tenant movement, authorities in the city became increasingly worried that they might not be able to keep the peace. At the same time, petitions from landlords and small property owners to the governor for protection from "tenant abuses" took on a greater tone of urgency.[30] Heightened concern over the protests also reached the governor's office when one of Tejeda's agents in Veracruz informed him that the Revolutionary Syndicate "had committed numerous crimes and offenses." Fearing that the number of police in the city would not be enough, the agent wrote, "Every day the situation appears to be getting more serious."[31]

In an effort to respond to these concerns, Rafael García ordered police to remove Proal's personal bodyguards from their post across from the syndicate headquarters. Hearing the police arrive around two o'clock in the morning to uproot his sentries, Proal complained loudly but could do little else. Slamming the door to his office in disgust, he quickly sent out messengers to alert union sympathizers throughout the city. Despite the hour, a sizable crowd soon gathered outside the union offices that eventually forced police to remove themselves from the scene. Addressing his followers, Proal declared that the mayor had initiated "a serious conflict." To protest the recent crackdown on tenant activities, he then asked them to take part in a special demonstration that would be held that night in Juárez Park.[32]

Yet, while members of the syndicate appeared to be successfully maintaining their position in the larger Veracruz political arena in early July, federal authorities began maneuvers to repress the tenant protest. Evidence that events were beginning to turn against Proal came in late June when the secretary of war ordered the transfer of federal forces to the port of Veracruz. On July 1, 520 soldiers arrived in Veracruz.[33] At the same time, intense disagreement between the Olmos and proalista factions within the tenant movement came to a climax.

The July Massacre

On the night of July 5, members of the syndicate met in Ferrer Guardia Park. Addressing his followers, Proal vigorously denounced Olmos as a "betrayer" of the tenant cause. Soon, a group of protesters, red banners in hand, made their way to his house. Not seeing Olmos there, they searched the neighborhood and eventually discovered him hiding at his sister's residence inside patio El Toro. When Olmos refused to meet with the crowd, several of Proal's followers began to tear off the outer bars covering the tenement door and windows. Once inside, militants attacked the dissident leader with stones, cutting his head and severely bruising the rest of his body. While Olmos was beaten, others trashed the room. According to the report in *El Dictamen*, a few tenants stole cash and lottery tickets lying on a table.[34] Five policemen arrived at the scene and fired several rounds into the air in an attempt to disperse the crowd. Eventually, the proalistas retreated to Ferrer Guardia Park while members of the Red Cross attended to Olmos.

Shortly thereafter, troops patrolled the city with orders to prevent any further disturbances. Officials also called in reinforcements stationed at a nearby barracks. Despite the heightened military presence, fighting soon broke out between protesters and armed troops on the Veracruz streets. One incident led to the death of an officer and several injuries when soldiers defended themselves against attacks by tenants who had ambushed them and attempted to take their guns. Later, military personnel positioned themselves on the corner of Madero and

Aquiles Serdán Streets, and around nine-thirty that night, police arrested six protesters, one of whom they charged with murder.

A short while later, followers of Proal gathered outside the Hotel Diligencias to hear what the Revolutionary Syndicate would do next. Addressing his audience, Proal delivered a harsh commentary against José Olmos, the police, and federal troops. After a brief rally, most of the protesters quietly left the scene. At one point, however, troops stopped tenants on their way through the city center and detained them for a moment before allowing them to pass. A few shouted insults at the soldiers once they had reached a safe distance. Soon they found their way home or to the syndicate headquarters for debriefing. An hour or so later, most people in the city had shut their windows and doors for the evening as what *El Dictamen* later called a "sad calm" descended upon Veracruz.

After midnight, orders from the district judge calling for the arrest of Proal sparked a violent conflict between tenants and federal forces. At one o'clock that morning, approximately one hundred troops commanded by Colonel Ezequiel Mateos, the soldier who had been beaten earlier in the month outside the cantina Las Brisas del Malecón, made their way toward the Revolutionary Syndicate's headquarters. Approaching the building, Mateo's men came across several proalistas in the street as they positioned themselves a short distance across from the headquarters. A second armed group was holed up outside the customs house about two blocks away.

Seeing the soldiers coming toward them, tenants inside the building took refuge and began to arm themselves with rifles, pistols, poles, sticks, and stones. As both sides fortified their defenses, Colonel Mateos approached the door of the headquarters and called for Proal to come out. Mateos shouted to those inside that he had orders for the tenant leader's arrest. In response, Proal and several others shouted back their decision to resist. Seconds later, shots rang out from inside the building, forcing Mateos to take cover. After securing his position, Mateos then ordered his men to open fire. In the street battle that followed, tenants exchanged several rounds with the soldiers.

Hearing the gunfire, the second military column advanced and joined in an exchange of fire that lasted for several minutes, until federal troops eventually overpowered the tenants. Inside the syndicate office, several tenants had been killed or seriously injured while at least one soldier had died and another had been badly hurt. Accused of homicide and sedition, Proal gave himself up to officials. Authorities also arrested ninety men and fifty women and took them to Allende Jail.[35]

"The City Is a Place of Terror and Pain"

In the morning hours of July 6, a hard summer rain fell on Veracruz as
residents slowly filtered into the streets seeking news of the previous
night's events. Many began searching for missing family members in
the streets, along the waterfront, and in local hospitals. According to
early reports, at least two individuals had been found dead. *El Dictamen* listed several women, police, and military hurt in the conflict.[36]
From Allende Jail, Proal dashed off a telegram to officials in Jalapa
demanding an investigation. At the same time, Mayor García and the
city council communicated their willingness to "get the details" to
Tejeda.[37] Responding immediately to the crisis, the governor dispatched
his staff member, Victorio E. Gongora, to begin an official investigation.[38] Local authorities issued orders restricting public gatherings and
prohibiting the carrying of arms as well as the use of firecrackers in the
port of Veracruz. The decree left little doubt about the strong desire by
local officials to repress the activities of the Revolutionary Syndicate.
By nightfall, martial law had been established in Veracruz.

While some residents complied with the soldiers' requests, many
others did not. Scouring the streets for missing members, several from
the Revolutionary Syndicate soon came in conflict with authorities. A
group of Libertarian Women, for example, immediately defied the
military crackdown by marching in front of army headquarters, shouting insults at the soldiers and calling for the release of Proal and other
syndicate members. In response, troops ordered the women to return
to their homes or risk arrest. Elsewhere, police arrested three women
who had attempted to rally tenants by shooting off firecrackers in Juárez
Park. At the corner of San Lorenzo and Allende Streets a small bomb
had exploded but caused little damage. At the same time, tenants in
patio Cuauhtémoc staged a temporary act of collective resistance by
parking themselves in the street and demanding the release of Proal
and "their other comrades." Nearby, approximately fifty women had
gathered at the corner of Guerrero and Cortés Streets before police ordered them to return to their homes. Later that morning, a standoff
between police and a group of tenants gathered near Infantil Park left
one policeman and one civilian injured. Prompted by these and other
protests, authorities engaged in a new round of arrests.[39]

While the morning of July 6 proved especially contentious, the afternoon passed without any further clashes between residents and
military forces. Soon, however, police received word that tenants had
decided to convene a secret meeting inside the Cámara de Trabajo that
evening. Responding to the rumor, officials again ordered troops to

circulate throughout the city. To their surprise, police encountered about fifty renters assembled at Ferrer Guardia Park. Refusing at first to cooperate with requests to dissolve the meeting, tenants grudgingly left in small groups only after federal reinforcements had arrived and threatened them with arrest.

That night, no meeting at the union hall was held, despite rumors to the contrary. Having been ordered by the secretary of war to maintain the peace in Veracruz, authorities doubled the number of guards at Allende Jail after hearing that tenants might try to secure the release of Proal. In the end, however, the possibility of a jailbreak proved false. *El Dictamen* claimed the next day that "the entire city [had] slept peacefully" during the night.[40] And Rafael García wrote to Governor Tejeda that "complete calm" now prevailed in the city.[41] Yet despite the many efforts to restore order and quietly bring the protest to a close, word of atrocities being committed by federal troops in the port of Veracruz quickly spread across the nation. Closer to home, many in Veracruz scrambled to make a precise accounting of exactly who and how many had been killed or injured on the night of July 5–6.

Initial estimates in the local communist paper, *El Frente Unico*, were that close to 150 individuals had died that night. In contrast, *El Dictamen* counted 15 wounded, including 5 soldiers and 10 tenant women.[42] Additional testimony about the night of July 5–6, however, creates a more complicated picture. Some said that several bodies had been seen throughout the city with others "mysteriously appearing" over the course of the following week.[43] Yet despite disagreement about the total number of dead and injured, most agreed that the killing of citizens by military personnel was a grievous offense that required immediate legal action.

For their part, justice officials questioned Proal and his colleagues José Martínez, Jesús Medina, Juan Calderón, Trinidad Cruz, Pedro García, and Donato Morales late into the night of July 7. Some of those interrogated denied being members of the tenant union and argued they had only been minding their own business when police arrested them. In contrast, Proal proudly stated his position as head of the Revolutionary Syndicate. Recounting the events of July 5–6, the anarchist claimed that he and his supporters did not resist military advances but instead had become the victims of violent repression. Proal also indicated that he and other members of the Revolutionary Syndicate wished to cooperate fully with authorities.

State congressional representative Carlos Palacios arrived in Veracruz and, during the afternoon of July 7, conducted his own interviews with Proal and López Manzano. In a public statement, the lawmaker declared that striking tenants had his support because theirs was a "noble and just cause." He even proposed a meeting in Juárez Park but was quickly discouraged by local authorities.[44] Observing his behavior, some joked that Palacios might be positioning himself to become the director of the tenant syndicate.

The next day, the lawmaker sent a telegram to Tejeda stating that many residents strongly resented the presence of federal forces in the city and wanted the governor to intervene. At the same time, Palacios helped substantiate claims that federal troops had deliberately terrorized residents by writing that several unidentified bodies had shown up on the Veracruz beach: "This terrible crime has violated the sovereignty of the state. The people are indignant and demand that justice be done. The city, at this time, is a place of terror and pain. As the representative for Veracruz, I make my protest against the bastard aggressors before the entire nation."[45] In addition to his public statements, one of Palacios's first proposals was to call for the removal of López Manzano as head of the federal forces stationed in Veracruz. A week or so later, Governor Tejeda responded that efforts had been undertaken to replace the colonel.[46]

Meanwhile, reporters in Veracruz interviewed a badly beaten José Olmos in Aquiles Serdán Hospital, who insisted that the activities of his dissident association would continue and that a full investigation of syndicate finances was their top priority. Yet despite action planned by Olmos and other individuals outside the syndicate's inner circle, Proal had carefully made provisions for new leadership by selecting Manuel Almanza for the union's top post. Almanza soon assumed responsibility for coordinating all public business while Proal and members of the executive committee strategized from within the jail.

By July 8 tenants had already established a temporary headquarters inside patio La Ilusión on Esteban Morelos Street. While no reports of confrontations between soldiers, police, and tenants took place that day, rumors circulated that certain militants who formed a special "commission in charge of removing obstacles" had been entrusted with the assassination of López Manzano. Apparently, officials had intercepted a letter that, in addition to insulting members of the local government and army, threatened that "those who had taken part in the events of early July 6 . . . would [soon] be dead."[47] The report in *El Dictamen* on July 9 also stated that tenant organizers planned to announce ways in which they wished to resume protest activities and reprinted an exchange of telegrams between Manuel Almanza, as he took over directorship of the tenant syndicate, and President Obregón. Almanza wrote: "The Revolutionary Tenant Syndicate, with all due respect, denounces and protests the following: Today at three in the morning, federal forces assaulted the [tenant] union's headquarters, jailed [our] director Herón Proal and secretaries Porfirio Sosa and Rodolfo Mercado. The people of Veracruz are indignant over this matter and confident that you will grant the prisoners their liberty and reopen our office." To this, President Obregón replied: "All the information available to this administration regarding the brutal assault on Citizen Olmos as well as the events that have taken place regarding Proal and his associates have been given to me by local justice officials. I have given military personnel orders to maintain order and protect the lives of citizens. While it is not within my jurisdiction to punish those responsible for these lamentable and bloody actions, I am sure that the proper authorities will administer justice in the energetic and diligent manner in which they are charged."

With this, Obregón expressed his desire to avoid direct involvement in the matter as well as any possible blame. Still, officials in Mexico City were bombarded with communications protesting military action in Veracruz. A message to Secretary of Government Calles signed by "an exploited tenant" decried the use of violence and demanded that justice be served on those responsible for "the monstrous assassination on the night of July 5."[48] Another letter to Obregón written a few days later stated that "the sea denounced the crime by washing up cadavers riddled with bullet holes on the beach."[49] Despite the many appeals, however, President Obregón continued to maintain his distance while deferring to local and regional authorities.[50] Meanwhile, down on the Veracruz waterfront, members of the stevedores union took action by calling labor organizations in the port to attend a general meeting regarding the tenant protest. Shortly thereafter, acting governor Angel Caserín took it upon himself to declare the immediate "public necessity" of construction of worker housing in Veracruz, Orizaba, Jalapa, Córdoba, Tuxpan, Puerto México, and Huatusco while provisionally approving Tejeda's rent law.[51] But, as events during the coming months would attest, the fate of the renters' movement had not yet been sealed.

Notes

1. Many of these individuals were also affiliated with the Federación Local de Trabajadores de Veracruz (FLTV). For information on the port's labor unions, see Gema Lozano y Nathal, *Catálogo del Archivo Sindical del Puerto de Veracruz "Miguel Angel Montoya Cortés"* (Mexico City: Colección Fuentes, Instituto Nacional de Antropología e Historia, 1990), as well as Gema Lozano

DQ: What does this chapter say about public perceptions of federal involvement in public protests? (i.e. militerily)

y Nathal, "La negra, loca y anarquista federación local de trabajadores del puerto de Veracruz," *Antropología* 30 (April–June 1990): 10–19.

2. *El Dictamen*, June 2 and 3, 1922.

3. Ibid., June 5, 1922.

4. Ibid., June 8, 1922.

5. Daniela Spenser, "Workers against Socialism? Reassessing the Role of Urban Labor in Yucatecan Revolutionary Politics," in Gilbert Joseph, ed., *Land, Labor, and Capital in Modern Yucatán: Essays in Regional History and Political Economy* (Tuscaloosa: University of Alabama Press, 1991), 236–37.

6. *El Dictamen*, June 11 and 14, 1922. See also Octavio García Mundo, *El movimiento inquilinario de Veracruz, 1922* (Mexico City: Sep-Setentas, 1976), 147.

7. *El Dictamen*, June 11, 1922.

8. Ibid., June 13, 1922.

9. Ibid., June 12, 1922.

10. Ibid., June 13, 1922.

11. Ibid.

12. Ibid., June 14, 1922.

13. Ibid., June 15, 1922.

14. Calles to Tejeda, June 11–13, 1922. Quoted in Roman Falcón and Soledad García Morales, *La semilla en el surco: Adalberto Tejeda y el radicalismo en Veracruz, 1883–1960* (Mexico City: Colegio de México, 1986), 140.

15. Obregón had recently sent a delegation to Yucatán to help mediate labor conflict there.

16. García Mundo, *El movimiento*, 18.

17. Several skirmishes between members of the tenant syndicate and police earlier in the month gave officials sufficient cause for alarm. See, for example, *El Dictamen*, June 6, 9, 14, 1922.

18. Subsecretary of Government to Ministry of Foreign Affairs, June 13, 1922, AGEV, gobernación, "circulares," no. 116, letter "C," 1922.

19. Subsecretary of Government to Tejeda, June 16, 1922, Summerlin to Secretary of State, June 16, 1922, RDS, reel 161. The Spanish Embassy had also complained of tenant threats in Veracruz in early June. AGN, gobernación, box 24, c. 2. 51. 107, "Procedimientos del Sindicato de Inquilinos del Puerto de Veracruz."

20. Excerpt from Tejeda's report printed in *El Universal*, quoted in George Summerlin to Secretary of State, June 23, 1922, RDS, reel 161.

21. *El Dictamen*, July 1, 1922; García Mundo, *El movimiento inquilinario*, 154.

22. *El Dictamen*, June 17, 1922. On June 17 the city again witnessed a major conflict between workers and police when a crowd of laborers still on strike tried to disarm federal forces on the corner of Arista and 5 de Mayo Streets.

23. Later, a group of approximately three hundred tenants attacked the house of Inés García on Canal Street. After several minutes of intimidation by tenants, police arrived and eventually restored order. Ibid., June 21, 1922.

24. Fearing a new offensive by striking tenants, property owners met at the Hotel Diligencias on June 25 to form a new, more inclusive association headed by Salvador Campa. According to *El Dictamen* (June 27, 1922), the new association saw itself as a kind of resistance league.

25. Looking at individual relations among radicals in the Orizaba area in 1920–21, Bernardo García Díaz writes that affiliations tended to be quite fluid between anarchists and communists. García Díaz, "Acción directa y poder

obrero en la CROM de Orizaba, 1918–1922," *Historias* 7 (October–December 1984): 24.

26. *El Dictamen*, June 30, July 1, 1922.

27. Ibid., June 30, 1922; García Mundo, *El movimiento inquilinario*, 153.

28. Quoted in Paco Ignacio Taibo II, *Bolshevikis: Historia narrativa de los orígenes del comunismo en México, 1919–1925* (Mexico City: Editorial Joaquín Mortiz, 1986), 177.

29. *El Dictamen*, July 3, 1922.

30. See, for example, Isabel Dubois de González Marron to Tejeda, July 1, 1922, AGEV, gobernación, 1922.

31. Public Ministry Agent #1 to Tejeda, June 30, 1922, AGEV, gobernación, 1922. A few days later, Angel Casarín responded by saying that officials in Jalapa had sent a new rent law to the legislature and that hopefully this would remedy the situation. Casarín to Tejeda, July 2, 1922, AT, vol. 75, no. 99.

32. *El Dictamen*, July 1, 1922.

33. Ibid., July 2, 1922. García Mundo, *El movimiento inquilinario*, 156.

34. *El Dictamen*, July 7, 1922.

35. Ibid.

36. Ibid. See also Arturo Bolio Trejo, *Rebelión de mujeres: Versión histórica de la revolución inquilinaria de Veracruz* (Veracruz: Editorial "Kada," 1959), 142, and Leafar Agetro (Rafael Ortega), *Las luchas proletarias en Veracruz: Historia y autocrítica* (Jalapa: Editorial "Barricada," 1942), 86.

37. M. López to Tejeda, July 7, 1922, AGEV, gobernación, "Circulares" no. 116, letter "C," 1922.

38. Angel Casarín to confidential agent Juan Fortuny, July 6, 7, 1922, AGEV, gobernación, 1922.

39. Ibid.

40. *El Dictamen*, July 7, 1922.

41. García to Tejeda, July 7, 1922, AGEV, gobernación, "Circulares," 1922.

42. *El Dictamen*, July 7, 1922.

43. Bolio Trejo, *Rebelión de mujeres*, 142; Agetro (Ortega), *Las luchas proletarias*, 86; Taibo II, *Bolshevikis*, 178–79. Later government reports registered four dead and twenty-two wounded. Moisés González Navarro, *Población sociedad en México, 1900–1970* (Mexico City: UNAM, 1974), 1:182. Another report, generated the following October by a special committee made up of representatives from various local labor unions, stated that twenty-one women and nine men had sustained serious injuries. Letter from Comité Pro-Preso to Ministry of Government dated October 11, 1922, AGN, gobernación, box 24, exp.107.

44. *El Dictamen*, July 8, 1922.

45. Palacios to Tejeda, July 9, 1922, AGEV, gobernación, 1922.

46. Tejeda to Palacios, July 15, 1922, ibid.

47. Ibid.

48. Letter to Calles, July 7, 1922, AT, vol. 75, no. 99.

49. "Un inquilino que se ve imposibilitado de firmar" to Obregón, July 10, 1922, AT, vol. 75, no. 99.

50. For their part, state Justice officials sent messages to Tejeda hoping to prevent "similar developments" in Jalapa. Procurador General de Justicia del Estado de Veracruz to Tejeda, July 8, 1922, AGEV, gobernación, 1922. The governor indicated that protection had been arranged for residents there. Tejeda to Procurador General, July 14, 1922, AGEV, gobernación, 1922. Outside the state, tenant protest also grew increasingly controversial. On the night of July 7—just one day after the shoot-out in Veracruz—nearly four thousand tenants

had marched in Mexico City to protest the death of a renter who had been killed in the capital resisting eviction proceedings. Summerlin to Secretary of State, July 8, 1922, RDS, reel 161.

51. *Gaceta Oficial: Organo del Gobierno Constitucional del Estado de Veracruz-Llave*, July 11, 1922, 1–3. *El Dictamen* printed the text of the law on July 14, 1922. See also González Navarro, *Población y sociedad*, 1:182–83, as well as Falcón and García Morales, *La semilla*, 142. Tejeda obviously supported the law and encouraged Casarín to go forward with it. Early in July, for example, the governor sent messages about how properties should be taxed while also voicing his support for rents based at 6 percent. Tejeda to Casarín, July 2 and 4, 1922, AT, vol. 65.

7

"Behind the Words and 'Advanced Posturing' of Public Officials"
The Debate over State Housing Reform

Compañeros: Viva universal love!
Viva the emancipation of women!
Up with communism!
Viva free humanity!
Women, to the struggle!
—María Luisa Marín, *El Frente Unico*

[handwritten note: Same anger that poor showed toward police in The Slum]

On the night of July 8, 1922, a rally took place in the port across from the house of Veracruz state representative Carlos Palacios. After a number of speakers had addressed the crowd, including Palacios, who again energetically declared his commitment to the tenant movement, renters marched to Juárez Park.[1] Along the way, some shouted, "Death to the military!" and "Down with the bourgeoisie!" while distributing a special edition of *El Frente Unico*.[2] The next day, Governor Adalberto Tejeda informed President Alvaro Obregón that workers in the port had threatened to launch another general strike in protest of the July 5–6 massacre.[3] If those responsible for the killing were not brought to justice, many porteños agreed, the city would have to be shut down.

At the same time, direct action and other forms of public agitation taken by tenants in Jalapa, Orizaba, and Córdoba pressured state politicians. Along with members of the tenant syndicate in the port, many had traveled to the state capital to lend support to Governor Tejeda's rent law. Although Herón Proal and other leaders remained in jail, coordinated efforts by renters throughout the state eventually helped realize passage of the country's only significant housing reform legislation in the 1920s.

Reaction to the Massacre

In the aftermath of the July 5–6 shooting, authorities had ordered federal forces to remain on alert in Veracruz. Governor Tejeda requested that Secretary of Government Plutarco Elías Calles send an "impartial commission" to investigate the situation, which he said now caused a "great dissatisfaction among the people."[4] At the same time, Tejeda dispatched one of his aides, Juan Fortuny, to Veracruz.[5] Arriving in the port, Fortuny found that a cloud of darkness had descended on the city. Following the massacre, federal troops had taken the opportunity to evict several tenants from their homes.[6] Rumors circulated that accused members of the tenant syndicate of stealing from stores and homes of Spaniards.[7] Meantime, others tried to revive the idea that Proal was a "pernicious foreigner" who had "extended his influence to other cities and towns in the nation."[8] Despite these difficulties, however, many residents maintained their commitment to the protest.

Two days after the massacre, tenants wrote directly to President Obregón demanding the release of Proal and other syndicate members:

> The tenant strike has proved a blessing because, if for no other reason, it has alerted workers to the fact that behind the words and "advanced posturing" of public officials lies an abuse of power. The "revolutionary liberalism" of government officials has fallen like a miserable house of cards. And in its place they ostentatiously have shown us how they are "friends" of the "people" by shoving the barrel of a gun down our throats. In "respecting the [workers'] right to strike," they have sent in a military force to protect the go-getters and guarantee the "rights of workers and industrialists." We lament the fact that bayonets continue to sustain the bourgeoisie of the country [while] they miserably exploit the sweat of the Indian in the countryside and the blood of the proletariat in the cities.[9]

The petition revealed the deep frustration and anger felt toward the military and government officials. Soon, others across the country would express their solidarity with the striking tenants.[10]

On July 10 members of the tenant syndicate sent their account of the massacre to Calles in Mexico City. The testimony claimed that, in repressing the syndicate, members of the military had disregarded "the most rudimentary principles of justice." To begin to rectify this situation, tenants demanded the immediate release of Proal and other syndicate members, the return of all materials confiscated from tenant headquarters, and a full investigation. Over one hundred sympathizers signed the letter.[11] Soon, tenants Julián García and Pedro González left for Mexico City to meet with Calles.[12]

On July 11, port workers took the day off to honor the men and women killed.[13] Then, three days later, Mayor Rafael García issued a "manifesto" defending himself against accusations in the press that he was responsible for "recent disturbances in the city." He stated his support for the "heroic struggle of the tenants against property owners" and declared that landlords as well as the editors of *El Dictamen* had viciously tried to discredit him. "Property owners' recent refusal to pay city taxes," he said, "was an economic attempt to kill the municipality. Now, as the people judge who exactly was responsible for recent events, the hour of justice will soon arrive."[14]

Tejeda tried again to mediate talks between embattled tenants and landlords. On July 14 he met with delegations of both property owners and tenants.[15] Three days later, syndicate representative Manuel Almanza relayed Tejeda's message to tenants in the port. Almanza told the renters he had presented three major demands during his conference with the governor. First, members of the syndicate must be released from jail. Second, restrictions on tenant meetings and demonstrations must be lifted. Finally, all confiscated articles from the renters' union headquarters must be returned immediately. According to Almanza, Tejeda appeared sympathetic to these demands but had informed tenant representatives that only federal officials could authorize the freeing of Proal and the others. "The governor," Almanza assured the crowd, "will use his influence to achieve a solution in our favor."[16]

While federal officials collected information on the incident, members of the tenant syndicate had formed their own investigative commission. In a letter to Secretary of Government Calles describing the events of that night, renters argued that little doubt remained about the degree to which the military had been responsible for "so many dead and injured." "Ask those who lie injured in the hospital, in the jail, in their own houses, or buried in the cemetery," the tenants suggested, "[and] they all will certify that their wounds were the result of the troops firing on the people."[17] Thus, despite an official report issued in October 1922 declaring that twenty-one women and nine men had sustained serious injuries, the exact number of fatalities remained unclear. Residents, in collaboration with local labor, compiled a list of the injured, dead, and missing. According to information collected from the forty-three testimonials gathered by the defense committee, several observers saw nearly sixty unidentified men, women, and children injured or killed during the incident.[18]

Fearing a violent retaliation from militant renters, authorities soon stepped up their surveillance of city streets and neighborhoods. At the same time, police announced that public gatherings by the tenant syndicate would not be allowed until further notice. Justifying the decision, Rafael García later wrote to Governor Tejeda and officials in Mexico City explaining the ban:

> The city council has declared meetings by the syndicate prohibited [for the reason that] demonstrations organized by members of that group have taken on a violent character. Speakers [have] incited crowds against not only those they opposed [the landlords] but also authorities. Given my duty as mayor, I do not wish to issue strict measures to repress the expression of ideas. The regrettable events that took place on the night of July 5–6 and subsequent protests in which insults, threats, and intimidation have been employed to try to secure the release of Herón Proal require me, however, to prohibit tenant meetings until further notice.[19]

Although residents initially complied with the ruling, Carlos Palacios wrote to Tejeda in late August calling the continued crackdown "a fundamental violation" of citizens' rights and complaining of police circulating through the city making what he saw were arbitrary and unnecessary arrests.[20] The governor replied that he would recommend to Rafael García that authorities comply with Article 9 of the Constitution, which guaranteed citizens the right to assemble peacefully for the purpose of protesting or petitioning authorities.[21] A few days later, Tejeda received a petition from sixty prisoners held in Allende Jail expressing their outrage over the massacre and recent measures taken against the tenant syndicate.[22] More than fifty inmates also wrote to Secretary of Government Calles, blaming the military for the events of July 5–6 and asking, "What are our wives and children to do while we remain in jail?"[23] Two weeks later, Proal and the others wrote to Subsecretary of the Interior Gilberto Valenzuela demanding that "justice be served."[24] Yet while authorities considered these and other petitions, tenants had decided to launch a new initiative by organizing a statewide renters convention to be held in early August.

The Tenant Convention

When representatives from tenant unions in Orizaba, Santa Rosa, Nogales, Córdoba, Soledad de Doblado, and Veracruz arrived in Jalapa on August 4, 1922, scores of local sympathizers welcomed them with enthusiasm. Prior to the convention, tenant groups around the state had called for the release of Proal but had also been locked in their own struggles with property owners. For their part, members of the Orizaba syndicate had written to Tejeda earlier in the summer, informing him of their frustrations over local landlords' "intransigence" as well as the "ruinous state of almost sixty percent of the city's houses."[25] Tenants in neighboring Santa Rosa had also informed Governor Tejeda that they had come to no agreement with property owners.[26] Likewise, militants in other cities brought similar concerns to Jalapa, so that once assembled, renters largely agreed on the need for a statewide federation of tenants.

In a letter to Secretary of Government Calles, delegates first repeated their demands for the release of Proal and members of the Veracruz syndicate: "The charges against our nearly eighty compañeros are totally false. The only crime that these people have committed is to profess their ideological beliefs regarding the betterment of society. [As a result,] justice in Mexico has been corrupted and the working class of this country has suffered a serious deception at the hands of judicial officials."[27] Then, in a manifesto sent to Governor Tejeda, they made a broad appeal to the Mexican people: "The tenant syndicates [have presented] a serious challenge to the insatiable greed of the property owners. The people of Mexico have been double-crossed at this moment in history and deprived of any real justice, which for ten years has remained asleep until now."[28] Arguing that the movement had been born of "popular necessity," organizers called for the immediate release of all jailed tenants as well as the full passage of housing reforms. The manifesto commented specifically on the proposed rent law by saying that tenants wanted the law "to be charged with a spirit of conciliation and equilibrium between the two hostile classes." Judges, they argued, who "favor the interests" of the state's propertied classes should be immediately dismissed. No faction or minority should benefit above all others. Finally, renters resolved that the new state tenant federation be recognized by judicial authorities, that a housing reform law be passed requiring that rents be based at 4 percent of property values, and that all back rents be canceled.[29]

A few days later, Tejeda replied to leaders of the newly formed tenant federation that he would take their demands into careful consideration but that it would be difficult to grant all that they wanted. On the issue of back rents, Tejeda stated that under the law, the matter would have to be taken up directly with property owners themselves. Additionally, rents fixed at 4 percent of property values might prove difficult given the economic situation the state faced. Instead, the governor argued that rents based at 6 percent of property values would prove feasible and fair. Finally, while Tejeda praised convention-goers for their "honorable conduct," he made it clear that the release of tenant prisoners would have to wait for further discussion by state officials.[30] Meanwhile, incarcerated militants Herón Proal and María Luisa

Marín had wasted no time in resuming their "revolutionary" activities from within Allende Jail.

Strike within the Strike: The Tortilla Makers

Since the night of July 5–6, encouraged by Proal and Marín, tenants held in Allende Jail loudly sang songs, decorated the cells with their red banners, and made a regular practice of intimidating prison staff and other inmates. Defying federal efforts to discourage them, Proal and Marín tirelessly organized inside the jail, where they remained committed to their revolutionary ideology. On September 16 the two gained permission to hold a "Red dance" celebrating Mexican independence. Dramatically, Proal and Marín ordered the inside of the jail decorated with red banners and pictures of Russian leaders to express their solidarity with the international communist movement. According to *El Dictamen*, Allende director Andrés Andrade even lent them his phonograph for the occasion.

That night, male and female prisoners gathered in the women's section where they ate and drank while dancing to music. Tenants also sang communist hymns and shouted slogans praising revolutionary ideals. To the surprise of many outsiders, the dance marked the first time such a "Red" gathering had taken place within a Mexican jail. Reaction in the press remained cool, however. The editors of *El Dictamen* charged that tenants had been given "too much freedom" in being allowed to continue their "communist" organizing.[31]

A few days later, Marín organized a work stoppage by tortilla makers in the jail to protest what she claimed was a lack of adequate drinking water as well as other grievances. At first, the tortilla strike seemed to unify the female inmates. Soon, however, some grew disillusioned with the effort. Then, after a week of nearly constant contention, the staff of *El Dictamen* characterized Marín as a "boss" (*cacique*) and suggested she had ordered prisoners to "commit abuses" within the jail. In an editorial they wrote that she "has turned into a tyrant who demands that everyone answer to her" and noted that a sizable group of women were not willing to cooperate with Marín's desire to continue the tortilla-makers' strike.[32] Indeed, of those who claimed they had no interest in the strike, some said their only wish "was to regain their sacred liberty in order to return to their homes and children, who now live in a frightening state of abandonment."[33]

Disagreements within the women's section exploded on October 5 when a nearly three-hour battle broke out among female prisoners. According to one account, Marín had challenged a few women who intended to break the tortilla-makers' strike. The confrontation reached a high point when, after shouting insults at the inmates as well as members of their families who had been visiting, Marín and her followers took up sticks and stones to attack the challengers. After a period of intense fighting, one woman broke away and managed to call for help. Soon, ten prison staff intervened to restore order and Marín and two others were put in solitary confinement for fifteen days. The next morning, female prisoners returned to the business of tortilla making.[34]

Despite these and other difficulties in the prison, labor organizers in the city generally maintained their support for the jailed tenants. On October 11, workers who had recently formed a "pro-prisoners committee" (Comité Pro-Preso) wrote to Governor Tejeda requesting that Proal and the others be released. They stated that the imprisonment of tenants represented "a great injustice" because many had small children who needed to be cared for. The real crime, the letter read, "was the robbery carried out by unscrupulous landlords in the port." [35] The committee gave Tejeda three days to consider the matter. If the governor did not use his "intelligent powers" to reply after that point, they suggested "there would be negative consequences." Five days later, a member of Tejeda's staff issued a reply stating that the governor could not act in the matter, because it "remained in the hands of judicial authorities."[36] Still, the committee continued to lobby Tejeda.

On October 23, labor leader José Mancisidor wrote to the governor informing him that members of the prisoners' support committee wished to secure the release of Proal and "other workers and women held in Allende Jail even if it meant launching another general strike." Additionally, Mancisidor recommended that Proal and his closest associates be taken to Jalapa to consult with state officials on the proposed rent law. "If matters are left unresolved for some time," he warned, "things will only get worse and more dangerous."[37] Indeed, as October came to an end and residents prepared for the traditional Day of the Dead holiday in early November, another major confrontation between residents and local police proved Mancisidor's prediction true.

March on the Day of the Dead

Outside the jail, porteños did not remain quiet for long after the massacre of July 5–6.[38] During summer and fall 1922, tenants continued their battle against landlords and administrators. On October 1, for example, renters of patio 123 Revilagigedo Street attacked the owner, José Rivero Cueto. Police arrested two individuals and charged them with assault.[39] Two weeks later, syndicate members announced that they had begun a new campaign of direct action.

As one might expect, some residents had grown tired of public confrontations between renters and police, even though a few tenants had managed to negotiate agreements with their landlords. But militants continued to write to President Obregón, boldly asserting themselves and asking for the release of Proal and his colleagues. One petition charged that if officials did not employ effective measures to free their leader, protesters would again shut down the city by calling a general strike.[40] Yet as tenants persisted in their petitioning of government officials, one of the many street battles that took place during fall 1922 resulted in the death of an unidentified tenant organizer on October 16. According to *El Dictamen*, a delegate of the syndicate had been shot while trying to stop the payment of rent by a group of uncooperative tenants.[41]

Then, on November 1, port workers and local labor confederation members met to discuss the tenant protest.[42] The following day, the tenant syndicate announced that a Day of the Dead procession would make its way to the city cemetery. After gathering downtown, hundreds of residents traveled through the streets of Veracruz carrying flowers, candles, and mementos of family members as well as several red banners. As they arrived at the cemetery, the situation grew tense. According to the police report submitted by Commander Manuel Zamudio:

> [Members of] the tenant syndicate [then] went into the cemetery. Soon, groups of women arrived carrying banners but without committing any offenses. I then talked with Syndicate Secretary Miguel Salinas, warning him that tenant demonstrations had been banned by the police chief. [Salinas] then told me that they had permission from the mayor. After trying to confirm whether this was true, additional police arrived. About thirty minutes later, tenants began to leave the cemetery led by someone named Bolio, two Spaniards, and a few others who began to agitate the people there. We waited and tried to dissuade the crowd from becoming excited but they continued to harass us. While we talked with a couple of protesters a shot suddenly rang out, killing one member of the syndicate. Seeing this, the crowd looked at us, believing we had fired one of our guns. Tension between the protesters and police then erupted as individuals called for us to be lynched. Shooting broke out and I was forced to take cover.[43]

In the fray, one renter, Angel Marín, died, and several others, including three policemen, suffered serious injuries. In his letter to Mexico City officials, Mayor García explained that the confrontation had been sparked by "agitators" who had "mixed with" syndicate members in order to start a conflict with authorities. While who had been responsible for the violence remained a mystery, the damage had already been done and two more renters were dead.[44]

The next morning, port workers walked off their jobs at eleven o'clock in protest. Later that afternoon, many gathered for another march to the cemetery in honor of Angel Marín. This time, residents again traveled from the city center, carrying a casket draped in red-and-black fabric down Zaragoza Street, crossing over to Independencia to 20 de Noviembre and then to the cemetery. By the time everyone had gathered at the site, the crowd amounted to nearly three thousand people. Proudly displaying their organization's banners, representatives from most of the major labor unions attended. In the mix, marchers waved red-and-black flags that carried the inscriptions "Anarchy" and "Revolutionary Tenant Syndicate." Once Angel Marín had been buried, several speakers addressed the crowd and pledged to maintain the protest.[45]

On November 6 tenants again defied authority by marching through the city, shouting slogans and criticizing local authorities before gathering at Ciriaco Vázquez Park. According to a letter Rafael García sent to President Obregón and Governor Tejeda, protesters had fired a number of pistol shots before dispersing around 11:00 P.M. The police report of the same incident read, "Tenants had resumed their nightly meetings as before, organizing tumultuous demonstrations in the city's main streets, insulting authorities and residents whom they encounter by calling them 'bourgeois,' and moving through the city armed, shooting off their pistols anywhere without respect for anyone."[46] As a result, the governor soon ordered that syndicate meetings in the port again be prohibited.[47] Yet despite the ruling, authorities found they could not enforce such an order. Mayor García claimed he had been powerless to control the tenants.[48] Part of the commotion had been caused by a new organization in town calling themselves the Communist Youth. Members of this group ignored the ban on public demonstrations and had begun to conduct their own marches and direct actions.[49]

At about this same time, a staff member of the Veracruz Labor Department wrote to authorities in Mexico City saying, "State officials do not seem concerned about resolving this troublesome [tenant] problem any time soon." He continued, "the daily incidents that take place are truly shameful given that so many foreign visitors pass through the port."[50] Of course, many of those who complained most vigorously were landlords.

Rallying against Reform: The Property Owners

Aside from dealing with belligerent tenants, landlords viewed Governor Tejeda's proposed housing reform with great suspicion, often suggesting that it could never be successfully applied.[51] In particular, Article 3—which set the percentage at which rents would be calculated—stood as one of the main points of contention. Thus, when landlords throughout the state learned that the Veracruz state legislature had provisionally approved the reform in early July 1922, many quickly organized in resistance. Determined to block application of the law, they filed amparos against the governor, the legislature, and local officials, declaring that the reform stood in "violation of their constitutional rights."[52] Responding to these attacks, Tejeda sent a telegram to the district judge in Orizaba suggesting that actions intended to destroy laws passed by the state represented a "danger to the people of the state, not to mention tenants whose situation the law is designed to improve."[53] Soon, other challenges to Tejeda's law followed.

In late July, an editorial printed in *El Dictamen* complained that provisions in the reform that allowed for the appropriation of real estate by the state essentially meant the confiscation of private property.[54] "Although the measure was approved by the legislature," another editorial stated a few weeks later, "as many are not cooperating with the law now as the day it was passed."[55] Thus, with landlords arguing that the law should be ruled unconstitutional and tenants continuing to insist on the release of Proal and the other prisoners before they would seriously consider legal reforms, successful application of the measure seemed a remote possibility. Thus, state leaders began considering possible modifications.

Negotiating Housing Reform

In late September 1922, Herón Proal and Jalapa tenant leaders Moisés Lira and Isidro Polanco met in Allende Jail to discuss possible revisions to the rent law. Considering the different formulas at which rents would be refigured, they agreed that rates should be based at only 6 percent of property values. Then, in a message forwarded to Governor Tejeda by acting tenant syndicate head Manuel Almanza in early October, the three leaders declared that "while six percent is onerous for the producing classes of the state at this time because of the tough economic situation we find ourselves in, it is nevertheless not an obstacle to resolving the housing crisis."[56]

Responding to overtures issued by state lawmakers, a group of landlords headed by Salvador Campa agreed to meet with tenants in Jalapa to discuss revisions to the proposed law in early November.[57] Shortly thereafter, Campa informed a group of landlords in the port of possible changes. He suggested that proposed revisions would involve a reconsideration of the percentage at which landlords figured rents. "Certainly," Campa declared, "nowhere in the world have landlords been required to accept rents this low."[58]

Then in December, Campa and other members of the Veracruz Property Owners Association again traveled to Jalapa to meet with legislators.[59] Groups in Córdoba, Orizaba, Puerto México, Minatitlán, and other cities in the state also sent representatives. After a series of discussions, delegates reported back to their local organizations. The Veracruz group, according to testimony printed in *El Dictamen*, expressed a general feeling of satisfaction with the negotiations.[60] Following the meeting with property owners, Governor Tejeda and other lawmakers called members of the Veracruz tenant union to Jalapa on December 9 to discuss a new rate at which rents would be based.[61] Afterward, Tejeda wrote to officials in Mexico City, saying that he and tenant leaders had agreed to keep urban rents in the state based at 6 percent of property values.[62] Yet, while the governor and tenants were in accord on this point, members of the Revolutionary Syndicate of Tenants still held fast to their demand that Proal and the others be released before they would fully cooperate with state officials.

Just as efforts to realize a legal settlement to the rent strike by politicians appeared to be making headway, negotiations suffered a major setback in mid-December when landlords again accused the governor and state legislature of "attacks on private property," "violations against the Constitution," and a general "politics of expropriation."[63] In an interview printed in *El Dictamen*, Salvador Campa gave further indication of the position that many property owners throughout the state had recently taken regarding the reform. Fundamentally, Campa asserted, landlords' view of Tejeda's proposal had changed because they now believed the law would restrict new investment in housing as well as continue to make rental housing an unattractive business venture. Campa then commented that "very few people in the state appear willing to comply with the new law." And, he wondered, "even if the legislature gave final approval to the reform, how could state officials ensure compliance from either landlords or tenants?"[64]

Despite strong criticisms of the reform by both landlords and tenants, lawmakers Salvador González García, Juan Ochoa Díaz, and

Cristoforo Redondo presented the bill to the state legislature on December 26. The measure attempted to please all sides of the conflict by fixing rents at 6 percent of property values while adding various tax exemptions for individuals who constructed new housing.[65] After learning the details of the proposal, the editors at *El Dictamen* immediately took a negative view of the legislation, calling it "a law that will resolve nothing and satisfy nobody."[66]

In an interview printed in *El Dictamen*, Salvador Campa stated that the problem lay simply in the shortage of housing in the port. If additional construction could be facilitated, landlords throughout the city would be obliged to lower rents solely because of competition. "In Veracruz," he told interviewers, "there are approximately two thousand families without a place to live and naturally this makes the housing expensive."[67] For their part, lawmakers Aurelio Pavón Flores and Alfredo Serrano speculated that if belligerent landlords began evicting tenants after the first of the year, a "great number of renters would flood the streets in protest."[68]

The Legislative Debate over Tejeda's Housing Reform

Men and women from tenant unions all over the state attended the legislative session held on December 31, 1922, watching as lawmakers carefully read each article of the reform. Upon hearing politicians discuss a possible end to the moratorium on rents, tenants shouted their disagreement: "No, we don't want this! The strike will continue!"[69] Although lawmakers scolded them, the tenants again shouted their disapproval and began banging chairs to disrupt the assembly. After several minutes of confusion, legislators managed to restore order. Then, amid sporadic shouts from the crowd, Representative Juan Ochoa Díaz again took the floor. Criticizing the tenants, he asked for an increase in the percentage by which rents were to be figured:

> These people do not represent the interests of all veracruzanos. Our society is not simply composed of working-class elements, and it is the middle class who are the ones who will suffer. If lawmakers do not study the problem carefully, this measure will resolve nothing. With rents based at six percent, there will be no businessman in the entire republic who would be willing to build houses in our state. The bill will become a dead letter and is basically only a measure that confiscates property and nothing else. With the growing population here in Veracruz the situation is only going to get worse.[70]

Taking offense at the remarks of Ochoa Díaz, Representative Antonio Jiménez Bravo responded: "The working class has made a tremendous sacrifice in the past few years only to be faced with rents that have doubled since 1915. No state authority has attempted to do anything about the problem and for this reason we find ourselves involved in the present conflict. I am not proposing the destruction of capital, but the people have to eat. Six percent is fair."[71]

Hearing this, tenants inside the assembly cheered, confident that the rent law with rates fixed at 6 percent would soon be passed. On January 2, 1923, lawmakers again gathered at the capital and, after some discussion, approved Article 3, which based rents at 6 percent of the property value, and sent the bill to the governor for signing.[72] Across the street, tenants displayed their red-and-black banners and cheered the decision.

On January 5 militants in the port distributed a special edition of *El Frente Unico* that described the activities of the union delegates in Jalapa and announced their return that afternoon. When the group arrived, renters organized a demonstration outside the railroad terminal to welcome them. The assembled crowd then left the station area and made their way toward syndicate headquarters, singing and shouting along the way. Shortly thereafter, organizers announced a meeting to be held later that night "to celebrate the tenant victory."

Beginning at eight o'clock, tenants gathered in the plaza with their banners and fireworks before jubilantly parading through the streets of Veracruz.[73] Yet while this enthusiasm marked a victory of sorts for striking tenants, it did not detract from their main concern: securing the release of Proal and his comrades.[74] To the surprise of many, word came of a possible pardon in mid-January 1923.

Amnesty for Proal

On January 15, 1923, a local judge signed preliminary orders for the freeing of Herón Proal and the other tenant prisoners.[75] The same day, hundreds sympathetic to the tenant syndicate in the city as well as other peasant, worker, and tenant organizations visiting from the neighboring towns of Carrizal, Santa Fé, Tejar, Soledad de Doblado, Córdoba, Puente Nacional, Rinconada, Salmoral, Palo de Cabo, Santa Rita, Playa de Vaca, and Mexico City rallied to demand amnesty for the jailed tenants.[76]

Learning of the pending release, the editors of *El Dictamen* offered a word of warning: "We must note the fact that the Revolutionary Syndicate has represented an active seditious force. Until the day Proal is released, the power of this syndicate will figure, in one way or another, as a political force in the development of Veracruz politics. Proal and

El Frente Unico, January 2, 1923. *Courtesy of AGN*

El Frente Unico, January 4, 1923. *Courtesy of AGN*

his union already have attained a degree of political influence. And while Proal never tires of repeating his desire to distance himself from politics [and] his hatred for politics and politicians, inevitably [he] and his organizations remain within a political arena."[77] Other groups in the state also feared the potential political power of a reinvigorated tenant movement. Yet while *El Dictamen* cautioned readers about the release of Proal, legal complications kept him in jail.[78]

On January 24 the editors of *El Dictamen* again lashed out at Proal, questioning his rejection of "bourgeois justice" in the light of the current proceedings. Echoing earlier statements, one editorial asked, "What will happen if Proal is released?" In an article responding to these questions, Proal's lawyer, Gustavo Lortia Casanova, analyzed the politics of Proal's release and argued in favor of amnesty for the tenants.[79]

Meanwhile, in Allende Jail, the conflict escalated. Reflecting a growing tension between inmates and staff, tenants in the jail wrote to Obregón to complain about the treatment they were getting from prison authorities and to plead for their release. Claiming they were "unjustly being held," they demanded "protection and justice after being incarcerated wrongly for six months—the victims of landlord treachery and crimes committed by federal forces."[80] Of course, not everyone inside the prison sympathized with the tenants. On January 29 the city council read a complaint from several prisoners against Proal and the tenants that accused them of having "disrespected national institutions."[81] A few days later, word spread that prisoners in the women's section had filed a complaint against tenant leader María Luisa Marín.[82] In fact, included among those who objected to Marín's use of "abusive language" were now other members of the tenant union.

Nevertheless, efforts to secure the release of incarcerated tenants continued. On January 13, 1923, Manuel Almanza had written to Governor Tejeda requesting that he "take whatever measures are necessary to free our prisoners."[83] The same day, Proal's lawyer wrote to state justice officials asking that a general amnesty be granted to the tenants.[84] A month later, Proal and the other prisoners wrote another appeal to the governor. "As workers," their petition read, "we have a high expectation of the men responsible for administering justice."[85] Yet while Governor Tejeda sought to avoid touching off another round of heated criticism from his detractors, either by allowing for the release of Proal or through some other means, accusations against him came nonetheless.

At the end of January 1923, *El Dictamen* initiated a new round of editorials criticizing Governor Tejeda and Mayor García. In a long piece printed on January 31, editors accused the two politicians of denigrating federal authorities, business, and "everything decent and civilized in this country." The editorial went on to say that Tejeda and García acted as advocates of "bolshevism and political savagery," encouraging "the masses" to follow them. When port workers sided with Tejeda and declared a boycott of the paper beginning in February, *El Dictamen* editors responded that "[workers] can choose to quit buying our paper but we will continue to publish what we think is right."[86] Supporting *El Dictamen*, other papers, including *El Informador* in Guadalajara and *Excélsior* in Mexico City, printed editorials that backed the Veracruz paper while sharply criticizing Tejeda's politics.

On February 9, *El Dictamen* printed another editorial again accusing the governor of "bolshevism" and "censorship." In the midst of this political bickering, President Obregón received a number of telegrams railing against Tejeda and García. Aside from attacking the governor and Veracruz mayor, one communication also suggested that a tenant celebration in early February had disturbed the peace. As it turned out, the occasion proved to be the first anniversary of the Revolutionary Syndicate.

On the Syndicate's First Anniversary

On February 5, 1923, porteños celebrated the first anniversary of the founding of the Revolutionary Syndicate of Tenants. For the event, organizers printed a special edition of *El Frente Unico* with pictures of male and female tenants held in Allende Jail, under the headline, "The Greatest Injustice in the Pages of Veracruz History." For many in the port, the February 5 anniversary called for a dramatic celebration. During the day, countless groups of tenants paraded through the streets of Veracruz while members of the syndicate sold pictures of Proal to raise money for the prisoners. At various points, sympathizers passed by Allende Jail, where they expressed their solidarity with those held inside. In the center of many patios, renters set up altars with pictures of Proal, political pamphlets, candles, and flowers. Several of their banners denounced the government, imploring residents not to obey public authority. Some tenements hosted banquets where tenants discussed the apparent success of the movement and what they thought would be the upcoming amnesty of Proal.

That night, tenants came out of the neighborhoods and made their way to Juárez Park, where a large crowd gathered. Speakers declared February 5 "a great day for all tenants" and encouraged renters to continue their struggle for social justice. Following the rally, a group of men and women gathered near the syndicate headquarters to attend a dance hosted by the union. The festivities continued well into the night.

Peaceful celebration notwithstanding, complaints against the tenant syndicate continued in February 1923.[87] On February 7 residents wrote to Ministry of the Interior officials asking for protection and help in resolving the housing conflict. The petition stated that members of the syndicate had "restarted their program of marching through the city, interrupting traffic, threatening property owners, and shouting provocative phrases in front of the federal barracks." They also complained that "protesters congregating each night carry with them all types of weapons without permission from authorities."[88]

Meanwhile, deliberations concerning the issue of amnesty for Proal and the others dragged on in the courts during early February as many throughout the city prepared for the popular Veracruz celebration of Carnival.[89] On February 9 porteños learned that the Supreme Court had determined that no amnesty law existed that could be applied in Proal's case.[90] In protest, Proal wrote to Obregón asking for a chance to relate his version of the events of July 5–6. Making his plea for amnesty, he stated, "I have no political aspirations, I only wish to be useful to those who suffer, hunger, and thirst for justice in this region."[91] Despite his appeal, officials saw fit that he remain in jail for the time being.

On February 14 a state judge met with officials in Allende Jail concerning Proal's case. The magistrate listened to complaints from the tenant leader while also discussing the matter with a representative of the pro-prisoner committee.[92] For their part, Proal and two other tenants complained of the conditions in the jail, the lack of decent food, and the alleged corruption of prison staff.[93] While authorities made no further determinations regarding Proal's case, tenants outside the jail expressed their solidarity with the prisoners the next day when they informed their landlords that rent payments would be withheld indefinitely. Strikers also indicated that they had taken it upon themselves to change the name of Landero y Cos Street to Victimas del 6 de Julio in memory of the conflict.[94]

Elsewhere, members of property owners associations in Orizaba, Córdoba, Jalapa, and Veracruz learned on February 22 that the Supreme Court had issued a ruling on amparos filed against Governor Tejeda and the state housing reform proposed the previous summer.[95] In the decision, justices declared that amparos could not be applied to a bill still in the process of becoming law. Furthermore, the housing reform did not necessarily violate the individual rights of the claimants, as was required to justify application of the measure. This rather favorable ruling by the Supreme Court suggested that the movement had gained new legitimacy.

Shortly thereafter, tenants again decked their patios with red-and-black banners, paraded through the city, and held a special meeting in Juárez Park to commemorate the first full year of the rent strike, which had actually begun on March 5. During the day, protesters circulated throughout the city's patios urging residents to sign a petition to be sent to Secretary of Government Calles. The document stated, "Our daily protests are justified as they are the only way in which we can express our outrage with the exploitation that we have had to put up with for so many years." In addition to speaking out about the night of July 5–6, they blamed "foreigners [and] members of the [state's] Cooperative Party . . . who, with pistols in hand, threaten us constantly." Approximately 325 residents signed the petition.[96]

María Luisa Marín, writing from prison, added her voice by contributing two articles to an issue of *El Frente Unico*. The first, simply titled "The Fifth of March," celebrated the "ideal of communism" and the founding of the tenant syndicate the year before. The other expressed her commitment to equality between men and women, arguing that "women are the owners of the world because of their caring, limitless self-denial and incredible generosity." She explained that her enthusiasm for the tenant cause stemmed from her tremendous love of humanity and for Proal, whom she saw as the "liberator of the Veracruz people." She ended with a passionate call to her readers:

> Compañeros: Viva universal love!
> Viva the emancipation of women!
> Up with communism!
> Viva free humanity!
> Women, to the struggle! [97]

In endorsing a somewhat romanticized notion of women as self-sacrificing caregivers, Marín nevertheless advanced a blend of communist and feminist ideas as well. Although she would remain in jail for another two months, her articles in El Frente Unico certainly distinguished her in the eyes of the Veracruz public as one of the movement's visionaries.

In honor of the anniversary, Proal issued an official communication in which he vigorously denounced any formal political activity by union members as well as others who considered themselves true revolutionaries. "If we remain well organized," he urged his readers, "we can do anything we want."[98] In response, property owner representatives Salvador Campa and Francisco Rúiz Murillo wrote to members of Tejeda's administration, complaining of the usual "insults" and "offenses" committed by tenants. Campa sent along a copy of the March 5 issue of *El Frente Unico* as "proof" of the protesters' "disrespectful" attitude toward authority.[99]

Reaction to recent tenant advances continued on March 12, when *El Dictamen* reported that small property holders, "many of them widows," had sent a petition to Governor Tejeda and President Obregón asking that back rents be accounted for and that tenants be required to resume payment. Not surprisingly, the document railed against the tenant syndicate:

> [Many] small property owners in the port wish to end the abuses we
> have suffered at the hands of the group known as the Revolutionary
> Syndicate of Tenants. The people we refer to are led by bosses who
> use any means available to further their aims and who receive daily
> dues that by now have amounted to considerable sums. If one con-
> siders who is truly suffering in all of this, in all actuality it is the small
> property owner, [many of us being] old and lacking the ability to
> work and earn a living. Not only do we suffer, but so too do many
> workers because there is no construction taking place. Every night
> groups parade through the streets of Veracruz, screaming insults and
> yelling, "Death to the bourgeoisie!" This so-called strike and the rent
> reductions the legislature has approved are proof that state politi-
> cians have become prisoners of the Red bosses. [Mr. Governor,] the
> little capital that we have managed to earn is difficult to acquire and
> too easy to lose. In all other civilized countries there are laws that
> protect [an individual's] right to do business. We demand that you
> do something that will end this critical situation.

The petition, signed almost exclusively by women, appeared to have been written with the advice of the property owners association. Then, on March 26, landlords met to discuss what more could be done to stop the daily meetings of tenants and better secure the rights of property owners. Subsequently, they sent a message to Secretary of Government Calles, which said, in part, "The current legislature has created a rent law that is a disaster."[100] Yet, despite criticism, the governor and his staff in Jalapa went forward with a final review of the law.

Approving Housing Legislation, April–May 1923

On April 1, 1923, a large group of renters again filled the legislative galleries in Jalapa to witness the final deliberations over Tejeda's housing reform. After one representative had argued that "workers already had plenty of rights" and that rents based on 6 percent would prevent both new construction and the proper maintenance of existing properties, renters loudly applauded the testimony of Representatives Andrés Pérez Cadena and Alfredo Serrano, who defended the figure of 6 percent. Yelling "Sellout!" and other criticisms at the politicians who sought to increase the percentage at which rents would be set, protesters caused such a commotion that legislators eventually had to end the session. The following day, some representatives asked that police be prepared to intervene in case tenants attempted to interrupt the proceedings. Meanwhile, landlords in the port again rallied in opposition.

On April 8, *El Dictamen* printed an editorial by Manuel Díaz Cueto, who claimed that certain aspects of the new law favored only "irresponsible tenants." He went on to say, "If the government is not willing to take our needs into account, then landlords are capable of fighting back." That same day, property owners also considered undertaking their own brand of direct action by refusing to pay city taxes.

In an attempt to appease the landlords, Governor Tejeda again met with them on April 11. He tried to reassure the group that if any deficiencies in the law arose, certain adjustments would be attended to.[101] These promises, however, did little to quiet property owners. Moving against the rent law, landlords from Orizaba, Jalapa, Córdoba, and the port met on April 22. After much heated discussion, they decided that reassurances from the governor meant nothing. Upset over a detail in the new law that granted tenants rent concessions in case of illness, they pledged to "match tenants' direct action with their own." In other words, they had decided to follow through with their threat to withhold tax payments.[102]

At the same time, the tenant syndicate in Orizaba sent out a call to workers. In a communication that circulated in the popular neighborhoods, organizers urged residents to fortify their commitment to the rent protest: "The purpose of this bulletin is to ask all the renters of patios, [workers in] factories, and [members of] unions to maintain the boycott against all the scabs who have tried to obstruct the movement."[103] The communication then outlined the manner in which rents, union dues, tenant propaganda, and other matters would continue to be handled.

Anticipating the passage of the rent law, property owners again discussed their differences with Governor Tejeda on April 28. Not a group to mince words, they advised him to "expect difficulties" in applying the new law. Then, in a last-ditch effort to stave off final approval of the bill, they offered to pay higher state taxes to fund the construction of popular housing if Tejeda agreed to table the reform.[104] Taking their position into consideration at the last minute, Tejeda, surprisingly, raised the rate at which rents would be based to 9 percent before tenants had a chance to react.[105] Soon thereafter, members of the legislature approved the bill. A few days later, following the popular celebrations of May 1 throughout the state, Tejeda declared the new Ley de Inquilinato effective as of May 2, 1923. Despite the last-minute change in the rate at which rents would be figured, architects of the reform nevertheless sought to reduce rents to slightly more than 1910 levels, donate land for the construction of new housing, and provide for the supervision of landlord-tenant relations. Additionally, Tejeda's reform unofficially provided for the freeing of Herón Proal and the other members of the tenant syndicate.

Notes

1. In the next few weeks, Palacios began an investigation into the events of July 6 and regularly lobbied Tejeda on behalf of tenants. See telegrams between Palacios and Tejeda, July 31, August 1, 6, 8, 1922, AGEV, gobernación, 1922.

2. *El Dictamen*, July 9, 1922.

3. Tejeda to Obregón, July 9, 1922, AT, vol. 65.

4. Tejeda to Calles, July 9, 1922, AGN, gobernación, vol. 24, file 107; Tejeda to Obregón, July 9, 1922, AT, vol. 67.

5. Calles to Tejeda, July 10, 1922, AGN, gobernación, vol. 24, file 107.

6. Provisional Governor Angel Casarín received several messages regarding troops evicting tenants that he passed on to Secretary of Government Calles. Casarín to Calles, July 12, 1922, ibid.

7. J. Ramírez, general in charge of military operations in the state of Veracruz, to Calles, July 4, 1922. Subsecretary of the Interior Gilberto Valenzuela to Secretary of Foreign Affairs, July 20, 1922, AGN, gobernación, vol. 24, file 107.

8. Jalapa businessman Gaspar Uriarte to Obregón, June 27, 1922, AGN, gobernación, vol. 24, file 107. Uriarte included examples of tenant posters and handbills from Jalapa.

9. Petition signed by approximately 190 residents (many of them women) from patios San Francisco and Consuelo to Obregón, July 8, 1922, AGN, gobernación, vol. 24, file 107. A note attached to the back of the petition states, "There are many more from other vecindades who wish to sign but are afraid."

10. See, for example, letters from workers in Oaxaca, Puebla, and Yucatán, AGN, gobernación, box 26, C.2.51. 258.

11. Letter from Revolutionary Syndicate to Calles, July 10, 1922, AGN, gobernación, vol. 24, file 107. In the same file, see also letters from Abel Mendoza, José Martin Martínez, and Luz María Troncoso to Calles, July 16, 1922, and communication from Julian García, Antonio Guzmán, José Reyes, and M. Ramírez in Mexico City to Calles, July 8, 1922. At the same time, several other citizens sent letters to authorities in Mexico City.

12. *El Dictamen*, July 15, 1922.

13. Workers of the Liga Zona Marítima to Calles, July 11, 1922, AGN, gobernación, vol. 24, file 107.

14. Rafael García, "Manifiesto al pueblo veracruzano," July 14, 1922, ibid.

15. Tejeda to Calles, July 14, 1922, ibid.; Tejeda to Property Owners, July 13, 1922, and Tejeda to Manuel Almanza, July 13, 1922, AGEV, gobernación, 1922.

16. *El Dictamen*, July 18, 1922.

17. Members of the Revolutionary Syndicate Commission to Calles, July 28, 1922, AGN, gobernación, vol. 24, file 107. The report from the Chief Justice (Procurador General de Justicia) signed July 17 states that Colonel López Manzano has remained "well within the law." Report of the Procurador General de Justicia to Tejeda, July 17, 1922, AGEV, gobernación, 1922.

18. Letter from Comité Pro-Preso to Secretary of Government Calles, October 11, 1922, AGN, gobernación, vol. 24, file 107.

19. M. López for García to Tejeda, August 22, 1922, AGEV, gobernación, 1922.

20. Palacios to Tejeda, August 22, 1922, ibid.

21. Tejeda to Palacios, August 22, 1922, ibid.

22. Gustavo Luna, Marcos Gutiérrez, and fifty-nine others to Tejeda, August 31, 1922, ibid.

23. Prisoners of Allende Jail to Calles, August 31, 1922, AGN, gobernación, vol. 24, file 107.

24. Members of Tenant Syndicate of Veracruz to Gilberto Valenzuela, September 20, 1922, ibid.

25. Tenant Syndicate of Orizaba to Tejeda, July 4, 1922, AGEV, gobernación, 1922.

26. Tenant Syndicate of Santa Rosa to Tejeda, July 7, 1922, ibid.

27. Executive Committee of the State Tenant Convention to Secretary of Government Calles, August 4, 1922, AGN, gobernación, vol. 24, file 107.

28. Delegates to the State Tenant Convention to Tejeda, August 4, 1922, AGEV, gobernación, 1922.

29. Ibid.

30. Tejeda to Executive Committee of the State Tenant Convention, August 10, 1922, ibid.

31. *El Dictamen*, September 18, 1922.

32. Ibid., September 27, 1922.

33. Concepción Pérez and over twenty others to Tejeda, September 29, 1922, AGEV, gobernación, 1922.

34. *El Dictamen*, October 6–7, 1922.

35. Comité Pro-Presos to Tejeda, October 11, 1922, AGEV, gobernación, 1922.

36. Secretary of Government to Comité Pro-Presos, October 16, 1922, ibid.

37. José Mancisidor to Tejeda, October 23, 1922, AT, vol. 68.

38. On July 8 and 9, 1922, the *New York Times* printed a short piece describing clashes between tenants and the military in Veracruz. The article on July 8 stated, "The rioters yesterday were led by women radicals who insulted the soldier guards and attempted to incite the syndicalists to storm the prison and free Proal." The same day the *Times* ran a different report titled "Red Coffin for Mexican Funeral" that briefly noted a funeral procession for the tenant striker killed in Mexico City. The description read: "The funeral of an anti-rent payer killed on Wednesday passed through the main streets today, the body being carried in a bright red coffin. Red and black flags were carried by the mourners, the majority of whom were women."

39. *El Dictamen*, October 2, 1922.

40. Ibid., October 14, 1922.

41. Ibid., October 17, 1922.

42. Ibid., November 2, 1922.

43. Rafael García to Ministry of the Interior, November 3, 1922, AGEV, gobernación, 1922.

44. Ibid.

45. *El Dictamen*, November 4, 1922.

46. Police report of events on November 6, 1922, sent to Tejeda by García, November 18, 1922, AGEV, gobernación, 1922. García to Obregón, November 17, 1922, AGN, gobernación, vol. 24, file 107.

47. *El Dictamen*, November 7, 1922.

48. Rafael García to Tejeda, November 13, 1922, AGEV, gobernación, 1922.

49. *El Dictamen*, November 10 and 11, 1922; Rafael García to Tejeda, November 10, 1922, and Tejeda to García, November 23, 1922, AGEV, gobernación, 1922.

50. Inspector Genaro Castro to Department of Labor, November 11, 1922, AGN, trabajo, vol. 496, exp. 1.

51. See editorials in *El Dictamen*, July 1–2, 1922.

52. Tejeda to Procurador General, August 1, 1922, AGEV, gobernación, 1922. Full copies of several of these amparos are held at the AGEV.

53. Tejeda to First Judge of the 1st Instance, Orizaba, July 31, 1922, ibid.

54. *El Dictamen*, July 26, 1922. As another way to resist the new law, many property owners also continued to neglect tax payments.

55. Ibid., August 16, 1922. Political trouble arose not only for Tejeda but also for Mayor García. In mid-September, the state legislature decided that García had interfered with local elections and suspended him as mayor of Veracruz. The mayor quickly responded that he had been elected for a period of two years and the ruling represented a violation of his constitutional rights. The next day he filed an amparo in protest. AGEV, gobernación, 1922.

56. Manuel Almanza to Tejeda, October 1, 1922, AGEV, gobernación, 1922.

57. *El Dictamen*, November 9, 1922. About the same time, the Veracruz City Council discussed measures that would donate urban lots for the construction of new housing. See *El Dictamen*, November 13 and 15, 1922. Despite a recent extension of the moratorium on rents, eviction requests continued to be processed by local courts.

58. Ibid., December 1, 1922.

59. Ibid., December 7, 1922.

60. Ibid., December 9, 1922.

61. Ibid.

62. Tejeda to González García, December 4, 1922, AT, vol. 93, no. 69.

63. *El Dictamen*, December 12, 1922.

64. Ibid.

65. Ibid., December 27, 1922.

66. Ibid., December 28, 1922.

67. Ibid.

68. In the meantime, syndicate members involved themselves in a new conflict between owners and vendors in the city's Fabela Market. *El Dictamen*, December 30 and 31, 1922.

69. Ibid., January 1, 1923.

70. Ibid.

71. Ibid.

72. Ibid., January 3, 1923.

73. Ibid. Tenant direct action continued during the early part of January 1923. See ibid., January 7–11, 1923.

74. For complaints about Proal and members of the Revolutionary Syndicate in Allende Jail, see Prisoners of Allende Jail to Obregón, November 18, 1922, AGN, gobernación, vol. 24, file 107; Prisoners of Allende Jail to Tejeda, November 20, 1922, AGEV, gobernación, 1922; Andrés Andrade to Obregón, November 20, 1922, AGN, gobernación, vol. 24, file 107; and *El Dictamen*, December 4, 13, 16, 1922.

75. *El Dictamen*, January 16, 1923.

76. Telegram received by Gilberto Valenzuela, Subsecretary of the Interior, January 15, 1923, AGN, vol. 24, file 107.

77. *El Dictamen*, January 17, 1923.

78. Ibid., January 19, 1923.

79. Ibid., January 26, 1923.

80. Tenant prisoners to Obregón, December 17, 1922, AGEV, gobernación, 1922.

81. *El Dictamen*, January 30, 1923. Manuel Mújica, Ladislao Menéndez, and other prisoners to Tejeda, December 9, 1922, AGEV, gobernación, 1922. Tenant prisoners friendly to Proal had countered with a letter to Tejeda stating that Director Andrade, Councilman Faustio Mateos, and other prison officials had treated them unfairly from the time they had entered the jail in July. Prisoners to Tejeda, December 15, 1922, AGEV, gobernación, 1922.

82. *El Dictamen*, February 4, 1923.

83. Almanza to Tejeda, January 13, 1923, AGEV, gobernación, 1923.

84. Lortia Casanova to Procurador General, January 13, 1923, ibid.

85. Proal and other prisoners to Tejeda, February 20, 1922, AGEV, gobernación, 1922.

86. *El Dictamen*, February 2, 1923.

87. See, for example, letters from the property owners association dated February 3, 5, 7, 1923, complaining of tenants carrying weapons, "giving them the horse," and attacking their houses. Property owners to Tejeda, February 1923, AGEV, gobernación, "Union de Propietarios, Veracruz," 1923.

88. Letter signed by approximately seventy residents to Ministry of the Interior, February 7, 1923, AGN, gobernación, vol. 24, file 107.

89. *El Dictamen*, February 8, 1923.

90. Ibid., February 9, 1922.

91. Proal to Obregón, March 14, 1923, AGN, gobernación, vol. 24, file 107.

92. *El Dictamen*, February 15, 1923.

93. Ibid.

94. Ibid., February 10, 1923.

95. Ibid., February 22, 1923.

96. Members of the tenant syndicate (and residents of various patios) to Calles, March 6, 1923, AGN, gobernación, vol. 24, file 107.

97. *El Frente Unico*, March 5, 1923.

98. *El Dictamen*, March 8, 1923.

99. Salvador Campa and Francisco Rúiz Murillo to Secretary of Government in Jalapa, March 5, 1923, AGN, gobernación, vol. 11, file 365.

100. *El Dictamen*, March 27, 1923.

101. Ibid., April 12, 1923.

102. Ibid., April 23, 1923.

103. "Sindicato de Inquilinos: Llamamiento a los sindicatos y trabajadores en general." Poster, Orizaba, April 23, 1923, AGN, gobernación, vol. 17, file 353.

104. *El Dictamen*, April 29, 1923.

105. Mario Gill, "Herón Proal," in *México y la revolución de octubre (1917)* (Mexico City: Ediciones de Cultura Popular, 1975), 74; Olivia Domínguez Pérez, *Política y movimientos sociales en el tejedismo* (Jalapa: Universidad Veracruzana, 1986), 62; Paco Ignacio Taibo II, *Bolshevikis: Historia narrativa de los origenes del comunismo en México, 1919–1925* (Mexico City: Editorial Joaquín Mortiz, 1986), 183.

8

The Firecracker Wars
Closing Political Opportunity
for the Revolutionary Syndicate

The temples of justice were not easily controlled by the young
revolutionaries.
— José Mancisidor, *La ciudad roja*

On April 23, 1923, Herón Proal had written to Governor Adalberto
Tejeda from his cell in Allende Jail asking to be released: "My
associates and I have been held prisoner unjustly and arbitrarily for
ten months. The only crime we have committed is surviving the vile
and cowardly massacre perpetrated by federal forces. Today the un-
armed people say there is no justice in the country. You should give us
our freedom."[1] Governor Tejeda responded that he had begun to make
arrangements to grant them amnesty.[2] Upon hearing the news, porteños
sympathetic to the renters' cause decorated the fronts of their houses
with banners and organized dances in anticipation. Then, on May 11,
state officials allowed the prisoners to walk free.[3]

As they left the prison, members of the Revolutionary Syndicate
marked the occasion in dramatic fashion as well-wishers jubilantly set
off firecrackers, applauded their peers, sang songs, and shouted slogans. In groups of ten, the men wearing white cotton shirts and pants
made their entrance into the street first. The women followed, dressed
in cream-colored dresses and straw hats with red ribbons. Proal and a
group of his most intimate compañeros came out last, to a warm reception. Addressing the crowd, the tenant leader announced that a demonstration would be held in Juárez Park that night. The cheering renters
then loudly paraded through several of the city's main streets before
eventually arriving at the offices of the Revolutionary Syndicate.

In an interview given shortly after leaving the jail, Proal said that he intended to tour the republic in the interest of solidifying a national renters movement. On the syndicate's plans in the port, he told reporters, "We will restart our open air cultural conferences, demonstrations, and public meetings and, of course, our commitment to direct action."[4] Thus, despite federal repression and a ten-month incarceration, the radical spirit of the movement had apparently survived.

While Proal's pronouncements came in the wake of sympathetic state legislation, they also marked the beginning of the end for the Veracruz Revolutionary Syndicate of Tenants. In the coming months, Proal and members of his organization would face fierce opposition from local property owners as well as rival renter and labor associations. Then, beginning in December 1923, a major military rebellion involving over half the army threatened to topple the administrations of Alvaro Obregón and Adalberto Tejeda. The revolt had serious repercussions for the tenant movement. As both the federal and state administrations closed ranks to defend themselves, political opportunities for continued tenant protest diminished significantly.

Responses to the Rent Law

Earlier that year, members of the Revolutionary Syndicate in Jalapa had issued a series of public statements defending the strike, commenting on the proposed rent law, and declaring the need for a united front. One poster urged tenants to consider the plight of a woman who could not meet the price set by her landlord and subsequently found herself homeless, struggling to support her children. To the "bourgeois men" the authors warned:

> The state government can see that all the tenant syndicates agree to the same principles and have formed a confederation of more than eighty thousand renters in Veracruz. We have also [worked to] unite all the peasants in the state. Together with like-minded individuals elsewhere, we observe that the rent law will soon see the light of day. While it does not completely meet our expectations, we see it as a move in the direction we are all working toward. The Red Syndicate of Tenants is a powerful organization if it is united. Reds in the republic and in the entire world will not be defeated.[5]

As evidenced here, Jalapa militants saw themselves as part of a larger confederation of renters throughout the state. Subsequently, they wrote to the governor proposing that an emergency fund be established to help the poorest tenants and that to administer it, a commission or special office consisting of members of the tenant syndicate be created in each city. In turn, the new department would report to state officials and provide regular progress reports regarding application of the rent law.[6]

Property owners throughout the state interpreted the law as a threat and quickly mobilized to block its implementation. Some in Orizaba, unhappy with the constant demonstrations and direct actions organized by tenants, complained to government officials of "threats and abuses" committed by renters.[7] One woman, named María de Jesús Campos, wrote to Obregón declaring that tenant syndicate members had committed crimes against her with impunity: "Because of the lack of protection offered by local officials many other small property owners like me have also suffered greatly at the hands of the tenant protesters who march through the city streets nightly denouncing landlords and the bourgeoisie and shooting off firecrackers."[8] She added that tenants who refused to join the syndicates had been threatened with water cut-offs, blocked access to bathrooms, and other humiliations. For these reasons she implored the president to intervene and "stop this evil."[9]

Members of the Orizaba Property Owners Association also claimed that the governor's actions had created "trouble he was unwilling to take responsibility for." Manuel Lira, writing for the association, sent their complaints to Obregón:

> The problem in question, raised in an antisocial and pernicious manner, as we have seen, has now gained the attention of the entire state. [The tenant syndicate has made] innumerable threats and [carried out] violent acts [many of which] we have been victim to. There may well have been more except for the fact that we have maintained our just and indignant resistance to them. The repeated tragedies that have occurred in the port of Veracruz are well known and we believe that the group responsible is the tenant syndicate. Of course, the main instigator of their actions and the only one to blame goes by the name of Herón Proal.[10]

Lira's letter left little doubt that, for many, Proal represented a serious threat to the well-being of Veracruz. In the meantime, tenants in the port accelerated their attacks on landlords.

Direct Action and Changing Public Opinion

From the beginning, direct action had been an important part of the syndicate's repertoire. Events in winter 1923, however, suggested a new level of militancy. Evidence that the protest was spreading to other areas had appeared earlier, in mid-February, when tenants in several guesthouses declared themselves on strike. The renters in one *pensión*, called El Bosque, had sent a message to members of the tenant syndicate expressing a desire to join the organization as well as their plan to discontinue payments to the owner, José Couce. They announced their participation in the tenant strike one evening just before the nightly renters meeting by displaying a red-and-black banner from the guesthouse balcony while below, a contingent of union members cheered the action and shot off firecrackers in the street. Speakers took the opportunity to denounce local elites and sing a few of their favorite songs before proceeding to Juárez Park.[11] Yet after more than a year of regular public rallies, marches, and agitation, continued fighting between proalistas, dissidents within the tenant movement, and members of the Communist Youth frustrated those who had hoped that a spirit of cooperation would prevail.

Landlords in both Orizaba and the port of Veracruz agreed to meet with representatives of the tenant syndicate in early June.[12] Those who participated in the talks in both cities managed to achieve a degree of success. Generally, small property owners made agreements with tenant representatives while more powerful landlords remained intransigent. Of this group, *El Dictamen* reported that many complained that the housing law destroyed them economically while others simply asserted that the reform violated their constitutional rights.[13]

On June 12 property owners and tenants met in the port's People's Library. Landlords argued that the reduced rates did not leave them sufficient resources to pay utilities. While they suggested rents be set at higher levels, Proal said it would be difficult to persuade tenants not only in Veracruz but also in Orizaba, Córdoba, and Jalapa to pay increased rates. After almost two hours of discussion, the two groups came to no agreement other than to reconvene in a few days.[14] Even after a second meeting, property owners and tenants remained deadlocked.[15] Frustrated, landlords asked President Obregón for federal government protection. In their petition they stated that tenant protest and Tejeda's law would lead to the loss of "every idea of liberty [while] sovereignty and individuality [will become] only a myth."[16]

Meanwhile, tenants in the port had begun preparations for another statewide convention with renters not only from Veracruz, Orizaba, Jalapa, and Córdoba but also Minatitlán, Puerto México, Santa Rosa, Soledad de Doblado, Huatusco, and other smaller towns scheduled to attend. As the date for the meeting grew near, tenants circulated the following schedule:

July 5
10:00 A.M.
Tenant demonstration in the streets of Veracruz
7:00 P.M.
Procession with a cavalcade of Veracruz campesinos
July 6
11:00 A.M.
March with campesinos, tenants, and workers
7:00 P.M.
Evening gathering in Principal Theater with singing and speeches[17]

Before the meeting began, however, Proal announced a new round that he termed "people's actions" (*actividades del pueblo*). One of the first expressions of the new campaign came on the night of June 30 when rent protesters declared their opposition to local political parties. Issuing a call to tenants warning against "corrupt politicians," proalistas sacked mayoral candidate Manuel Caldelas's office. They burned records, destroyed campaign materials, and apprehended and injured Caldelas and his brother Juan before police could intervene.[18]

The following day, the well-known Mexican militant Enrique Flores Magón arrived in the port to help inaugurate the tenant convention. Because Flores Magón had just recently returned from the United States, he was given an enthusiastic reception at the train station and then escorted to Juárez Park, where he and Proal addressed a rally. Eager to accommodate the radical hero, tenants installed Magón and his female companion in a room at patio La Tripolitania. Shortly thereafter, porteños as well as guests from around the state marked the first anniversary of the July 5–6 massacre. Firecrackers, singing, and occasional gunshots testifying to the popularity of the tenant movement must have left some people wondering how much longer the protest would last.[19]

As the gathering came to a close, renters staged assaults on two local guesthouses where they claimed "Spanish landlords lived off the misery of their tenants." In this action, some seventy tenants armed with sticks, clubs, rocks, knives, and a few guns first approached the cantina and guesthouse Santo Domingo, property of Jesús Castañón. Soon they had the place surrounded. With red banners in tow, they formed a semi-circle on Aquiles Serdán Street, stopped traffic, and sent a "commission" inside to talk. Demanding the room keys from Castañón, they told him that they intended to "take over this *posada* and unionize those who are living here!" They shouted, "Houses, we want houses and rooms!" The proprietor resisted briefly but soon gave in. The protesters then seized the guesthouse, rushed upstairs, and hung banners from the windows looking out onto the street while a crowd below began shooting off firecrackers.

Seemingly unstoppable, the assemblage moved down the street to the pension El Cosmopólita. By this point, the number of those united under the union's banners had grown to nearly one hundred men and women. Moving closer to the building, they encountered mounted police. As a standoff developed, some protesters managed to get inside the building, where they began breaking bottles, glasses, light fixtures, furniture, and windows in the downstairs bar. In the mêlée, the owner's wife and their two children escaped out a back entrance but were closely followed by three or four female protesters. Eventually, police intervened and managed to disperse the crowd but not before considerable damage had been done to the establishment. Later that evening, a group of tenants briefly returned to the scene and triumphantly shouted, "¡Gachupín!" and "¡Viva Proal!" Searching for someone to hold responsible for the incident, authorities eventually arrested several individuals associated with the renters union.[20]

A few days later, tenants and police tangled again. This time, members of the tenant syndicate tore down a Mexican flag displayed outside a private residence.[21] The incident, which took place on July 18, the day Mexicans commemorate the death of their national hero Benito Juárez, caused such a commotion that a visiting reporter from the *New York Times* sent the story back to readers in the United States. Under the headline "Vera Cruz Tenants Riot," the story read, in part: "Ten persons, including two policemen, were wounded yesterday in a street battle between police and members of the Red Union of Revolutionary Tenants. The trouble had its inception partly in an attempt by the tenants to haul down the flag of the republic that a landlord had hoisted over his building. When patrolmen started to take the troublemakers to jail, the tenants left behind began to shoot and throw stones, bringing down three of the police from their horses. The population is in a state of great excitement."[22]

As the altercation renewed fears about the tenant protest, an exchange of telegrams took place between members of the tenant syndicate and President Obregón. One syndicate member, Marcos Gutiérrez, concerned about what he saw as a growing military presence in the city, told the president: "At this time the police are overrunning the city with guns and swords. We urge guarantees and immediate liberty since already several compatriots of the city have been wounded, beaten, and imprisoned."[23] Apparently unperturbed, Obregón responded that he had forwarded the tenant complaint to the "respective authorities":

> The executive officer under my charge sincerely regrets that the directors of that union recognize authorities and laws only in those cases in which they seek guarantees from the former granted by the latter, but do not equally recognize the one or the other when there is a call for respect of their decisions and the rights of others granted by these same laws that you invoke on account of violations. The case under reference will be made known to the respective authorities and they will determine those responsible and impose the corresponding punishment.[24]

Soon, local authorities arrested Aurora "La Chata" Ramírez and María Luisa Marín, among others.[25] A few days later, an editorial printed in *El Dictamen* pointed out that although Proal had been heard earlier saying that strikers sought to promote reforms in the most peaceful way possible, recent direct action tactics by the syndicate threatened the lives of Veracruz residents. In agreement with these comments, city councilmen soon requested that army troops again be brought in to help support local police and prevent any further disturbances by tenants.[26]

On July 22 property owners asserted themselves by communicating to President Obregón their frustration over failed negotiations with renters as well as recent "hostilities" committed by protesters. They argued that federal intervention could—and should—expedite a resolution to the conflict. [27] The next day, a landlord delegation led by Alejandro Sánchez headed to Mexico City to discuss the matter further with federal authorities. About the same time, an editorial printed in the Mexico City paper *El Universal* under the title "The Cancer of Veracruz" expressed the feelings of many people outside the state about the troubled political situation:

> [One does not see] in Yucatán, nor in Puebla, nor in the Federal District such occurrences as take place in Veracruz. What is happening in Veracruz does not resemble a furious madness. It resembles Saint Vitus' dance. Together with the great irregularities charged against the misgovernment reigning in Veracruz, which seriously affect the industrial prosperity of the state, we must note others, however, which deal with actual anarchy and which signify an insult not only for Veracruz but for the republic. We refer to the scandalous abuses committed in the port.

Focusing on the components of this proverbial "dance of death," the editorial goes on to criticize the members of the tenant syndicate, calling them a "social ulcer":

> That singular and queer Syndicate of renters established there, does
> not limit itself to not paying rent; it has organized itself into a state
> within a state. The chief of the clan assumes power equal to the judi-
> ciary, giving orders to the agent of the public minister. In order that
> this social ulcer may be seen in all its alarming putrefaction, the council
> of the port sought guarantees from the executive of the republic be-
> cause these were not to be had from the state government.

And, finally, "it is time to settle this anomaly, the established situation
of anarchy in Veracruz. And this, we insist, cannot be settled by the
local Veracruz government, which is incapable of deciding anything,
but by the government of the republic so that chaos may cease."[28]

With this appeal to federal authorities, the editors at *El Universal*
attempted to stir up as much resentment as possible by characterizing
the rent protest and Tejeda's administration as the antithesis of things
"Mexican." Yet despite mounting pressure to end the strike, many tenants in the port continued to withhold payment, while landlords, seeing their attempts to evict belligerent renters remain stuck in local
courts, felt they had been left with few legal options. Meanwhile, a
group of Veracruz tenants made their way to Mexico City.

A Visit with the President

At the end of July, approximately forty members of the syndicate
boarded a train headed to Mexico City. Once in the capital, rent strikers from the Federal District welcomed the Veracruz brigade with a
colorful reception. Porteños then paraded through sections of the city,
carrying their banners while singing revolutionary songs and chants.
Later, they met with President Obregón, who told them that their requests for federal land to build houses in the port could be handled
only by state authorities.[29] Nevertheless, Obregón assured them that
he would send a commission to Veracruz to survey the land situation,
guarantee tenants' right to assemble in public, and continue to investigate certain matters still unresolved regarding the events of July 5–6.
After what seemed like a constructive interaction, however, army personnel searched the delegates' car at a rail station outside Mexico City.
"It makes one wonder about the president," declared one of the delegates at a rally in Veracruz the next day, "when one day he assures us
of his support for our protest while the next he orders soldiers to stop
and inspect us."[30] Surely the incident only encouraged the militants'
cynicism regarding the political motivations of Obregón. The next day,
Proal sent an official complaint about the search to Mexico City. Hearing of the tenant syndicate's exchange with the president, the editors

of *El Dictamen* took the opportunity to comment on stalled negotiations between tenants and landlords:

> No one has complied with [Tejeda's rent law], which was enacted for the purpose of bringing an end to the conflict. [Things might have been different] if [members of] the syndicate had acted as an organization properly oriented toward working effectively for the improvement of renters in this city, promoting affordable and clean housing. They should have dedicated themselves to ensuring that landlords maintain their properties instead of following Proal. Now, after more than one year, it is quite reasonable to suggest that this group conducts itself in a way that violates the law and threatens our social security. They are capable of nothing but criticism and pretense.[31]

The editorial concludes by calling their tactics a "communist game" that threatened so-called law-abiding citizens in the state and criticizing Tejeda's administration for supporting the tenant syndicate.

Yet while it seemed that conservative forces in the state might be gaining the upper hand in the conflict, acts of sabotage undertaken by members of the electrical workers union in early August signaled the beginning of a new citywide strike in Veracruz. As authorities put local police and federal troops on alert, the port was again occupied and placed under martial law. Rather than unifying renters, however, this event would help accentuate divisions already present within the tenant movement.

The 1923 General Strike

On the night of August 9, electrical workers, frustrated in their negotiations with the Mexican Light and Power Company, cut the power lines to the city, leaving Veracruz in darkness. The following day, federal forces and forty hired laborers from Puebla arrived to restore service. During the next week, as talks stalled between union officials and company representatives, workers continued their campaign of direct action, sabotaging electrical cables and clashing with police. On the morning of August 11, for example, strikers derailed a streetcar headed south to the seaside Villa del Mar resort.[32] Although no one had been hurt, authorities suspended trolley service throughout the city. As the situation worsened, representatives from several businesses in the city called on Governor Tejeda and President Obregón to intervene.[33] In response, authorities sent for members of the state labor relations board to negotiate a settlement.

On August 20 people affiliated with the Veracruz Local Federation of Workers (FTLV) joined the strike. This meant that office workers, millers, bakers, masons, and others who made up the organization had walked out in solidarity with the electrical workers. Employees at the local ice factory, candleworks, and brewery also got involved.[34] A citywide committee, like the one established during the general strike of June 1922, soon took shape to enforce the terms of the stoppage, and women affiliated with the tenant syndicate rose to the occasion by patrolling streets, markets, and neighborhoods throughout Veracruz.[35]

The Libertarian Women again focused their organizing efforts on domestic workers, whom they viewed as "slaves of the bourgeoisie." In their campaign they began unionizing maids, hoping to "leave the bourgeoisie without anything to eat." After a few days of fierce "recruitment" by the Libertarian Women, many domestic workers refused to visit the city markets for fear of being harassed by the militants. Indeed, on August 24, *El Dictamen* complained that direct action taken by the tenant women had contributed to the "exorbitant" price of food in the port. They made it clear that to them the campaign to unionize domestic workers constituted a wrong-headed approach, especially since female tenants generally tended to "make more money than most of the house servants." The editorial also joked that "one day Proal and María Luisa Marín's cook and maid will tell us the intimate history of the happy life enjoyed by the syndicate leaders."

Members of the tenant syndicate organized demonstrations and marches in support of the general strike, just as they had the year before. Often these gatherings ended with Proal addressing an audience in Juárez Park or outside the Hotel Diligencias. During this period, Proal's speeches sharply denounced state and federal authorities' support for the local power company while also encouraging his audience to renew their commitment to direct action.[36]

On August 15 police fought with four soldiers who had been drinking in the cantina El Aguila de Oro. In the crossfire, a prominent member of the tenant union named Lucio Marín and a military officer, José Contreras, were killed and eight others were injured. The following day, members of several of the port's labor unions as well as supporters of the tenant strike gathered to honor Marín.[37] Ten days later, 250 mounted troops together with a number of infantry arrived in the port with orders to "protect the citizens of the city." Shortly after their arrival, authorities arrested several of the Libertarian Women and sent them to jail for disturbing the peace.[38] Then, in the days that followed, the presence of federal troops and police further discouraged strikers from continuing their campaign of direct action. The troop presence combined with food shortages and worsening economic conditions in the city moved labor leaders to call off the strike during the last week of August.[39]

The ending of the general strike did not neutralize conflict in the port. The labor and tenant protest persisted well into fall 1923, when business leaders finally complained to federal officials that labor organizing and unrest was crippling the regional and, to some extent, the national economy. Members of the National Chamber of Commerce, Mexico City office (Cámara Nacional de Comercio de la Ciudad de México) in a letter to President Obregón claimed that "millions of pesos have been lost by the paralyzation of the Port of Veracruz." Other businessmen told federal authorities that the situation in Veracruz had seriously affected the economy of other cities. Some suggested that officials use their power to rid the country of "foreign agitators" and help end "dangerous" labor organizing in the port. In response, the Veracruz Maritime Workers League (Liga de Trabajadores de la Zona Marítima) sent a letter to President Obregón in which they defended the recent strike action in the port and claimed the constitutional right of all Mexicans to collective action.[40]

By this time, a few ambitious militants once affiliated with the Revolutionary Syndicate had turned away from the city to concentrate on rural areas. After receiving tenant union funds to begin organizing rural workers, militants Ursulo Galván, Manuel Almanza, Sóstenes Blanco, and José Fernández Oca started a campaign to organize a statewide peasant association.[41] Frustrated with the seemingly uncontrollable character of the urban protests, Governor Tejeda had also turned his attention to rural areas in search of popular support. His backing of *agrarista* efforts came in part as a response to challenges from conservative forces in the state that had intensified earlier, in January and February 1923.

Tejeda under Fire

A shoot-out in the small Veracruz town of Puente Nacional (located between the port and Jalapa) on March 9, 1923, had brought political tensions in the state to a boil. The clash between members of the state civil guard and private militia forces funded by local landowners (*guardias blancas*) left seven dead and four wounded. More important, the episode sparked a major confrontation between Tejeda and Obregón, who at the time supported the governor's archrival, General Guadalupe Sánchez. Following the incident, Obregón had ordered all state civil guard and rural organizers disarmed. Yet while authorities arrested members of the civil guard involved in the incident, they managed to neutralize only part of the force loyal to Tejeda. The remaining guard, who kept their weapons, according to one historian, "showed an even greater determination to use force against the landowners."[42]

A little more than a week after the Puente Nacional incident, Tejeda presided over an agrarian congress in Jalapa that included more than one hundred delegates, many from the state's central region, as well as officials from the National Agrarian Commission (Comisión Nacional Agraria). Local labor unions also participated in the talks, hoping to gain influence. After a series of discussions, Tejeda and representatives of peasant and labor organizations founded the League of Agrarian Communities and Peasant Syndicates of the State of Veracruz (Liga de Comunidades Agrarias y Sindicatos Campesinos del Estado de Veracruz) on March 23, 1923. Ursulo Galván subsequently became its president and immediately began organizing efforts in the field.[43]

Then, in August, several newspaper columns criticizing the policies of Tejeda appeared when the governor traveled to Mexico City to meet with federal officials. Two, printed in the Mexico City papers *Excélsior* and *El Universal*, accused Tejeda of championing the cause of the working classes to a dangerous and "immoral" degree. The editors at *Excélsior* claimed he had taken advantage of a "federal government incredibly weak and overly tolerant of radicals" in freeing "dangerous criminals" who sometimes took part in "obscure political activities." Furthermore, the Veracruz administration had initiated programs "more dangerous than those of Governors Múgica in Michoacán and Sánchez in Puebla," making "the sly fellow [of Veracruz] an obstacle to the reconstruction of the nation."[44] Similarly, the editors of *El Universal* called Tejeda's government "confused" and singled out Proal and the tenant movement as a threat to social stability. "How many scandals, how much more energy will be wasted, how many more lives will be lost," they asked, "before the federal government will intervene?" They continued their attack, saying, "For eighteen months property owners in Veracruz have been caught between a rock and a hard place: the turbulent and arbitrary actions of Proal's organization, and the inept favoritism of local and state officials." The governor had whipped up "delirium" among the Veracruz working classes; and, because of his politics, "not only have the principles of the Constitution been cast aside but so too have the basic rights of any civilized society."[45] Thus, the editors argued, the federal government needed to take immediate action. They proposed that with the Veracruz leader in town, President Obregón should seize the opportunity to dispense a heavy dose of political discipline.

An opinion piece printed early in September adds another colorful example of the growing opposition, suggesting that "the ghastly work of Señor Tejeda" and the ringleaders of the so-called Veracruz Soviet had begun to assume an alarming character: "Veracruz is now under the control of a worker dictatorship that has broken with our constitutional system and condones the use of violence to achieve its justice. Moreover, the control of the federal government has been given over to more ambitious and powerful forces. The one who has benefited from these events has been the governor of Veracruz, Adalberto Tejeda. Tejeda thrives among the strikers like a fish lives in water." According to the text, it remained unclear what Obregón would do about the situation, though "probably he will only smile and say something about the sovereignty of the states" when he should consider "public opinion" in this serious situation and intervene directly.[46] Like this piece, other criticisms of Tejeda identified the Veracruz tenant syndicate as a prime example of "unconstitutional activities" taking place within the republic. After a flurry of critical remarks sparked by the visit to the capital, similar criticisms came later in the month from a variety of sources including another Mexico City paper, *Cronos*.[47]

Responding to these and other criticisms, President Obregón visited the port in early September and declared that "the government of Veracruz has not done what it should."[48] Meeting with various members of the Veracruz elite, including a commission of women from the port's Spanish community, Obregón tried to assure disgruntled residents that order would soon be restored. In the meantime, however, forces opposed to Tejeda had been readying for a full-scale attack on the governor.

Polarizing State Politics

As the political environment in the state again entered turbulent times during early fall 1923, the future of Tejeda's political career lay in the balance. New difficulties had begun in August when the state held elections for local and federal representatives. In order to maintain political power, Tejeda needed to keep a majority in the legislature. At the same time, however, his chief political rival, Guadalupe Sánchez and the state Cooperatist Party (affiliated with the Partido Nacional Cooperatista, or PNC), had gained the support of many regional landowners, businessmen, and urban property owners.[49] Mounting tensions between these competing groups soon led to a major confrontation.

In September, one group of *anti-tejedistas* gathered at the Hotel México in Jalapa while another group gathered at the Hotel Veracruz

in Mexico City.[50] At the meeting in the nation's capital, property owners Alejandro Sánchez, Antonio Revuelta, Severo Ordoñez, Enrique
Melgar, and several other Veracruz elites came together to plan a major protest. The invitation to the meeting read: "Longtime resident of
the port of Veracruz Enrique Melgar, along with members of the Property Owners Association, invites you to attend a meeting of veracruzanos on September 5 at eight o'clock in the evening at the Hotel
Veracruz. The purpose of the meeting is for us *jarochans* to address the
distressing and urgent situation that we currently face in the state and
particularly in the port of Veracruz."[51]

In a letter encouraging a friend to join their effort, a member of the
group explained the reasons for their action against Tejeda:

> We have already celebrated two meetings with the purpose of decid-
> ing how we should voice our unhappiness about the anarchistic situ-
> ation that now exists. [It is our opinion that] those bad elements who
> today govern Veracruz have virtually ruined the state. And, because
> of such bad government, we feel it is necessary to intervene. To help
> us decide what form this action should take to save Veracruz from
> the evil that threatens it, please join us on September 13 at seven in
> the evening at the Hotel Veracruz.[52]

Yet, while this group of disgruntled veracruzanos sought to address
what they saw as a problem of "bad government," dissident forces
headed by General Guadalupe Sánchez began making plans to oust
Tejeda.

Meanwhile, actions in the port initiated by individuals affiliated
with the tenant movement made it clear that many citizens had not
lost their enthusiasm for the rent protest. In fact, when followers of
Proal observed a solar eclipse in early September 1923, they took the
event to be a sign that they would soon triumph in their struggle against
local landlords.

The Sun and the Moon

On September 10 nearly 150 tenants gathered to witness the eclipse in
the Veracruz city square. As Herón Proal addressed the large number
of women assembled across from the parish church, he referred to the
tenant syndicate as the "soul" of Veracruz. Then, as the moon began to
pass in front of the sun around half past two that afternoon, Proal waxed
poetic as he told his audience that the sun represented communism
and the moon, capitalism: "For a moment, the moon will obscure the
light of day, but soon the brilliance of the sun, like the light of com-

munism, will return in all its magnificent splendor." As rays of light gradually returned to illuminate the plaza, women in the crowd began singing. Proal told them that the crossing of the sun and the moon represented a natural progression, "just like our evolution toward communism." Then turning to more immediate affairs, he said that although the property owners worked to have Tejeda's rent law declared unconstitutional, he wondered whether "any law [was] constitutional." Even if the Supreme Court rules that the law is unconstitutional, he shouted, "Who cares, because we are united!" Wrapping up his speech, Proal instructed the crowd to march around the plaza, singing the hymns that so "disgust the bourgeoisie."[53] After circling four or five times, he led the group into the street, where they continued the demonstration.

Proalista theories of history and nature notwithstanding, residents soon heard reports of landlords carrying out a new round of evictions in the port as well as other difficulties faced by the tenant syndicate, compounded by continuing criticism.[54] An editorial in *El Dictamen* blasted Proal and his followers for turning the strike "into a business" sustained by funds collected from patio residents, while Public Minister Eligio Hidalgo Alvarez informed Proal that he would be held responsible for "abuses committed by his followers."[55] Angered by accusations of mismanagement and irresponsibility, tenant syndicate secretary Marcos Gutiérrez wrote to Governor Tejeda complaining of "arbitrary acts" committed by property owners and municipal officials.[56]

Tenant syndicates elsewhere in the state also faced renewed pressure in mid-October. In Córdoba, for example, the local business association (Asociación Patronal de Córdoba) issued a statement denouncing the renters movement as a threat to city residents: "As it has been almost two years since tenant syndicates in Veracruz, Orizaba, Jalapa, and Córdoba have been in existence, [we have been subject to] constant tumultuous demonstrations that have injured our society in general and property owners, businessmen, and industrialists in particular. While Article 123 of the Constitution guarantees workers and tenants the right to strike, it does not afford anyone the right to force his own personal justice on society." The businessmen went on to argue that rent strikes throughout the state amounted to a severe attack on individual rights and that tenant demonstrators "had disregarded the idea of authority on many occasions." Following up on these complaints, the association decided in an emergency meeting that "order and morality" needed to be reestablished in Córdoba. Anything less, they suggested, would spell the loss of constitutional rights for all the residents of the city, and therefore the first move in restoring public civility would be to prohibit any further activities by the local tenant syndicate.[57]

Meanwhile, justice officials in the port had begun their own campaign against the protest. On the morning of September 28, fifteen mounted police traveled to the red light district on Guerrero Street to carry out evictions ordered by local judge Martín Maldama. When police confronted a group of prostitutes on the street, several announced they would not cooperate and immediately sought support from members of the tenant syndicate. A group of syndicate women soon arrived and encouraged the sex workers to resist. As police moved in to begin eviction proceedings, however, many of the women agreed to resume payment.

The next day, police closely monitored the Guerrero Street area, pressuring tenants to sign new agreements with landlords or move out. According to *El Dictamen*, only two or three women openly resisted, complaining that their accesorías lacked ventilation, light, and basic sanitary conditions. On one occasion, local officials visited the room of a belligerent female tenant who loudly exclaimed that she would continue to strike and then slammed the door in their faces. A while later, Proal rode through the area in a new red automobile that the syndicate had recently purchased. Seeing this spectacle, some openly criticized him for owning his own house and car while they continued to scrape by.

At the same time, *El Dictamen* printed a feature article entitled "The Hardships We Suffer." Written as a native son's return to the port, the article lamented recent changes in the social atmosphere of the city. It recounted a conversation between two men as they entered the La Huaca neighborhood. As they walked around, one complained that some now called Veracruz the "Mexican Moscow." When the other man charged that the local "bourgeoisie" should be held responsible for many of the city's social problems, his friend disagreed: "What hypocrisy! While it is true that they are not all veracruzanos, the people's attitude has changed. One can see a loss of dignity, of the pride that those well born here once possessed. At one time we were altruistic, generous, affectionate with our families and neighbors. Now things are quite different."[58] Although the atmosphere in the city had changed, this imaginary encounter offered a nostalgic view of Veracruz. As the second speaker would have it, the city's popular classes needed to be more respectful of their "social betters" rather than so assertive of their rights. But Proal and the tenant syndicate continued to maintain their notorious "Moscow" militancy. In early October 1923 renters dusted off a tactic they had used the year before to establish the Colonia Comunista: land invasion.

Appropriating Revolutionary Ideology

Although land reform up to that point had taken place primarily in rural areas, certain sites that lay at the periphery of cities also came under the purview of state officials. In the port, Rafael García and other municipal authorities had first targeted the property of Spanish businessman Antonio Revuelta for expropriation in June 1923.[59] Encouraged by this process, tenants hoped redistribution would lead to the establishment of several new popular settlements.[60]

While authorities worked through official channels to help resolve the housing problem in the state, residents in the port engaged in several creative activities to acquire new urban land—especially in the southeastern section of the city. There, property held by a Spanish resident of the port connected with the Spaniards' welfare league, Beneficencia Española, had first been occupied in spring 1922. Subsequently, squatters named the area Colonia Flores Magón after well-known anarchist Ricardo Flores Magón. As the strike wore on, the site hosted increasing numbers of residents. Then, during summer 1922, many tenants in the area broke off relations with Proal and formed their own organizing committee, calling themselves the Tenant Syndicate of Colonia Flores Magón. The new committee's leadership took charge of assigning lots, collecting dues, and general policing of the area.

The following March, sixty-eight residents of the settlement complained to President Obregón that the Spanish owner had demanded that they leave within twenty-four hours. "In view of this threat," the squatters wrote, "we are prepared to defend ourselves against the possibility of violence, so we ask that you protect us and help us defend our noble struggle to emancipate ourselves."[61] Continuing to occupy the land, tenants maintained their dispute with the owner through that spring and early summer. Then, in mid-June, members of the settlement issued a formal complaint to justice officials against Proal, arguing that Proal had tried to interfere with the administration of their tenant syndicate since his leaving Allende Jail. In particular, they objected to Proal's suggestion that "among the colonia there existed many tramps, dope smokers, and prostitutes."[62]

In fact, members of the city council had addressed the occupation question at a meeting on July 19, 1923. They decided to order an eviction, giving colonists six days to clear off the land. An area in the northeastern section of the city, officials suggested, would be more appropriate for resettlement.[63] Despite the order, however, squatters continued to occupy the colonia. Then, in September, the Veracruz City Council granted permission to residents of the Colonia Flores Magón to introduce water and drainage service in their neighborhood. A few days later, Faustino Díaz Caneja, president of the Sociedad Española, filed an amparo against the decision. Díaz Caneja argued that the council's determination violated the constitutional rights of the property owners. He added that individuals occupying the land had done so without permission and should be expelled.[64]

Noting the controversy, a group of proalistas invaded the properties adjacent to the settlement in early October. By October 10, Proal and his associates had commandeered a large area, charging one peso per month for access to the land. Within days, many squatters had constructed primitive shelters out of wood and tin. Characteristically, *El Dictamen* asserted that new acquisitions by the tenants had been achieved through the use of threats.[65] The editor's dark suspicions about the tenants soon proved true elsewhere in the city.

The La Vencedora Incident

Tensions between police, landlords, and tenants in the port ended in bloodshed a few days later outside the La Vencedora store. The conflict began when the store's owner, Antonio Laso, issued an eviction notice to Trinidad Olivares, a tenant in his nearby patio. Members of the syndicate came from surrounding tenements to block the eviction and a fight ensued. According to a telegram Proal and his associate Arturo Bolio Trejo sent to Governor Tejeda the following day, tenants believed "local police had attacked residents in the port without reason." They claimed that "Spanish landlords took part in the exchange of fire [that resulted in] five persons being injured, fourteen women arrested, and two left dead." For the rest of the day, fifteen mounted police patrolled the neighborhood to keep the peace.[66]

Another street confrontation over an attempted eviction prompted the Veracruz City Council to issue a ban on all public gatherings by members of the tenant syndicate. They justified the move by saying that recent behavior by Proal involved "acts outside the law and clear violations of the Federal Constitution."[67] Then residents received more bad news when they learned that Pioquinto Morales, one of several injured in the La Vencedora incident, had died the night before in Aquiles Serdán Hospital.

Immediately, Proal violated the city council's order by organizing a meeting in the city square for Morales's funeral. Angered by her death,

Proal blamed local landlords: "There is [for the bourgeoisie] still plenty of cannon fodder and we will fight to the death for the liberty we desire. If the landlords want to fight us, they had better be careful because we are willing to die just as we are willing to kill them by whatever means we can." Hearing this, a woman in the audience shouted out her hatred for those "bourgeois bastards who suck the life out of the worker." She continued, pointing to a small group of people who stood in front of the storefronts and cafés across the plaza listening: "They live comfortably with their cars, their houses full of nice things, maids, and whatever they need." As the group began their procession to the cemetery, they first passed by the onlookers and shouted insults and threats. Along the way, they stopped in front of La Vencedora, where they harangued a group of streetcar workers who had made the mistake of standing in front of the store. *El Dictamen* described Proal's fiery words as some of "the most violent and subversive" since his release from jail in May 1923.[68] On the night of October 17, police managed to break up a syndicate meeting in Juárez Park. Earlier that day, court authorities in Veracruz had declared Tejeda's rent law to be in violation of Articles 14 and 29 of the Constitution.[69] Unfortunately for the tenant movement, these and other events would soon lead to the apprehension of Herón Proal.

The Arrest of Proal

On October 28 renters sent a petition to Governor Tejeda complaining that Rafael García had again denied them the right to conduct public meetings: "Neither threats, shootings, slashings, deaths, injuries, nor imprisonment is the way to stop the struggle against the landlords' exploitation, much less attend to the needs of the people who rightly demand justice, land, and liberty. We have been denied not only the right to meet and demonstrate as we are accustomed but also to do the work of the patio commissions. [In denying us our rights] Rafael García is the one responsible."[70]

State officials received several other communications complaining about the Veracruz mayor. On the street, several posters circulated in late October that boldly accused García of being "the eternal traitor to the proletarian classes." One poster, which carried the endorsements of almost eighty individuals, charged García with forging alliances with landlords in order to bring the rent strike to an end.[71] In the midst of these charges, García revoked the ban on tenant gatherings.

Then, in early November 1923, disagreement between dock and rail terminal employees initiated a new phase of labor unrest in the port that required military intervention to keep the peace. Fearing negative consequences for the national economy, President Obregón asked labor leaders to resolve their differences.[72] As the tumultuous situation gradually came to an end, Mayor García suggested that representatives of the city's major worker associations help bring the tenant movement under the "legal" leadership of local labor affiliated with the Regional Confederation of Mexican Workers (CROM). This move by García would soon spell trouble for Proal and his associates.

On November 7 the city council issued another ban on syndicate meetings. Labor leaders responded by calling for the "reestablish[ment] of the tenant movement on fully legal grounds." While their proposal came, in part, out of frustrated attempts to control independent strike activities, it left no doubt that many in the city—including several worker organizations—had little idea about how to end the strike.[73]

The following day, however, nearly thirty tenants led by Porfirio Sosa and María Luisa Marín visited with Mayor García. When Marín realized that García would never change his mind about the ban on public meetings, she accused him of being a "traitor" to the workers' cause. Tenants soon appealed to the governor, asking that he intervene to nullify García's order. Refusing to be silenced by García or any other politician, members of the syndicate made even more noise as the sound of firecrackers could be heard coming from the direction of their headquarters later that afternoon. A newspaper report the following day stated that military officials had heard the commotion renters had caused as well as their "insults of President Obregón, the army, and [every other] authority."[74] Aware of opposing forces closing in on them, Proal and other members of the Revolutionary Syndicate began to feel that time was running out for them.

On November 11 a local judge ordered the arrest of Herón Proal after charging him with libel and intent to harm public officials. At first, the tenant leader resisted by hiding in the back of the syndicate office. A few hours later, however, he gave himself over to police and loudly declared, as he entered Allende Jail, that he had grown accustomed to being imprisoned and that this time would be no different. Upon hearing of their leader's incarceration, members of the tenant syndicate clashed with police, who eventually took two members of the Libertarian Women into custody.[75] *El Dictamen* informed residents the next day that members of the local labor federation had temporarily taken over leadership of the tenant syndicate.

Gathering across from the Cámara de Trabajo the next day, proalistas held a rally to protest the arrest of their leader. Of the several speakers who addressed the crowd, many denounced Mayor García. In contrast, an editorial in *El Dictamen* complained that "the tyranny [established by] Proal has been similar to that required in primitive societies [and] now we are heading in the same direction" unless something is done soon. For their part, property owners wrote to Rafael García and state justice officials expressing their desire to bring a quick and final end to Proal's influence in the city. The release of Proal on November 20, however, did much to discourage those who believed the strike would end soon.[76] Shortly thereafter, Mexicans went to the polls. In Veracruz, residents elected police inspector Miguel Melche as the city's new mayor.[77]

As veracruzanos prepared for a change in local government on December 1, *El Dictamen* reminded them that "the tenant problem represents one of the first issues the new officials will have to face." Yet while renters and landlords continued to do battle over housing, members of the military opposed to President Obregón conspired to launch a major rebellion under dissident former minister of finance Adolfo de la Huerta.

On December 6, *El Dictamen* informed residents that de la Huerta and the Cooperatist Party president, Jorge Prieto Laurens, had arrived in the port the day before. A pre-candidate for the presidency, the paper indicated that de la Huerta intended to spend a few restful days at the Hotel Imperial before moving north to continue his campaign. As it turned out, the former minister of finance and his friends had more in mind than a tropical vacation. On December 7, de la Huerta declared himself in opposition to Obregón. As a direct challenge to Adalberto Tejeda, de la Huerta took advantage of deep divisions in the state legislature and named José Pereyra Carbonell as provisional governor. Not surprisingly, the Cooperatist Party faction in Jalapa heartily approved of the move while also giving their support to the rebels. With Guadalupe Sánchez leading the dissident force in Veracruz, de la Huerta and his supporters launched an armed revolt that soon spread to include nearly two-thirds of the Mexican army.

Responding to the crisis, Governor Tejeda quickly mobilized a collection of armed peasants and workers throughout the state. Meanwhile, Obregón worked to consolidate support in the Mexican Senate as well as to gain assurances and arms from U.S. President Calvin Coolidge so that by late January 1924 the rebellion had been defeated.[78] In the process, however, tolerance for striking tenants in Veracruz was significantly diminished as Tejeda increasingly turned his attention to mobilizing support in the countryside. This shift in the governor's focus left Herón Proal and the Revolutionary Syndicate of Tenants especially vulnerable.

Notes

1. Herón Proal to members of the Congress, April 25, 1923, AGEV, gobernación, 1923.

2. Tejeda to Pedro M. González, April 13, 1923, AGEV, gobernación, 1923.

3. Procurador General de Justicia to Tejeda, May 11, 1923. *El Dictamen*, May 12, 1923. AGEV, gobernación file "Sindicato de Inquilinos, Veracruz," 1923.

4. *El Dictamen*, May 12, 1923.

5. Tenant Syndicate of Jalapa, January 17, 1923, AGEV, gobernación, 1923. Shortly thereafter, tenants in Orizaba issued a formal complaint against President Obregón while publicizing their grievances throughout town. Handbill circulated in Orizaba, February 1923, AGN, gobernación, vol. 11, file 365.

6. Moisés Lira to Tejeda, May 17, 1923, AGEV, gobernación, 1923.

7. Marcos Ramírez and other residents of Orizaba to Obregón, April 11, 1923, AGEV, gobernación, 1923.

8. María de Jesús Campos to Obregón, April 30, 1923, sent to Tejeda by Subsecretary of the Ministry of the Interior on May 31, 1923, AGN, gobernación, vol. 18, file 396.

9. Ibid.

10. Manuel Lira to Obregón, May 31, 1923, AGN, gobernación, vol. 17, file 353. Calles's subsecretary of the interior circulated the petition in the national Congress during late May. See Subsecretary of the Interior to Members of the Permanent Commission of the Congress, May 24, 1923, AGN, gobernación, vol. 17, file 353. Adolfo de la Hoz and the Liga de Defensa de Propietarios de Casas in Orizaba sent similar letters to Obregón on June 27, 1923, and June 29, 1923, respectively. See other letters from Orizaba Property Owners Association to Obregón on August 15, 22, 1923, September 8, 1923, February 16, 1924, AGEV, gobernación, 1923, 1924.

11. *El Dictamen*, February 20, 1923.

12. Ibid., June 8 and 9, 1923.

13. Ibid., June 9 and 10, 1923.

14. Ibid., June 13, 1923.

15. Ibid., July 11 and 12, 1923.

16. Property Owners Association of Jalapa to Obregón, July 25, 1923, AGEV, gobernación, 1923.

17. Handbill circulated in Veracruz, June–July 1923, AGN, Obregón/Calles, 407-v-17.

18. *El Dictamen*, July 1, 1923.

19. Ibid., July 7, 1923.

20. Ibid., July 11, 1923.

21. Ibid., July 18, 1923.

22. *New York Times*, July 20, 1923. See also reaction in *El Demócrata*, July 23, 1923, and mention in Summerlin to Secretary of State, RDS, reel 161.

23. Marcos Gutiérrez to Obregón, July 18, 1923, RDS, reel 161.

24. Obregón to Gutiérrez, July 19, 1923, ibid.

25. *El Dictamen*, July 18, 1923.

26. At the same time, many in support of the tenant cause wrote to state and federal officials demanding that urban land be made available for workers housing. In August, authorities received several requests asking that property owned by Antonio Revuelta in the southern part of the city named Terrenos Collado be expropriated by the state and sold. One letter signed by over 170 market vendors in the port accused Revuelta of monopolizing ownership

of local lands and claimed he owned almost half the municipality. Sindicato Revolutionario de Locatarios de los Mercados del Puerto to Obregón, August 4, 1923; Confederación Sindicalista del Estado de Puebla to Obregón, August 6, 1923; Unión de Estibadores de Veracruz to Obregón, August 8, 1923; Federación de Sindicatos de Obreros y Campesinos de la Region Jalapeña to Obregón, August 11, 1923. Many others, including municipal leaders in Cuernavaca, Morelia, Guadalupe, Zacatecas, Progreso, Yucatán, and Izamal, Yucatán, as well as the governor of Hidalgo all called for the selling of Revuelta's land. AGN, gobernación, 423-v-6, "Terrenos Collado."

27. *El Dictamen*, July 23, 1923. In late July the Property Owners Association elected a new board with Alejandro Sánchez as president. Executive Board to Ministry of the Interior, July 23, 1923, AGN, gobernación, vol. 10, file 252.

28. *El Universal*, July 23, 1923. Translation by the staff at the U.S. consul's office in Mexico City.

29. *El Dictamen*, July 31, August 3, 1923.

30. Ibid., August 5, 1923.

31. Ibid., August 8, 1923.

32. Ibid., August 10, 11, 1923.

33. Rosa María Landa Ortega, "Los primeros años de la organización y luchas de los electricistas y tranviarios en Veracruz, 1915–1928" (Bachelor's thesis, Universidad Veracruzana, 1989), 108.

34. García to Obregón, August 21, 1923, AGN, Obregón/Calles, 407-v-28.

35. Landa Ortega, "Los primeros años," 109–10. See also Bernardo García Díaz, *Puerto de Veracruz* (Jalapa: Archivo General del Estado de Veracruz, 1992), 210–14.

36. Landa Ortega, "Los primeros años," 115.

37. *El Dictamen*, August 15–17, 1923.

38. Ibid., August 26–29, 1923.

39. Ibid., September 1, 1923.

40. AGN, Obregón/Calles, 407-v-28. See other letters to Obregón filed under "El problema obrero," AGN, Obregón/Calles, 407-v-28, file 4, annex 2.

41. For good reason, Mexican historian Mario Gill later called the state peasant league "the daughter of the tenant movement." Mario Gill, "Veracruz: Revolución y extremismo," *Historia Mexicana* 2, no. 8 (April–July 1953): 631. The life and work of Galván is chronicled in Sóstenes Blanco, *Ursulo Galván, 1893–1930, su vida, su obra* (Jalapa: Liga de Comunidades Agrarias y Sindicato Campesino del Estado de Veracruz, 1966).

42. Heather Fowler-Salamini, *Agrarian Radicalism in Veracruz, 1920–30* (Lincoln: University of Nebraska Press, 1971), 40.

43. Fowler-Salamini, *Agrarian Radicalism*, 40, 92.

44. *Excélsior*, August 14, 1923.

45. *El Universal*, August 16, 1923.

46. Unidentified newspaper clippings stamped September 6, 1923, AGN, Obregón/Calles, 407-v-28. See also "Los laureles del señor Tejeda," Obregón/Calles, 407-v-28, annex 1.

47. *Cronos*, August 25, 1923. Also see August 28, 30, September 12, 30, October 1, 4, 1923.

48. *El Dictamen*, September 3, 1923.

49. Veracruz Property Owners Association to Tejeda, July 29, 1923, AGEV, gobernación, 1923, "Veracruz quejas."

50. Report to Tejeda from "El Comisionado," September 12, 1923, AT, vol. 86, 1923.

51. September 3, 1923, ibid.

52. "El Comisionado" to Tejeda, September 14, 1923, ibid.

53. *El Dictamen*, September 11, 1923.

54. Ibid., September 12 and 23, 1923.

55. Ibid., September 22, 1923.

56. Marcos Gutiérrez to Tejeda, September 23, 1923, AGEV, gobernación, 1923.

57. *El Dictamen*, October 16, 1923.

58. Ibid., September 30, 1923.

59. Ibid., June 17 and 18, 1923. The initiative to expropriate the Revuelta land came first from the mayor, who argued that the family had purchased the property but had failed to build on it in the amount of time stipulated by an 1888 state law. Authorities approved the expropriation of Revuelta lands on June 22, 1923. *El Dictamen*, June 23, 1923. The state eventually expropriated another Revuelta property (Collado y Boticaria), long the site of informal popular settlement in the port (known by residents as the Colonia Flores Magón), from Revuelta for the construction of additional worker housing on May 7, 1931. Veracruz Registro Público de la Propiedad, December 15, 1932.

60. In 1926 new worker settlements—Adalberto Tejeda, Francisco I. Madero, Alberto Pastrana, and Vicente Guerrero—would be organized under the banner of the Unión Cooperativa de Colonias Obreras 22 de Marzo. Veracruz Registro Público de la Propiedad, AGEV, October 7, 1926.

61. Residents of Colonia Flores Magón to Obregón, March 10, 1923, AGN, gobernación, vol. 18, file 355.

62. *El Dictamen*, July 10, 1923.

63. Ibid., July 20, 1923. That same month, Proal reapplied for city land. On July 26, for example, he asked the city council to donate lots 55 and 69 on Cuauhtémoc Street and others on neighboring Sánchez Tagle to the syndicate. While they delayed their response to Proal, the paper reported four days later that local authorities had given nearly forty-eight blocks (*manzanas*) to the carpenters union (Sociedad Cooperativa de Artesanos Carpinteros) for colonization. *El Dictamen*, July 27 and 30, 1923.

64. Ibid., September 18, 1923.

65. Ibid., October 10, 1923.

66. Ibid.

67. Ibid., October 8–12, 1923. Rafael García to Obregón, October 16, 1923, AGN, gobernación, vol. 4, file 114. See also Property Owners Association to Tejeda, October 11, 1923, AGEV, gobernación, 1923.

68. *El Dictamen*, October 13, 1923.

69. Meanwhile, in Orizaba, a group of two hundred tenants again created controversy when they assaulted the house of lawyer Emilio J. Ordóñez. Ibid., October 24, 1923.

70. Petition signed by more than thirty residents sent to Tejeda, October 28, 1923, AGEV, gobernación, "Veracruz Ayuntamiento, quejas," 1923.

71. *El Dictamen*, October 24, 1923. See also October 25, 27, 28, 1923.

72. Ibid., October 28–31, November 1–5, 1923.

73. Ibid., November 6, 1923.

74. Ibid., November 8, 1923.

75. Ibid., November 11, 1923.

76. Ibid., November 13, 14, 16, 21, and 22, 1923.

77. Melche had been one of the founding members of the Mexican Confederation of Labor Unions in 1912. Leafar Agetro (Rafael Ortega), *Las luchas*

proletarias en Veracruz: Historia y autocrática (Jalapa: Editorial "Barricada," 1942), 154–55.

78. Soledad García Morales, "Cotidianidad, cultura y diversión durante la ocupación delahuertista del puerto de Veracruz," in *Actores sociales en un proceso de transformación: Veracruz en los años veinte,* ed. Manuel Reyna Múñoz (Jalapa: Universidad Veracruzana, 1996), 103–28. For a full account of the rebellion in Veracruz, see Soledad García Morales, *La rebelión delahuertista en Veracruz* (Jalapa: Universidad Veracruzana, 1986).

9

The Fall of the
Revolutionary Tenant Syndicates

Is Bolshevism over?
—*El Dictamen*, December 27, 1926

The December 1924 inauguration of Alvaro Obregón's successor, Plutarco Elías Calles, soon spelled the end of the tenant movement. That same month, a series of public confrontations between Herón Proal and members of a new dissident renters group provided the pretext for federal officials to have Proal arrested and brought to Mexico City.[1] In his place, María Luisa Marín took over leadership of the Revolutionary Syndicate. Under her guidance, militant renters continued to strike while also devoting a great deal of time working to secure the release of Proal. Despite many petitions, the tenant leader would remain in jail for the remainder of Calles's term while divisions within the tenant movement allowed labor organizations allied with the state to incorporate the housing issue into a larger, albeit much less controversial, framework.[2]

Against the "Despotism" of Proal

For the first part of 1924, the de la Huerta rebellion overshadowed the rent strike in Veracruz. Nevertheless, as many tenants throughout the state continued to deny rent payments to their landlords during the winter months, resentment felt by various members of the Revolutionary Syndicate of Tenants toward Herón Proal grew intense. That spring, several militants openly broke with the anarchist.

On April 5 a group calling itself the Unión Inquilinaria (later changed to Organización Inquilinaria) held a public meeting in the port to condemn what it called the "despotism" of Proal and announce the formation of a new tenant organization.[3] In a letter to Governor Adalberto Tejeda, the group stated that "since the passage of the rent law, there [has] no longer [been] a reason to prolong the conflict." The letter, signed by José Olmos and two of Proal's former sidemen, Arturo Bolio Trejo and Porfirio Sosa, ended with a jab at their old friend, saying that their group stood against "the tyranny of one individual."[4]

Independence Avenue, mid-1920s. *Courtesy of AGEV, José Pérez de León Collection*

Proal responded a few days later in a syndicate poster that circulated in Veracruz:

> Members of the Revolutionary Tenant Syndicate: Beware of Olmos and other traitors. This other organization wants tenants to pay rents again and participate in politics. I don't want to condemn anyone, I only want tenants to remain united. In Jalapa there has appeared the Sindicato Evolutivo to counter the Revolutionary Syndicate there. In Córdoba [a group has formed] named Pro-Ley. Here in the port there is now the Unión Inquilinaria. What has happened to the men who only yesterday shouted, "Don't pay rent!"? How could they change their minds so quickly? Power to the Tenant Syndicate! Up with the Social Revolution! The loyal and committed ones always triumph. Up with the revolutionary women, up with the strong and dignified youth who hear the revolutionary call, *Revolución pro-comunismo!*[5]

In the coming months, tensions between Proal and his former colleagues continued to escalate. In the meantime, lawmakers in Jalapa considered some of the problems that had arisen regarding application of the rent law.

Syndicate handbill, 1925. *Courtesy of AGN*

State officials, landlords, and tenants testified before the state legislature. On May 13, 1924, *El Dictamen* reported: "A state official commented that the poor interpretation of the law by a large number of
tenants and landlords [in the state] had caused numerous difficulties.
These mishaps have come [to put it more precisely] because of the bad

faith of some and the ignorance of others." The next day the paper informed readers that Governor Tejeda had criticized local judges who had issued eviction notices in an "irregular fashion." To remedy the situation, Tejeda insisted that proceedings be standardized according to the law. The paper also reported that Tejeda had requested the services of several lawyers in Veracruz to determine which tenants and landlords had cooperated with the law. The editors saw the reform, however unsatisfying as it might be, as better than no law at all: "Many tenants as well as landlords have said that this law is bad. Indeed, while it is difficult to defend it, the law, if obeyed, will at least help to reestablish the concept of rights and obligations as compared to the disgraceful situation that we currently face. It is something that will help set responsibility and judicial order while avoiding new catastrophes."[6]

Calling Veracruz "ungovernable," the editors nevertheless saw several difficulties in applying the law, while landlords around the state complained to government agents.[7] Then, on May 30, federal officials received a petition from property owners in Mexico City regarding what they saw as the "anguished situation" in Veracruz. They were appealing to the politicians' "basic sense of justice" and respect for law and order because "protesting tenants were destroying the rich state of Veracruz."[8] Officials received other letters complaining about the rent strike in Veracruz, including one sent by the Property Owners Association in Torreón, Coahuila, that stated: "Events in Veracruz initiated by Herón Proal are shameful not just for the state but also for the entire republic."[9] With similar denunciations being made elsewhere in Mexico, it seemed as though the syndicate's luck was running out.

In fact, Veracruz Mayor Miguel Melche informed property owners that city officials had decided to cooperate with tenants associated with the new Organización Inquilinaria but not with Proal and members of the Revolutionary Syndicate.[10] Yet when a commission composed of municipal staff and Organización delegates visited patio Ilusión to make their first evaluation, Proal and a few of his colleagues also appeared on the scene and declared that they had formed their own delegation to determine property values.[11]

Shortly thereafter, Veracruz Property Owners Association representatives José García Suero, José Cano Rosas, and Antonio Ramos proposed a meeting of all landlords in the city. At a gathering held on May 22, many members loudly complained that Proal and "his women" continued to obstruct tenement evaluations. In the commotion, one member shouted out that even local sanitation officials had come out against patio assessments "because many of the buildings were completely run-down." After landlords delivered a strong note of protest to officials in Jalapa regarding the manner in which assessments were being carried out, state commissioner José Almaraz canceled all appraisals until further notice.[12]

In contrast, some declared their willingness to restart rent payments. An article printed in *El Dictamen*, for example, listed residents of several tenements who had already embraced the Organización Inquilinaria's more reform-minded position.[13] Yet while some appeared willing to cooperate with state officials, animosity toward the Red syndicates who continued their boycott increased. In Orizaba, tempers flared on May 31 when angry renters attacked Alberto de la Llave, a prominent businessman and vice president of the property owners association.[14] Elsewhere, syndicate leaders Moisés Lira, Isidro Polanco, and Ignacio Palacios informed *El Dictamen* that their office in Jalapa had been ransacked by nearly seventy members of the Sindicato Evolutivo.[15]

Meanwhile, as residents in the port increasingly confronted a choice between eviction or resumed payment according to guidelines established by the rent law, a growing number of tenants affiliated themselves with the Organización Inquilinaria.[16] Proalistas, however, wanted no part of a negotiated settlement that, among other things, did not stop evictions. Thus, a June 2, 1924, poster issued by the tenant syndicate declared: "Protest continued evictions, don't forget our fallen brothers in July 1922 and other victims. We'd rather die than live as slaves! *¡Revolución pro-comunismo!*"[17] Two days later, Proal wrote to Tejeda asking the governor to consider a prohibition on evictions.[18]

Yet while syndicate members balked at the prospect of a mediated settlement in the port, negotiations monitored by Tejeda's staff between landlords and tenants from Jalapa and Orizaba appeared to make significant strides. In early June, landlords and tenants from Jalapa announced that they had reached a provisional agreement.[19] A communication to Secretary of Government Calles on the situation in Orizaba included a copy of an agreement between tenants and landlords made in the city's Llave Theater on June 7, 1924. A portion of the text read: "Property owners have agreed to the following clauses proposed by the Tenant Syndicate: for houses renting for less than 100 pesos per month, rents [will be] based at 6 percent. For houses constructed after 1921, value will be established by Juntas Avaluadoras [and set accordingly]. Landlords agree to forgive back rents if the state will also agree to cancel back taxes since the first of May 1922. Landlords will also agree to make repairs and sanitize patios once they begin receiving rents."[20] More than a year after passage of the rent law, the document represented the first successful negotiation between a renters union and landlords in the state. Yet while the accord appeared to pave the way for a resolution to the conflict statewide, other problems soon clouded such possibilities.

Complaints and Concessions

In early June, Secretary of Government Calles and national labor leader Luis Morones attended a banquet in Orizaba held in their honor. While Calles offered details about his presidential campaign, Morones took the opportunity to chastise the city's tenant syndicate. He charged that rent protesters were "a bunch of thugs" and that their efforts amounted to little more than a series of "threats and plundering."[21] Yet while Morones's negative characterization of the rent strikers may have turned a few in the audience against the protest, it did not deter state officials from recognizing the demands of the statewide tenant movement through small but not insignificant land concessions.

Soon, citizens got word of new action by the governor when *El Dictamen* reported that the state had expropriated land near Jalapa on *rancho* San Nicolás for the purpose of building worker housing. In fact, tenants had already invaded the land and now planned to realize the settlement of the area in a way that would, as one person at the site told reporters, "serve as an example for the entire state."[22] While tenants made plans to hold a dance in honor of the new colonia, they also indicated that formal agreements with landlords in Jalapa would be signed in a few days.[23]

In the port, Proal and members of the tenant syndicate took the expropriation of the Jalapa rancho as encouragement for further action. On June 13 the anarchist led a group through the city to an area bordering Pino Suárez, Arista, Estéban Morales, and Jiménez Streets. After delivering a short speech at the site, Proal, with the others, proceeded to survey the land with the intention of establishing a popular neighborhood. However, owner Antonio Granes learned that members of the tenant syndicate had targeted his land for invasion and called the police. Shortly thereafter, a small group of soldiers arrived, telling Proal that he and his associates would have to leave. After a few minutes of foot-dragging and grumbling by the renters, the gathering disbanded without further incident.[24]

Then, around five o'clock on the morning of June 15, tenants again returned to the site and claimed that if the owner did not cultivate or build on the land he would necessarily forfeit the title to it. When Granes complained to Mayor Melche, he found out that Governor Tejeda had given the tenants permission to occupy his land and several nearby lots.[25] Having acquired the land for tenant use, Proal then asked the state legislature not to tax him for transferring ownership of the property. Finding this request particularly ironic, *El Dictamen* ran a story with the headline: "Proal Is Now a Property Owner and Wants to Be Exempt from Payment!"[26] Despite the usual bickering, renters celebrated the recent acquisition of appropriated urban lots by inviting the state attorney general, Hermenegildo Carrión, to dinner. Unable to attend, he sent three other justice officials in his place. After enjoying a meal with Proal and several union members, the tenants then sang a few communist hymns for the visiting officials.[27]

Yet while tenants tried to win favor with the judiciary, *El Dictamen* reported that state officials had made a change in the rent law regarding evictions. The revision stated that "delinquent tenants" who had previously been protected from property owners now could be forcibly removed for not paying rent without a judge's order. Interestingly, a large group of landlords who met in the port on June 15 reacted negatively to the amendment, suggesting that the ruling would only anger tenants and encourage them to continue the strike.[28] Nevertheless, as the change went forward it became all the more clear that reconciliation between renters and property owners would be extremely difficult. Matters became even more delicate when several property owners filed amparos in local courts contesting Tejeda's power to expropriate lands. Only a few days later, the number of these complaints filed against the state had risen significantly. [29] District Judge Alfonso Quitena Pérez further complicated matters when he ruled on June 20 that suits filed against Tejeda merited the suspension of urban land reform activities until further notice.[30]

With the expropriation of urban lands stalled, state justice officials soon conducted a review of city treasury records and estimated that Veracruz had lost some 530,000 pesos because of the rent strike. A little less than half of this sum represented back utility (principally water) payments while the remainder came from taxes not received by local landlords.[31] Armed with this new information, property owners sent another petition to the senate and President Obregón declaring their opposition to Tejeda's rent law and subsequent revisions regarding evictions. In their communication they characterized the changes as "true judicial nonsense [from which] we have suffered enormously."[32] In their own attempt to address the situation, city boosters called for the revitalization of sections of the city that had been colonized in recent years by the Veracruz urban poor.

An Appeal for Urban Renewal

On July 9, *El Dictamen* printed an editorial supporting the "urbaniza-tion" of federal lands along the city's coastline for the purpose of re-solving the housing problem.[33] "The formation of a new neighborhood," the editors suggested, "could help avoid many of the inconveniences and losses that the lack of housing has caused." The area, which to that point had been no more than a "refuge for garbage and people with-out homes, could be taken and turned into an attraction for the city." The editors, predicting that construction of three different kinds of hous-ing would help to create a viable solution to the problem, cleverly pro-posed that the new neighborhood be called Regeneración, a name that paid tribute to the Flores Magón brothers while also expressing city boosters' desire for local improvements. The only problem federal of-ficials would encounter, it seemed, would be to find the right construc-tion firm for the job. Nevertheless, they looked forward to federal assistance in resolving a problem that had "aggravated local leaders" for so long:

> With the generous cooperation of the federal government in helping to resolve the housing problem, we will be able to realize the value of this area. The houses that will be built there will help relieve the ter-rible crowding of renters in small and unsanitary tenements. [This project] will also provide an opportunity for those accustomed to liv-ing without paying rent to now take advantage of a situation that will provide them with their own house and thus avoid the problems that have [in the past] plagued property owners. Finally, this will help rid the city of a site occupied by weeds, rotting garbage, and dis-placed transients, making way for a modern, hygienic, and well-built neighborhood that can withstand the demanding climate of the port.

Indeed, the idea of urban renewal sponsored by the federal govern-ment must have encouraged civic leaders, possibly reminding them of the earlier times when railroad and port concessions produced tremen-dous growth and prosperity for local elites. For others, however, the project offered little real promise of urban reform. Consequently, orga-nized tenants resumed their attacks on local landlords.

In late July and early August, both landlords and tenant leaders throughout the state also continued to press state agents on the issue of housing reform. In Jalapa, tenants complained that city officials had confiscated furniture and other items belonging to the statewide ten-ant federation. In their correspondence to Tejeda, residents from nearly fifty patios had signed their names.[34]

In the port, Proal wrote to the governor on August 2, saying, "The people are in misery." He asked that civil codes be revised to prohibit evictions and complained that city officials had been selling land to "Spaniards" rather than donating it to "needy tenants."[35] Coming to the defense of landlords in the state, Orizaba businessman and property owner Alberto de la Llave warned officials that cancellation of back rents and continued toleration of the tenant syndicates meant economic disaster.[36] Responding to these claims, Mayor Melche ordered police to conduct a survey to see which tenants had resumed paying rents. He figured that if landlords had indeed received payment, they should have no excuse not to fulfill their responsibilities to the city. As information from *El Dictamen* suggests, tenants in a variety of patios indeed had begun to resume payment during fall 1924.[37] About the same time, landlords enjoyed some relief in late August when state officials decreed that back taxes owed by property owners for the period of the tenant strike would be forgiven.[38] Tenants also were granted certain concessions a month later when state justice officials sided with residents of Veracruz's popular Colonia El Cocal by deciding that amparos filed by property owners against state expropriation would be dismissed.[39] Yet with these accommodations both Obregón and Tejeda continued to receive letters from tenant and landlord groups. Many argued that Mayor Miguel Melche was refusing to comply with the rent law.[40] Monitoring the strike situation, U.S. State Department officials wrote:

> There is but little change in the [tenant strike] situation. It has been somewhat relieved by a few renters coming to an agreement with landlords to pay less rent. Others have taken up lots expropriated by state decree and built shanties thereon. It is believed 3,000 people are now living in the new addition to Veracruz, in a motley state. The Supreme Court of the Republic has overruled local judges granting injunctions against state authorities from expropriating private lands for housing purposes in the interest of the rent-strikers. Its decision was based on grounds that it was for the public welfare of the people. An inspection of the quarters on these lands would disillusionise [*sic*] any real friend of the people that it has been for their public welfare. Rather, the effect has been to retard their welfare by encouraging them to live in shacks in an unsanitary condition. It is certain that persons with capital will not put their money in what was considered to be the best security in the city. No houses are being built and old ones are not being repaired.[41]

Thus, despite government permission to colonize land for popular settlement, the housing situation in Veracruz remained largely unchanged.

In the nearly eighteen months since the rent law had gone into effect, crowding and sanitation had only grown worse. In addition, the city treasury had been nearly depleted. According to one source, Veracruz had "only eight police on duty, all of the rest having left on account of failure to receive any pay." At the same time, U.S. observers noted that the street-cleaning department was allowing the city to become "very unsanitary" and saloons were "thriving." Painting a particularly gloomy picture of Veracruz in late 1924, North American diplomats wrote: "State and municipal authorities are engaged in furthering their own personal ends with no thought of improving the welfare of the people. There has been a constant change for the worse during the last few years, and the best friends of Mexico in this district lament the existing state of affairs and see no change in the immediate future unless some unexpected radical movement takes place."[42]

Barring some new kind of political campaign, the account leaves little doubt that economic and social conditions in Veracruz were deteriorating. Revolution, popular protest, and subsequent state reforms, it seemed, had contributed to the degradation of the Veracruz urban environment rather than helping to improve it. There existed no shortage of testimony that year regarding the fact that the housing crisis had deepened, including the observation in *El Dictamen* that "some homes in the port are in such a state of disrepair that they constitute a serious threat to people's lives."[43]

Then, in the midst of growing chaos in Veracruz, newly elected president Plutarco Elías Calles and Veracruz governor Heriberto Jara both took office on December 1, 1924.[44] Seeing these leaders assume their posts, residents immediately wrote to them, voicing their concerns about the condition of the city and their specific complaints about the tenant protest.[45] By now, renters affiliated with the statewide renters association—including even Proal's former colleague Porfirio Sosa—denounced the anarchist leader for his unwillingness to cooperate with the rent law. It would not be long before the influence of the Calles administration would have an important impact on the tenant protest.

The December Clash: Marín Takes Over

Seeing the transfer of political power as an opportunity to advance their position, members of the Organización Inquilinaria wasted no time in writing to Governor Jara. In their communication, they attacked Herón Proal and former governor Tejeda, whom they saw as "overly tolerant" of radical activities.[46] Thinking Jara would take a tougher stand against the tenants encouraged several other groups critical of

Proal to call for harsher measures to be implemented against the Revolutionary Syndicate. Not surprisingly, members of the press joined in by vigorously attacking Proal. A clipping from an unidentified paper at the time reminds readers: "Remember that Proal, sustained by Tejeda, [was] responsible for the deaths of many on the night of July 5–6. Remember that he once was only a poor tramp who now has more than one thousand pesos to his name. If the governor does not do something about Proal, he will remain a hindrance to the progress and tranquility of Veracruz."[47] With these and other complaints, it appeared as if a full-scale assault against Proal was in the making. In December, differences between the syndicate and the Organización Inquilinaria became increasingly apparent. Tensions came to a head on December 16 when a fight between the two groups broke out in the port.

The origins of the conflict had taken shape a few days earlier when Organización leaders demanded that a resident of patio Dos Cocuites take down Revolutionary Syndicate banners and replace them with flags bearing the name of the Organización. When word about the switch reached Proal, he told two members of his group to reinstall the syndicate's red colors. Then, on the morning of December 16, nearly two hundred proalistas visited the patio to carry out Proal's instructions en masse. As they hung the banners, some shouted insults to Organización members while others shot off firecrackers.[48] In the fray, a few Organización sympathizers ran to nearby patio La Ilusión to gather support. Soon, they had assembled a crowd who, armed with clubs, rocks, and concealed guns, returned to confront the proalistas. A fight then ensued that left four people seriously wounded, including José Reyes, who would later die from his injuries. The next day, local officials called for the arrest of Proal.[49] On December 20, police found the tenant leader outside a local shoe store and took him into custody. That afternoon, tenants assembled to honor the dead tenant Reyes with a rally and a procession to the cemetery.[50]

Quickly, authorities charged Proal with rebellion and sent him to Mexico City.[51] In his place, María Luisa Marín took control of the tenant syndicate. Then, as one of her first acts as head, she issued a call to the public that urged Veracruz residents to demand the release of Proal: "We will do what we can so that our children will not denounce us as traitors and cowards. For them we will prove that with Proal and without him, the Veracruz renters will defend their rights. In view of the danger that now threatens us we issue an urgent call to the people: Don't wait for the powerful to help you because they will never appreciate the dignity and value of our solidarity, which some day

will triumph. The supreme hour of the people has arrived! People of
Veracruz, wake up and join the struggle!"[52]

In the weeks that followed, Marín coordinated a variety of efforts
all dedicated to the task of securing Proal's release. The syndicate petitions included one to President Calles and one to the Supreme Court
signed by nearly two hundred women.[53] Yet, despite these appeals, officials refused to allow Proal to go free while also ruling that syndicate
meetings would again be prohibited until further notice.[54] President
Calles defended this decision by declaring Proal a "nuisance to public
order," stating further that, despite requests by the Veracruz legislature to return the anarchist to the state, Proal would remain in Mexico
City.[55] In the meantime, Marín continued her campaign to liberate her
colleague while also dedicating herself to the union's day-to-day business of organizing demonstrations and direct actions. Determined not
to be defeated by either property owners or unsympathetic state officials, she continued to write to President Calles complaining about the
"intransigence" of local landlords and demanding the release of Proal.[56]

Meanwhile, property owners from Veracruz, Orizaba, Jalapa, Córdoba, Minatitlán, Puerto México, Soledad de Doblado, Río Blanco,
Nogales, and Santa Rosa met with Governor Jara in early January 1925.
At that time, they discussed bringing the tenant strike to an end by
establishing an informal agreement that proposed a moratorium on
both back rents and back taxes. Encouraged, participants in the talks
felt that a settlement satisfactory for both tenants and landlords would
soon be in the making.[57] Yet for renters in the state who supported
Proal, resolution of the strike still appeared to be only a distant possibility. While rival members of the Organización Inquilinaria continued to express their willingness to pay rents, renters affiliated with the
Revolutionary Syndicate defied the ban on public demonstrations and
took to the streets.[58]

The new governor offered his own perspective on the strike in late
January. In an interview with *El Dictamen*, he emphasized his desire to
see housing and sanitation conditions in the state improve and said
that tenants had the right to hold public meetings but that their gatherings must be conducted in a lawful and orderly manner. While he said
he would not tolerate exploitation, the new governor indicated that
the problem must be resolved, and, because a significant number of
landlords and tenants were still not talking, the government would
have to resort to "energetic measures to enforce compliance of the rent
law."[59]

Despite the governor's intention to mediate a solution, many landlords continued to resist state efforts. Representing property owners,

José Cano Rosas and Salvador Campa sent a letter to *El Dictamen* that the paper printed on January 29. Standing their ground, the landlords stated that they did not wish "to become the servants of tenants or the state." In the meantime, members of the Revolutionary Syndicate prepared to celebrate another anniversary of the union's founding.

"The Proletarian Women Will Make the Social Revolution"

February 5 marked the third anniversary of the founding of the Revolutionary Syndicate of Tenants. For the occasion, María Luisa Marín instructed tenants to deck their patios with red banners to show their commitment to the strike. In response, residents of patios El Obrero, Tanitos, La Malinche, and others arranged colorful displays. Expressing their loyalty to tenant leaders, renters hung two large red banners from the roof of Proal's house at number 33 Arista and decorated the union's headquarters on Landero y Cos. Members of the Organización Inquilinaria also joined in the celebration by hanging red-and-black flags outside patio Elena and their offices at La Ilusión. The two groups, each in their own way, communicated a willingness to hold out hope that negotiations with landlords and state officials might result in the passage of significant reforms.

On the afternoon of February 5, Marín and others spoke to a crowd assembled across from the Hotel Diligencias. Many in the audience held banners that read: "The Women of the Port Struggle for Progress," "In the Name of Humanity We Ask for the Freeing of Proal," "The Women of the Port Protest the Unjust Imprisonment of Compañero Proal," and "The Proletarian Women Will Make the Social Revolution." Marín attacked property owners and demanded the release of Proal. After finishing her address, she led a procession, fronted by a group of children playing tambourines and banging tin cans, to the offices of *El Dictamen*. Police asked the tenants to disperse, but, ignoring the order, protesters continued to mill outside the newspaper headquarters until police began pushing their way into the crowd.

As some took refuge outside the nearby cantina Blanco y Negro, authorities closed in to break up the gathering. Seeing the police approach, someone threw a rock that hit one of the officers in the shoulder. In the commotion, screams, pistol shots, and a tremendous noise followed before police eventually gained the upper hand. As renters grudgingly agreed to leave the scene, municipal officials ordered police to patrol city streets and closely monitor tenant activities in order to prevent any further disturbances.[60]

Two days later, *El Dictamen* commented on María Luisa Marín's directorship of the Revolutionary Syndicate:

> Herón Proal [has] sent his woman [to take] his place. [Since then, Marín has] brought new energies and enthusiasms to the tenant cause. With equal vigor [she has] directed the [syndicate's] business and, as in the past, collected dues that have made the protest such a prosperous enterprise for some time. María Luisa, as Proal has said, is an "intelligent" woman and one need only spend a short time here to become familiar with her activities: agitation in the patios, aggressive commentaries against the authorities, firecrackers, and a full range of other gestures that usually culminate in the tumultuous public demonstrations that are by now well known and recalled with horror by the long-suffering residents of this city.

In the weeks that followed, Marín continued to organize but preferred to avoid another major confrontation with local police.[61] This did not prevent her, however, from taking on state and labor leaders working to marginalize proalistas and bring the tenant strike to an end.

Toward Incorporation: The CROM Conference

At the beginning of March 1925, tenant and landlord union representatives met in Jalapa to resume negotiations. For the most part, both groups continued to make the same arguments: tenants claimed that landlords of large properties remained belligerent, while others insisted that the rent law violated their constitutional rights. Also present were a group of small property owners who presented their own request for a satisfactory resolution to the strike in a petition signed by nearly eighty individuals.[62]

A week later, tenant delegates from unions affiliated with the Regional Confederation of Mexican Workers (CROM) throughout the state met with landlords in Orizaba. On March 9, *El Dictamen* reported that a proposal had been drafted suggesting that houses renting for less than 50 pesos would be regulated by the 1923 rent law while those renting for more than 50 pesos would not. After a series of meetings between the two groups, the matter of how to revise the percentage of property values at which rents should be based stood out as the most contentious and unresolved issue. Finally, a heated debate on March 10 between CROM representative Martín Torres and landlord delegate Salvador Campa ended in an agreement that rents would be figured somewhere between 10–12 percent of property values rather than the 9 percent stipulated by Tejeda's law, until further negotiations could take place.

Reaction to the temporary CROM accord was immediate. Members of the state tenant federation, including proalista affiliates, fully rejected any agreement produced by the Orizaba talks. In fact, many renters complained that they had not been invited. Then, on March 23, tenants in Orizaba gathered in the Llave Theater to declare that revisions to the rent law were "onerous" and favored only "landlord interests."[63] The next day, labor leaders in the port announced a convention designed to bring an end to the housing conflict that would be held a week later.[64]

On April 1, 1925, delegates from various labor organizations affiliated with the CROM in Orizaba, Córdoba, Jalapa, Puerto México, Soledad de Doblado, Minatitlán, Alvarado, and Tlacotalpan met in the port of Veracruz. Determined to disrupt the proceedings because of her opposition to the CROM, María Luisa Marín and a handful of supporters attempted to stop the opening of the convention by barricading the entrance to the stevedores' union hall. Unsuccessful in their effort, Marín and the others then entered the hall, interrupting the proceedings by insulting speakers and yelling, "Death to the exploiters of the people!" and "Viva Proal!" Later that night, militants assembled outside the Revolutionary Syndicate headquarters to express their desire for the tenant strike to continue rather than be negotiated by "state-sponsored labor affiliates" such as the CROM. After they had paraded through the streets for a time, police eventually moved in to disperse the gathering. A fight broke out and by the end of the evening thirteen renters associated with the syndicate had been arrested.

The following day, authorities accused Marín of attempting to burn down the local caulkers and carpenters' union building. As a result, twenty-five police arrived outside the syndicate headquarters that morning to take her into custody but were unable to locate her. Searching the city, they found her a few hours later. As several tenants gathered around Marín to show their support, she told them that they should not abandon the strike because of negotiations that "betrayed the cause of the proletariat," and she reminded her compañeras that the government had "forgotten their responsibilities to the people and sold out to the bourgeoisie." Then she ran into the syndicate headquarters at the last minute to avoid the police. Several minutes of pushing and shoving on the street left a policeman and several tenants injured. During the fray, the tenant leader had somehow escaped—but not for long. Three days later, police finally managed to take her into custody.[65] Justice officials accused Marín of violating a ban on tenant meetings, sedition, and attempted arson. While authorities eventually dropped the charges, they now had little doubt that Marín was a dangerous element on the Veracruz political scene. If law and order ever were to be restored in the port, they knew her power would have to be neutralized.

The Containment of Proal and Marín

Meantime, in Mexico City, officials cleared Proal of any criminal charges and released him from prison. He immediately joined organizing efforts in the capital and took part in International Workers Day celebrations. Then, on May 2, ongoing conflict between the Confederación General de Trabajadores (CGT) and CROM members erupted into a street battle that left one woman, María Guadalupe Rangel, dead. Approximately two weeks later, police arrested Proal in connection with the incident. But when Mexico City police failed to produce sufficient evidence against Proal, they allowed him to go free, and he returned to Veracruz.

During the first week of May 1925, Governor Jara and other state officials promised revisions to Tejeda's rent law that would produce a resolution to the housing conflict would soon be forthcoming.[66] A month later, lawmakers made their deliberations public. One change (section "I," regarding eviction proceedings) promised to make it more difficult for landlords to remove tenants from their properties.[67] Yet while María Luisa Marín and other tenant leaders applauded the changes, landlords indicated that they would not cooperate.[68]

As some property owners met in Veracruz late in July to fortify their resistance, other landlords came to accept reduced rents (many based at 6 percent of property values) as long as tenants restarted payment. The following month, city officials increased pressure on landlords who had received rents but continued to neglect tax payments.[69] In response, a delegation of property owners traveled to Mexico City to talk with President Calles. Another group met with Governor Jara, who suggested that if back rents would be forgiven, so too would back taxes.[70]

Despite resistance by proalistas, *El Dictamen* reported that over four hundred tenants had resumed payment of rents by mid-November. Then, after assuming a less confrontational posture, Proal agreed to cooperate with sanitation officials, who now began a new tenement inspection and cleaning campaign in the city. Revolutionary Syndicate members soon joined in the effort to evaluate patio values. In an interview with the press, Proal told reporters in November that he hoped to help bring the strike to an end and write a book about his experiences.

Still, he indicated that significant tensions between tenants and a number of landlords remained.[71]

In late November, police threw Proal and Arturo Bolio Trejo in jail for a few days after the two had disagreed violently during the evaluation of a tenement, despite the fact that by this time a special Renters Department (Departamento Inquilinario) had been established in Veracruz.[72] *El Dictamen* reported the following month that city council members had warned, "Every day [drainage and sanitation] problems get worse and soon the day will come when Veracruz becomes a pestilent lagoon where only vultures can survive."[73] Indeed, conjuring dark images from the city's past signaled the truly dire situation that now confronted port residents. If urban reform remained a possibility, decisive action to end the tenant protest would have to be taken quickly. For municipal officials, the beginning of the new year provided a timely opportunity for imposing harsh measures against rent strikers.

New Year's Resolutions

On January 4, 1926, temporary Veracruz mayor Fernando García Barna, with the backing of state military commander Arnulfo Gómez, issued orders for all tenant organizations to remove their banners from the outside of city tenements. The next day, García Barna summoned Proal to his office and warned him not to interfere with negotiations taking place between landlords and tenants. Two hours later, fearing new acts of repression against the Revolutionary Syndicate, Proal asked state authorities for "protection."[74]

Having initially complied with police orders, protesters soon expressed their unhappiness with city officials by painting red stars on tenement fences, entrances, and outer walls. Infuriated, police arrested Proal in his home on Arista Street on January 12. Taken before a local judge, the tenant leader was charged with refusing to comply with García Barna's order as well as interfering with the assessment of tenement values. Hearing word of Proal's arrest in Veracruz, officials in Mexico City immediately issued orders demanding that Proal be expelled from the state. At the same time, local officials warned María Luisa Marín to avoid any action intended to interfere with the proceedings against Proal or property assessments geared toward promoting new rental contracts between landlords and tenants.[75]

On January 14 authorities put Proal on a boat that sailed for Frontera, Tabasco. Once at the Tabasco port, Governor Tomás Garrido Canabal refused to let him disembark. Ten days later, Proal was back in

Mexico City, where officials installed him in Santiago Tlatelolco Prison. Meanwhile, city officials had served María Luisa Marín with an ultimatum: Discontinue agitation in the tenements and help bring the strike to an end or be deported. Hoping to facilitate a truce between fighting tenants, Mayor García Barna called a meeting with Marín and her rival, Arturo Bolio Trejo. At four o'clock that afternoon, Marín, accompanied by a group of syndicate women, walked into City Hall. There, García Barna read orders issued by military commander General Arnulfo Gómez requiring the militants to comply with the rent law or face arrest. After hearing the ultimatum, Marín and Bolio Trejo faced each other. Then, García Barna told them that they were to combine their organizations in the interest of ending the strike.

Responding to this request, Bolio Trejo told Marín that he had no intention of causing trouble and would be prepared to leave the city if necessary. In contrast, Marín passionately declared that she would never agree to disband the Revolutionary Syndicate. Hearing this, García Barna informed Marín that if she did not relinquish her post within forty-eight hours she would be deported. And if her followers refused to "quit painting red stars on the doors and windows of their tenements," he warned, "they too would be apprehended and sent to jail."[76] The next day, Marín filed an injunction against President Calles, General Arnulfo Gómez, Mayor García Barna, and the Veracruz chief of police in an attempt to block her arrest and possible expulsion from the state. Upon receiving the request, a local judge temporarily suspended charges against Marín until a ruling could be made. Nearly two weeks later, city officials announced that the "fusion" of the two rival tenant organizations, proalista and Organización, had proved unsuccessful. In the light of this failure, they declared that tenants would be required to sign new contracts with their landlords or be evicted. In the agreements signed during the last week of January 1926, the name of María Luisa Marín appeared alongside members of the commission assigned to assess property values. Nevertheless, believing that militant tenants sought to renew their campaign against the signing of rental agreements, police soon arrested Marín.[77]

Then, on Friday, January 29, Mayor García Barna announced that María Luisa Marín would be given the opportunity to remain in jail or leave Veracruz. In response, Marín told officials that she would leave the city the following Monday after taking time to sell some of her belongings. Members of the tenant syndicate wished Marín good luck as she left and promised her that they would continue their protest until an agreement with landlords could be reached.[78] Following the departure of Marín, Inés Terán took over as secretary general of the syndicate. Yet while the remaining proalistas promised to keep the protest alive, maintaining independent tenant organizing would prove to be extremely difficult.

Marginalizing the "Super-Strikers": The Final Blow

As a growing number of renters in Veracruz continued to sign rental contracts with their landlords in early 1926, the appeal of the Revolutionary Syndicate began to fade, but state and local discourse regarding the problems of popular housing did not. During that winter, sanitation workers bleached patios and targeted substandard tenements while the staff of the newly created Veracruz Renters Department continued to register new rental contracts. Similar activities took place in Orizaba, Córdoba, and Jalapa.

Hoping to bring the strike to an end, municipal leaders in the port issued an order in February 1926 that required tenants and landlords to sign agreements within forty-eight hours. Despite this ruling, disagreement over patio evaluations persisted.[79] In March, for example, when members of the Revolutionary Syndicate complained to Governor Jara about continued "irregularities in the evaluation of tenements," Mayor García Barna strongly disagreed and sent his own message to the governor, saying, "Those complaining are outside the law." A few days later, he said that tenant leaders would "do anything to avoid paying." Organización leader Arturo Bolio Trejo agreed. He used the term "super-strikers" (*super-huelguistas*) to describe those elements within the tenant movement he had grown to despise and seconded García Barna's comment that some in the city would never restart rent payments under any circumstances.[80]

In an effort to add to a strike solution, in late March, Governor Jara introduced a proposal that provided state funds for the construction of inexpensive worker houses throughout the state. He received widespread support for the proposal, including from the editors of *El Dictamen*. About a week later, officials in Mexico City agreed to sell federal lands along the coast to the city. Many thought the area, as discussed in such hopeful terms the year before, would provide the necessary space for much-needed colonization.[81]

Laborers affiliated with the Federation of Sea and Land Workers (Federación de Trabajadores del Mar y Tierra) undertook another initiative to resolve the housing crisis, which gained public support. Working closely with city officials, members of the union organized a renters convention that took place in late April. Among the resolutions made during the meeting, delegates decided that "independent" renter associations would no longer "be tolerated." Labor-led efforts and not those advanced by members of the Revolutionary Syndicate or Organización Inquilinaria, in other words, were the only "legitimate" means to resolve the housing crisis. Adding the weight of their national organization, officials from the CROM approved the Mar y Tierra proposals to end the "old problem" in late April.[82] Not surprisingly, tenants in the city not affiliated with the CROM strongly rejected the Mar y Tierra accord.[83]

As debate regarding a resolution to the protest continued through spring 1926, Governor Jara again took matters into his own hands. On June 10 he issued a statement demanding that local judges enforce the rent law. Those not willing to sign agreements and resume paying rent, he declared, would be taken to court and evicted.[84] Still, problems enforcing the law at the local level continued as residents bickered over the evaluation of tenements, eviction procedures, and exactly who should oversee the negotiation process.

The last significant public gathering held by the proalistas came on the fourth anniversary of the July 5–6 massacre. The morning of July 5, many tenants in the port hung red banners outside their patios. Later, they assembled in front of the Revolutionary Syndicate headquarters, where they shot off firecrackers and prepared for a festive parade through the central streets of the city. Soon, however, they got word from police that their procession would not be allowed because municipal officials had decided that all public demonstrations would be strictly prohibited. That night, authorities again ordered all syndicate banners taken down.[85]

Despite increasing restrictions on the Revolutionary Syndicate, residents received good news in August when the Supreme Court ruled that land expropriation by the state government was a matter of legitimate "public utility" and not a violation of property owners' constitutional rights. A few weeks later, state officials announced that Colonias Flores Magón and El Cocal would soon be fully serviced with streets, drainage, and other amenities.[86]

At the end of September a tropical storm hit the Veracruz coast, causing tremendous damage and forcing many in areas surrounding the port to abandon their homes. By mid-October, however, state officials had responded to the damage by proposing a law that would provide additional funds for housing construction and repair—especially in rural areas washed out by the storm. Editorials printed in *El Dictamen* during the remainder of the year echoed lawmakers' concerns about the housing shortage throughout the state.[87]

Calavera del Inquilinato, published for Communist youth. *Courtesy of AGN*

Although tenants again gathered for another statewide convention in November, public officials declared in mid-December that "tenant threats would not be tolerated." Thus, when a December 27 editorial in *El Dictamen* asked, "Is Bolshevism over?" anyone observing the high profile of tenant organizing in Veracruz over the past few years could confidently answer "yes." By this time the enthusiasm that had once fueled the Veracruz movement had faded. And while sporadic resistance by independent renters in the port would continue for several years, state authorities, mainly through alternate uses of repression and co-optation, had finally gained control over the nearly ten-year-old urban popular movement.

Notes

1. *El Dictamen*, December 19–22, 1924.
2. Erica Berra-Stoppa, "Estoy en huelga y no pago renta," *Habitación* 1, no. 1 (1981): 39. For examples of tenant communications to federal officials, see letters (with well over one hundred signatures each) from members of the syndicate dated January 14, 1925, September 3, 1926, October 4, 1926. AGN, Suprema Corte de Justicia, vols. 2018–2034.
3. Numerous complaints regarding the tenant syndicates in the state are compiled in AGN, gobernación, vol. 17, file 353.
4. For a listing of the group's organizing principles (including the motto "Peasants and Workers of the World, Unite"), see Unión Inquilinaria to Tejeda, April 8, 1924, AGEV, gobernación, 1924.
5. Poster dated April 13, 1924, AGEV, gobernación, 1924.
6. *El Dictamen*, May 14, 1924.
7. Veracruz landlords to Tejeda, May 15, 1924, AGEV, gobernación, box 786, file 652, 1924.
8. Liga de Propietarios de Tacubaya, D.F., to Calles, May 30, 1924, AGN, gobernación, vol. 17, file 353, 1924.
9. Cámara de Propietarios in Torreón, Coahuila, to Calles, n.d., AGN, gobernación, C-28, 1924.
10. *El Dictamen*, May 15, 1924.
11. Ibid., May 18, 1924.
12. Ibid., May 23, 1924.
13. Ibid.
14. Ibid., May 31, 1924. For subsequent complaints about the syndicate in Orizaba, see AGN, gobernación, vol. 17, file 353, 1924, and AGN, gobernación, vol. 31, file 240, 1924.
15. *El Dictamen*, May 24, 1924.
16. Ibid., June 4, 7, 1924.
17. AGEV, gobernación, 1924.
18. Proal to Tejeda, June 4, 1924, ibid.
19. *El Dictamen*, June 8, 1924.
20. AGN, gobernación, vol. 17, file 353, 1924.
21. *El Dictamen*, June 10, 1924.
22. Ibid., June 11, 1924.

23. Ibid., June 14, 1924. For other conflict in Jalapa during the summer, see AGEV, gobernación, box 752, 1924, "Jalapa, Ayuntamiento quejas."

24. *El Dictamen*, June 14, 1924.

25. Ibid., June 15, 1924.

26. Ibid.

27. Ibid., June 18, 1924.

28. Ibid., June 16, 1924. *Gaceta Oficial*, the official paper of the state legislature, published the changes on June 16, 1924.

29. *El Dictamen*, June 19, 1924.

30. Ibid., June 21, 1924. Quitena Pérez was overruled by the Supreme Court in August 1926.

31. Ibid., June 23, 1924.

32. Ibid., July 3, 1924.

33. Continuing to battle local landlords, members of the tenant syndicate realized a number of direct actions to block eviction proceedings during the first week of July. *El Dictamen*, July 4, 1924.

34. Tenants to Tejeda, July 25, 1924, AGEV, gobernación, 1924.

35. Proal to Tejeda, July 26, August 2, 19, 1924, ibid.

36. Alberto de la Llave to Tejeda, July 19, 1924, AGN, gobernación, vol. 17, file 353, 1924.

37. *El Dictamen*, August 28, September 23, December 18, 1924.

38. Poster, "Decreto Gonzalo Vázquez Vela, gobernador constitucional internino del Estado Libre y Soberano de Veracruz," AGN, gobernación, vol. 17, file 353, 1924.

39. *El Dictamen*, September 23, 1924.

40. Organización Inquilinaria to Tejeda, September 3 and 19, 1924, AGN, gobernación, C-28, 1924; Organización Inquilinaria to Obregón, September 8, 1924, AGN, gobernación, 1924; Revolutionary Syndicate to Tejeda, September 11, 18, 19, 20, 1924, AGN, gobernación, 1924. See also the proalista poster reprinting telegrams to Tejeda, September 1924, AGEV, gobernación, 1924.

41. Memorandum to Secretary of State, November 3, 1924, RDS, reel 161.

42. Ibid.

43. For more on housing conditions, see reports in *El Dictamen*, May 14–17, 27–29, 1924.

44. Ibid., December 1, 1924.

45. Porfirio Sosa to Heriberto Jara, December 6, 1924, AGEV, gobernación, 1924.

46. Organización Inquilinaria to Jara, December 4, 1924, AGEV, gobernación, box 807, "Diversos," 1924.

47. Unidentified newspaper clipping, AGN, gobernación, 1924.

48. Although it probably mattered little to members of the Revolutionary Syndicate, municipal authorities had recently lifted a ban on the use of firecrackers in the city.

49. *El Dictamen*, December 17, 1924. See also AGN, gobernación, file C-28, 1924.

50. *El Dictamen*, December 21, 1924.

51. Ibid., December 22, 1924.

52. "Boletín del Sindicato Revolucionario de Inquilinos," December 24, 1924, AGN, gobernación, C-28, 1924. The same message (with over fifty signatures) had been sent to Calles the day earlier.

53. María Luisa Marín to Calles, December 25, 1924, and petition from Federación de Mujeres Libertarias to Presidente del Tribunal Superior de la

Justicia de la Nación, January 14, 1925, AGN, Justicia, vols. 2019–29, 1925. Petition from residents of patio San Ramón (twenty-five signatures) to Calles, January 26, 1925, and María Luisa Marín to Calles, February 20, 1925, AGN, gobernación, C-28, 1925.

54. *El Dictamen*, December 24, 1924.

55. Ibid., December 26, 1924.

56. María Luisa Marín to Calles, February 20, 1925, AGN, gobernación, C-28, 1925. Two weeks earlier, an article in *El Dictamen* on the lack of sanitation in the city's tenements (titled "Dante-esque Vision") testified to the fact that housing conditions only continued to deteriorate. *El Dictamen*, January 13, 1925.

57. *El Dictamen*, January 15, 1925.

58. Ibid., January 24, 1925. An editorial printed the same day suggested that residents needed to reestablish "the habit of paying rents" and "respecting authority."

59. Ibid., January 26, 1925.

60. Ibid., February 6, 1925.

61. In the meantime, a new organization called the Syndicate of Unemployed Workers (Sindicato de Obreros sin Trabajo) issued a manifesto and proposal regarding the tenant strike. They suggested to the governor that they would resume paying house rents if general living expenses could be reduced. Ibid., February 22, 1925.

62. Ibid., March 1–3, 1925.

63. Ibid., March 24, 1925.

64. Ibid., March 26, 1925.

65. Ibid., April 1–3, 1925.

66. See Jara's Report, portions of which *El Dictamen* reprinted on May 7, 1925. Hearing of tenant organizing in the state of Zacatecas, Alejandro Sánchez, a landlord, wrote to Calles that further protest in the country by renters would be "truly lamentable . . . after having witnessed the innumerable threats and abuses that have been committed by the tenants in this sad port." Sánchez to Calles, June 11, 1925, AGN, gobernación, C-28, 1925.

67. *El Dictamen*, July 6 and 9, 1925.

68. Ibid., July 20–21, 1925. María Luisa Marín to Secretario de Gobernación y Justicia, July 25, 1925, AGN, gobernación, C-28, 1925. Orizaba Property Owners Association to Secretario de Gobernación, August 3, 1925, AGN, gobernación, C-28, 1925.

69. *El Dictamen*, September 2 and 9, 1925.

70. Ibid., September 18, 1925.

71. Ibid., November 13, 1925.

72. Interestingly, the newspaper remarked that in the scuffle Proal sustained a cut to the left ear; it was the first injury to the tenant leader since the strike began four years earlier. *El Dictamen*, November 27, 1925. For reports on tenant-landlord negotiations, see *El Dictamen*, December 2, 3, 9, 12, 1925.

73. Ibid., December 22, 1925.

74. Ibid., January 6 and 10, 1926.

75. Ibid., January 13 and 14, 1926.

76. Ibid., January 15, 1926.

77. Ibid., January 28, 1926.

78. Ibid., February 1, 1926.

79. Ibid., February 20, 1926. On the new agreements, see ibid., March 5 and 14, 1926.

80. Ibid., March 18, 1926. Tenants in neighboring Orizaba and Nogales then added their own criticism of the situation by calling the recent application of the rent law "nothing more than an instrument of exploitation." *El Dictamen*, March 21, 1926.

81. See articles in ibid., March 29, April 2, 15, 16, 22, 1926.

82. Ibid., April 28, 1926.

83. Ibid., April 19–21, 1926. On April 22 the paper printed a statement by Arturo Bolio that denounced the Federación, calling their involvement in landlord-tenant negotiations "unjust."

84. Ibid., June 11, 1926.

85. Ibid., July 7, 1926.

86. Ibid., August 13 and September 12, 1926. A few days later, residents of Colonia El Cocal clashed with police when they attempted a land invasion in a neighboring area. *El Dictamen*, September 20, 1926.

87. Ibid., September 29, October 16, November 2, 6, December 6, 1926.

Conclusion
The Outcome and Legacy of
Inquilino Protest in Mexico

With good reason it has been said that, in the city, the revolution has not yet arrived. Still, a solution is badly needed for the many people who live in pigsties and in conditions worse than one finds in Belén Prison. Those casas de vecindad are sites of death that tenants occupy only out of necessity. There, they are forced to expose their bodies and spirits to an infamous exploitation that is by now legendary.

> —Aarón Sáenz, Federal District Department Chief, 1932

[Proal] worked in the warehouses of the Techo Eterno Eureka factory. Eventually, he had to quit because of poor health. Until he died, he maintained a passionate love for Veracruz but, sadly, lived in a small, broken-down wooden house whose value amounted to, including the lot, only about 2,700 pesos. Nevertheless, Proal's entire life had been a passionate struggle for justice. In his last years, he maintained a clarity and sense of humor. He felt resentment toward no one; nor was he bitter nor believed that he had failed. On the contrary, he showed himself to be a man proud and satisfied with his past. He lived peacefully in his house at 318 Hernán Cortés, respected and loved by the people of Veracruz.

> —Mario Gill, "Veracruz: Revolución y extremismo,"
> *Historia Mexicana*, 1953

By the time the tenant movement came to an end in the late 1920s, it was clear that the urban poor in Veracruz had established themselves as a new popular political force. Particularly important in this process were the many women who had gathered in markets, parks, streets, and other public venues to demand reforms. They, along with urban workers, middle-class groups, and rural peasants across Mexico, had joined a national struggle for influence in the postrevolutionary social order.

Herón Proal, circa 1950. *Courtesy of AGEV,*
Joaquín Santa María Collection

Reflecting a new revolutionary consciousness that included concerns over "consumer" issues such as housing, the actions of Herón Proal, María Luisa Marín, and others affiliated with the statewide movement called for revolutionary change not only in political and economic terms but also in matters related to gender. The Veracruz tenant newspaper *Guillotina* provides an interesting example. In a 1923 article titled "The Slave of the Slave" ("La esclava del esclavo"), author Estela V. Magón encouraged both men and women to "wake up" and "demand your rights." "It is time [men] see women as [their] equal, as a sister," she argued.

"Remember," Magón told her male readers, "if you are fighting to better your life, your dreams will never be realized until women are thought of as equals." Encouraging solidarity across gender lines, she declared that "without their help, your struggle against your enemies will be met with defeat." The liberation of women, the author concluded, was intimately linked to the goals of the revolution: "Emancipate her and then both men and women will assuredly find it easier to obtain LAND and LIBERTY."[1]

Assessing the Outcome of Tenant Protest

Given that tenant organizing did manage to help shape political discourse for a time, what can be said of the movement's lasting effect? Considering action taken by tenants in cities across the nation during the 1920s, the 1923 Veracruz rent law proved significant. On paper, it reduced rents to slightly more than 1910 levels and provided for the supervision of landlord-tenant relations. Given the highly contested matter of applying the law, probably one of its most tangible aspects came in the form of land concessions.

The 1923 law made provisions—based on Article 27 of the Constitution—for the expropriation of urban lands and the subsequent construction of worker housing. Thus, in addition to Tejeda's May 1922 granting of the Colonia Comunista area to Proal and his followers, residents of the port in 1926 saw the establishment of new worker settlements with such names as Adalberto Tejeda, Francisco I. Madero, Alberto Pastrana, and Vicente Guerrero. These areas came under the supervision of the March 22 Cooperative Union of Worker Neighborhoods.[2] Nine years later, state officials expropriated the property known to porteños as Colonia Flores Magón from Spanish businessman Antonio Revuelta for the construction of additional worker housing on May 7, 1931.[3]

Tenants in Jalapa, like those in the port of Veracruz, continued to strike between 1926 and 1930. Records from the municipal archive show considerable activity by organized renters about the time local officials established a property evaluation board (*junta calificadora*) in February 1929.[4] During 1929 and 1930, residents of patios Escojido, Ferrer Guardia, Cuauhtémoc, Sabino, San Roque, and Patio 15, among others, complained of landlords who refused to comply with Tejeda's rent law. Some registered their payments with local authorities, sometimes at the Tenant Department in City Hall.[5] Documents from other Veracruz cities also indicate that the law remained an everyday matter of contention for tenants, landlords, and government agents.

When tenants in Orizaba organized a convention in February 1928, the local paper *La Prensa* announced:

> Difficulties between landlords and the tenant syndicate as well as a number of evictions carried out in the last month have suggested the need for a renters convention. Representatives from both tenant and landlord organizations will take part under the supervision of authorities from the Cámara de Trabajo. Those invited from each group welcome the opportunity to resolve the much-debated question. One of the primary recommendations already mentioned is that renters continue to comply with the state law, paying rents and, thus, avoiding any cause for eviction. Unfortunately, observers have noted that some tenants, members of the Agrupación de Inquilinos, are refusing to cooperate. Their actions have led to the present troubles.[6]

By this late date, in Orizaba and elsewhere, achieving compliance with Tejeda's housing reform remained an extremely difficult task.

Information on the outcome of tenant protest in Córdoba presents a similar picture. Residents there, as in other cities, established a Renters Department to help mediate relationships between landlords and tenants in 1925. The staff of the new department considered a wide range of cases, often negotiating tenement values, payment rates, eviction requests, and related issues. In Córdoba during this time, the state tenants federation (Federación Inquilinaria del Estado de Veracruz) was the official organizing association for renters, though the independent Revolutionary Syndicate also continued its activities. During the late 1920s, many in the city signed new agreements with landlords.

Córdoba residents saw the establishment in 1926 of a new worker neighborhood called the Colonia Aguillón Guzmán.[7] Generally, the formation of new settlements in each of the state's major cities offered temporary relief for tenants while helping legitimate local revolutionary governments. Thus, despite many difficulties, Tejeda's 1923 rent law paved the way for a series of moderate concessions to the state's urban poor.[8] Renters in other areas outside the state of Veracruz would not be so fortunate.

The outcome of housing protest in the Federal District during 1922 contrasts with the Veracruz case in that legislators there made no move to realize official housing reform. The housing question, however, did not go unnoticed by elites. In December 1921, for example, President Obregón had asked Congress for 12 million pesos to finance the construction of popular housing. Then, in collaboration with Federal District governor Celestino Gasca, he issued a decree that allocated public lands on the outskirts of Mexico City for the construction of worker housing in September 1922. Yet rather than establishing a comprehensive reform, the decree began a practice of providing largesse to specific groups such as federal employees and organized labor.[9]

Obregón's September measure clearly favored propertied interests by including tax exemptions for new construction. In cases where new housing rented for no more than 20 pesos per month, officials declared that the property owners' tax-exempt status would remain in effect for ten years. And while the reform attempted to boost the housing supply in the Federal District, it made no provision for rent reductions.[10] Thus, despite the fact that "tenant interests" would later be incorporated into the official party bureaucracy in 1929, Mexico City residents saw no relief from rising urban rents until President Avila Camacho declared a wartime rent freeze on central city properties in 1942.[11]

In Guadalajara, concessions granted by the state of Jalisco after rent protests conducted in 1922 proved to be only a short-term remedy. In April 1924 protesters demanded that a law reducing rents to 6 percent of property values be instituted. Their initiative failed. In October that year, residents in the city of Ocotlán organized a renters union to demand housing reforms. Politicians again refused to act. Finally, in December 1929, the state workers' confederation (Confederación Obrera de Jalisco) formed a new tenant union in Guadalajara. Resurrecting the repertoire of the 1922 movement, they organized marches, demonstrations, and public meetings.[12] The results of their efforts, other than the construction of one hundred "nice houses" for Partido Revolucionario Institucional (PRI) workers in 1936, remain unclear.[13] In 1944 officials in Jalisco declared a willingness to monitor urban rents after several tenants had issued complaints.[14] Significant development of housing in Guadalajara would have to wait until the founding of the Popular Housing Commission as well as the State Housing Office and the Institute for Social Well-Being in 1948.[15] In the years that followed, most attempts to relieve poor housing conditions and high rents took shape sporadically and spontaneously. Occasionally, city residents invaded lands or illegally acquired property for housing construction. Echoing the substandard housing environment of earlier decades, a 1966 report stated that 40 percent of viviendas in Guadalajara lacked adequate water and cooking facilities while nearly 30 percent had little or no drainage.[16] Thus, tenant efforts in Guadalajara appear to have offered no more promising an outcome than many other areas in the country.

In cases of rent protest elsewhere in the republic, collective action remained limited to occasional demonstrations and temporary organizing efforts. Initiatives taken by renters in these areas resulted in no significant legislation during the 1920s.[17] With the exception of the Veracruz law, officials enacted no other state housing reforms until the mid-1930s, when measures were taken in response to popular protest.

In December 1935, renters in Mazatlán, Sinaloa, organized to protest high rents, high utility rates, and substandard housing conditions.[18] Incensed by the protest, the federal government responded harshly by declaring martial law. In a street confrontation that followed between troops and protesters, one person died and several were injured. After two days, the government ordered rents (for rooms in the city costing 8 pesos or less) reduced by 50 percent. Additionally, authorities mandated that rooms that rented for 20 to 25 pesos be priced at 20 percent less.[19]

To the south, tenants in Tepic, Nayarit, organized a protest in 1938 that led to the establishment of a new governmental department (Procuraduría Inquilinaria). Subsequently, state officials were called upon to mediate conflict and encourage the construction of new housing. By this point, politicians could draw upon a well-established repertoire of repression, co-optation, and concession as effective ways to deal with protest by the urban poor.[20]

Meanwhile, Marte R. Gómez, governor of Tamaulipas, issued a reform decree in November 1937 that declared the "public utility" of reduced rents for selected commercial and residential units.[21] Ten years later, the states of Tabasco and Yucatán each decreed minor rent reforms. In Yucatán, for example, officials determined that residential rents should not exceed 8 percent of property values. Authorities in Michoacán ruled in late 1954 that rental housing rates could not be increased. Three years later, the state government in Zacatecas enacted a rent freeze. The same year, officials in Sinaloa also capped rates for all tenement housing renting for less than 200 pesos per month. In 1963, lawmakers in Querétaro pro-rated rents on rental housing costing less than 250 pesos per month.

At the federal level, President Calles had created the Department of Social Security (Dirección de Pensiones Civiles) in 1926. Its responsibilities included making credit available for the construction or purchase of housing. The only state institution of its kind to help with housing finance, the department dispensed approximately ninety-six hundred loans between 1925 and 1947.[22] During that time, few of the recipients could be identified as being among those most deserving of such a program. Instead, "one of the most belligerent and dangerous sectors on the national political scene"—bureaucrats—benefited most handsomely from the program.[23] Thus, as revolutionary elites employed a repertoire of both concessionary and repressive means to achieve their political goals, their efforts proved quite successful in dealing with independent tenant protest and the politics of popular housing.[24] During this time, measures undertaken by Mexican elites reflected a general attitude in the Americas and Europe about the role of government in regulating popular housing.

In Germany, France, the Netherlands, Belgium, Sweden, Denmark, Portugal, Greece, Scotland, Wales, Ireland, the United States, Argentina, and Chile, lawmakers between 1880 and 1930 had established more stringent building codes as well as new finance schemes to promote home ownership and construction. Yet despite some temporary public initiatives, most politicians maintained a strong belief that private enterprise rather than state intervention was the most effective means to address housing issues.

Yet while several governments made popular housing more of a priority after the First World War, most saw government regulation as only a temporary measure. Scholars point out that the effectiveness of European government programs developed during the interwar years proved limited at best. In Portugal, for example, state-sponsored construction between 1910 and 1926 produced 1,145 units located entirely in Lisbon and Oporto. Once available, most of the dwellings were too expensive for the urban poor. A similar problem emerged in Scotland between 1919 and 1941 when rents assigned to a majority of the 241,000 new homes built with government help exceeded most working-class families' ability to pay. State-sponsored housing in Greece during the

1920s and in Ireland between 1880 and 1920, however, helped improve living conditions. Pursuing another strategy, some Europeans enjoyed positive changes in their home environment by joining housing cooperatives. Cooperatives established first in England and then in the Netherlands, Greece, and parts of Scandinavia offered an alternative to either renting or individual home ownership. Because of the small percentage of those involved, the cooperative movement contributed little to resolving urban housing problems.

Notable exceptions include the Weimar Republic during the 1920s, where politicians made provisions for state-sponsored housing development. Similarly, the government of republican Portugal (1910–1926) also supported public housing projects. Other situations where the government did intervene in the housing market include temporary legislation regulating urban rents in New York City, Buenos Aires, and Santiago, Chile.[25]

Thanks to the efforts of Jacob Riis, who published his seminal *How the Other Half Lives* in 1890, New Yorkers launched a national campaign for housing reform led by Lawrence Veiller. Although thousands supported the housing reform movement during the 1920s and 1930s, which lobbied for government regulation, most never wanted the state to intervene directly in the housing market. Nevertheless, in April 1920, the New York State Legislature passed a new set of laws (known as the April Laws) that gave tenants the right to contest rent increases. In September 1920 they created the Emergency Rent Laws, which established stronger guidelines against arbitrary rent increases and evictions. New initiatives that attempted to improve popular housing in New York City would have to wait until 1934, when Mayor Fiorello La Guardia promised to "take the profit out of the slums." Despite these and a few other exceptions, the majority of lawmakers throughout Europe and the Americas refused to intervene directly in the housing market.

Assessing the Tenant Movement in Veracruz

Given the degree to which house renters engaged in collective action during the 1920s, there is little doubt that the emergence, process, and range of protest outcomes illustrate the tremendous capacity of citizens to pursue the goals of improved housing and social justice. Yet while residents in Veracruz, Orizaba, Jalapa, Córdoba, Mexico City, Guadalajara, and elsewhere proved themselves to be highly capable of coordinated action, politics—rather than housing conditions—largely determined protest and reform trajectories.

Herón Proal and his family, circa 1950. *Courtesy of AGEV, Joaquín Santa María Collection*

From below, citizens sharing a common culture and a sense of moral outrage mobilized when they saw the political opportunity to do so. In this formulation, the history of each city and region offers a different context to be understood in the complex negotiation between civil society and the state in postrevolutionary Mexico. In cases where the urban poor "read" political circumstances as impractical and inopportune, they tended to remain silent or possibly engage in more clandestine forms of resistance. In cases where they thought the time was right to express their grievances, renters petitioned the revolutionary elite and sometimes engaged in collective action. High rents and poor housing conditions alone did not incite renters to strike, nor did Bolshevik agitators, the influence of foreigners, or the growing disparity in the international division of labor. Instead, renters in Veracruz and elsewhere, armed with the new political weapon of citizen rights, took to the streets to attack what they saw as arbitrary forms of social and economic control by landlords. Once they had a state authority that claimed to protect and represent their interests, they wasted no time in taking advantage of the new political situation to register their claims of injustice. Subsequently, the interaction between the tenant movement and state officials represented not only an urban rebellion against elements of the revolutionary elite but also an essential ingredient in the negotiation of the new social order.

Rent strikes in Veracruz took place because grassroots action initially motivated by moral outrage was then articulated through well-established social networks and stimulated by the discourse of the revolution. At the same time, tenant protest would not have developed to the extent that it did without the support of key political elites who helped provide the necessary political opportunity for mobilization. While housing conditions proved equally bad in most cities, alliances and divisions that emerged after the revolution between national, regional, and local elites in Veracruz helped set the stage for strike activity. Together, social forces developing both "from below" and "from above" explain the making of *el movimiento inquilinario*.

After the dust had settled, state intervention offered at least the promise of significant housing reform even if never fully realized. While producing some temporary gains for state residents, tenant mobilization is important today because it offers an important example of collective action by urban popular groups immediately after the revolution. And, although the old headquarters of Proal's Revolutionary Syndicate of Tenants on Landero y Cos is long gone, one can hope that more recent organizing among the urban poor will contribute to a new set of negotiations between the nation's power elite and members of civil society.

Notes

1. Estela V. Magón, "La esclava del esclavo," *Guillotina*, July 19, 1923.
2. Veracruz Registro Público de la Propiedad, October 7, 1926, AGEV.
3. Ibid., December 15, 1932.
4. Archivo Municipal de Jalapa, packet 28, file 69.1.
5. Ibid. See also files 69.2-12, and packet 26, files 69.12-16.
6. *La Prensa*, February 2, 1928.
7. Beatriz Calvo Cruz, "El movimiento inquilinario en Córdoba, Veracruz" (bachelor's thesis, Universidad Veracruzana, 1986), 4.
8. It remained on the books until Governor Miguel Alemán repealed the reform in 1937. Mario Gill, "Veracruz: Revolución y extremismo," *Historia Mexicana* 2, no. 4 (April–July 1953): 630.
9. Moisés González Navarro, *Población y sociedad en México, 1900–1970* (Mexico City: UNAM, 1974), 198.
10. Summerlin to Secretary of State, September 1922, RDS, reel 161. A project for a rent law for the Federal District was proposed in the Congress but not approved. For a copy of the initiative, see AGN, Obregón/Calles, vol. 731-I-5, and "Situación actual del arrendamiento de casas en la ciudad de México," AGN, Trabajo, vol. 503, file 5, December 31, 1922.
11. González Navarro, *Población y sociedad*, 191.
12. Jaime Tamayo, *La clase obrera en la historia de México* (Mexico City: UNAM/Siglo Veintiuno Editores, 1987), 7:140.
13. González Navarro, *Población y sociedad*, 221.

14. Ibid., 193.

15. Ibid., 219–20.

16. Ibid., 27.

17. González Navarro, *Población y sociedad*, 143–227; Manuel Perlo Cohen, "Política y vivienda en México, 1910–1952," *Revista Mexicana de Sociología* 41, no. 3 (July–September 1979): 769–835.

18. R. Henry Norweb to Secretary of State, December 5, 1935, RDS, 1930–39, reel 4.

19. William H. Schott to Secretary of State, March 6, 1936, RDS, 1930–39, reel 5.

20. After determining that little progress had been achieved, the Nayarit state government issued a law in 1943 that pro-rated housing expenses for renters.

21. González Navarro, *Población y sociedad*, 187.

22. Perlo Cohen, "Política y vivienda," 784.

23. Arnoldo Córdova, *La ideología de la revolución mexicana: La formación del nuevo régimen* (Mexico City: Ediciones Era, 1973), 358.

24. On lot concessions during the Cárdenas administration and after, see Alejandra Moreno Toscano, "La 'crisis' en la ciudad," in *México hoy*, ed. Pablo González Casanova and Enrique Florescano (Mexico City: Siglo Veintiuno Editores, 1979), 152–74.

25. Colin G. Pooley, "Housing Strategies in Europe, 1880–1930: Towards a Comparative Perspective," in *Housing Strategies in Europe, 1880–1930*, ed. Colin G. Pooley (London: Leicester University Press, 1992), 323–31. For an exposé on more recent New York City housing conditions, see the six-part series published in the *New York Times* in October 1996 titled "Barely Four Walls: Housing's Hidden Crisis." For commentary on revising housing regulation in New York, see Christopher Jencks, "Half-Right on Public Housing," *New York Times*, May 20, 1997.

Bibliography

Archives and Manuscript Collections

Archivo General del Estado de Veracruz, Jalapa
Archivo General de la Nación, Mexico City
Archivo Histórico de Salubridad, Mexico City
Archivo Municipal de Jalapa
Archivo Municipal de Orizaba
Archivo Municipal de Veracruz
Archivo Sindical del Puerto de Veracruz
    Archivo Tejeda
    Veracruz Registro Público de la Propiedad
Bancroft Collection, Berkeley, California
Hemeroteca Nacional, Mexico City
International Institute of Social History, Amsterdam
Mapoteca Manuel Orozco y Berra, Mexico City
National Archives and Records Administration, Washington, DC
    Records of the U.S. Department of State relating to the Internal
    Affairs of Mexico, 1910–1929 and 1930–1939
Port of Veracruz City Museum
Rockefeller Foundation Archives, Tarrytown, New York
UCLA Map Collection, Los Angeles, California

Newspapers and Periodicals

Antorcha Libertaria, Veracruz, Veracruz
Boletín Mensual del Departamento de Trabajo, Mexico City
Cronos, Mexico City
El Demócrata, Mexico City
El Dictamen, Veracruz, Veracruz
El Frente Unico, Veracruz, Veracruz
El Informador, Guadalajara, Jalisco
El Inquilino, Orizaba, Veracruz
El Obrero Comunista, Mexico City
El Universal, Mexico City
Excélsior, Mexico City
*Gaceta Oficial: Organo del Gobierno Constitucional del Estado de
    Veracruz-Llave*, Jalapa, Veracruz
Guillotina, Veracruz, Veracruz

Irredento, Mexico City
La Prensa, Orizaba, Veracruz
Luz, Mexico City
New York Times
Pro-Paria, Orizaba, Veracruz
Revista de Yucatán, Mérida, Yucatán
Washington Post

Books

Abud Flores, José Alberto. *Campeche: Revolución y movimiento social, 1911–1923.* Mexico City: Instituto Nacional de Estudios Históricos de la Revolución Mexicana, 1992.
Agetro, Leafar (Rafael Ortega). *Las luchas proletarias en Veracruz: Historia y autocrítica.* Jalapa: Editorial "Barricada," 1942.
Alarcón Martínez, Juana. *San Cristobal: Un ingenio y sus trabajadores, 1896–1934.* Jalapa: Universidad Veracruzana, 1986.
Anderson, Benedict. *Imagined Communities: Reflections on the Origin and Spread of Nationalism.* London: Verso, 1990.
Anderson, Rodney. *Outcasts in Their Own Land: Mexican Industrial Workers, 1906–1911.* De Kalb: Northern Illinois University Press, 1976.
Araiza, Luis. *Historia del movimiento obrero mexicano.* Mexico City: Editorial Cuauhtémoc, 1964–66.
Baldridge, Donald C. *Mexican Petroleum and United States-Mexican Relations, 1919–1923.* New York: Garland, 1987.
Bassols Batalla, Narciso. *El pensamiento político de Alvaro Obregón.* Mexico City: Editorial Nuestro Tiempo, 1967.
Basurto, Jorge. *El proletariado industrial en México.* Mexico City: Instituto de Investigaciones Sociales, UNAM, 1975.
Beezley, William H. *Judas at the Jockey Club and Other Episodes of Porfirian Mexico.* Lincoln: University of Nebraska Press, 1989.
Belmonte Guzmán, María de la Luz. *La organización territorial de Veracruz en el siglo X1X.* Jalapa: Universidad Veracruzana, 1987.
Benjamin, Thomas, and Mark Wasserman, eds. *Provinces of the Revolution: Essays on Regional Mexican History, 1910–1929.* Albuquerque: University of New Mexico Press, 1990.
Berins Collier, Ruth, and David Collier. *Shaping the Political Arena: Critical Junctures, the Labor Movement, and Regime Dynamics in Latin America.* Princeton: Princeton University Press, 1991.
Bethell, Leslie, ed. *Latin America: Economy and Society, 1870–1930.* Cambridge: Cambridge University Press, 1989.
_____. *Mexico since Independence.* Cambridge: Cambridge University Press, 1991.
Blanco, Sóstenes. *Ursulo Galván, 1893–1930: Su vida, su obra.* Jalapa: Liga de Comunidades Agrarias y Sindicato Campesino del Estado de Veracruz, 1966.

Blázquez Domínguez, Carmen. *Veracruz liberal*. Mexico City: Colegio de México, 1986.

_____, ed. *Estado de Veracruz: Informes de sus gobernadores, 1826–1986*. 26 vols. Jalapa: Gobierno del Estado de Veracruz, 1986.

Blázquez Domínguez, Carmen, and Emilio Gidi Villarreal. *El poder legislativo en Veracruz, 1824–1917*. Jalapa: Gobierno del Estado de Veracruz, 1992.

Bolio Trejo, Arturo. *Rebelión de mujeres: Versión histórica de la revolución inquilinaria de Veracruz*. Veracruz: Editorial "Kada," 1959.

Booker, Jackie. *Veracruz Merchants, 1770–1829: A Mercantile Elite in Late Bourbon and Early Independent Mexico*. Boulder, CO: Westview Press, 1993.

Brading, David, ed. *Caudillo and Peasant in the Mexican Revolution*. Cambridge: Cambridge University Press, 1980.

Brenner, Anita. *The Wind That Swept Mexico: The History of the Mexican Revolution of 1910–1942*. 1943; reprint ed., Austin: University of Texas Press, 1993.

Brime, E. M. *Directorio comercial de "Veracruz" para los años de 1913–1914*. Veracruz: Author's edition, 1913.

Brown, Jonathan. *Oil and Revolution in Mexico*. Berkeley: University of California Press, 1993.

Bustos Cerecedo, Miguel, ed. *Adalberto Tejeda Olivares: Dimensión del hombre*. Jalapa: Author's edition, 1983.

Carr, Barry. *El movimiento obrero y la política en México, 1910–1929*. 2 vols. Mexico City: Sep-Setentas, 1976.

_____. *Marxism and Communism in Twentieth-Century Mexico*. Lincoln: University of Nebraska Press, 1992.

Carroll, Patrick J. *Blacks in Colonial Veracruz: Race, Ethnicity, and Regional Development*. Austin: University of Texas Press, 1991.

Castells, Manuel. *The City and the Grassroots: A Cross-Cultural Theory of Urban Social Movements*. Berkeley: University of California Press, 1983.

Casteñeda, Jorge. *The Mexican Shock: Its Meaning for the United States*. New York: New Press, 1995.

Clark, Marjorie Ruth. *Organized Labor in Mexico*. Chapel Hill: University of North Carolina Press, 1973.

Coatsworth, John. *Growth against Development: The Economic Impact of Railroads in Porfirian Mexico*. De Kalb: Northern Illinois University Press, 1981.

Cockcroft, James. *Intellectual Precursors of the Mexican Revolution*. Austin: University of Texas Press, 1968.

Compañia Editorial Pan-Americana. *Verdades sobre México: El libro azul de México*. Mexico City, 1923.

Congreso de la Unión, Senado. *Diario de los debates*. Mexico City: Imprenta del Congreso de la Unión, September 3, 1919.

Córdova, Arnoldo. *La ideología de la revolución mexicana: La formación del nuevo régimen*. Mexico City: Ediciones Era, 1973.

Corzo Ramírez, Ricardo, José G. González Sierra, and David A. Skerritt. *Nunca un desleal: Cándido Aguilar, 1889–1960*. Mexico City: Colegio de México/Gobierno del Estado de Veracruz, 1986.

Cosío Villegas, Daniel, ed. *Historia moderna de México*. Mexico City: Editorial Hermes, 1957.

Cueto, Marcos, ed. *Missionaries of Science: The Rockefeller Foundation in Latin America*. Bloomington: Indiana University Press, 1994.

Daunton, M. J., ed. *Housing the Workers, 1850–1914: A Comparative Perspective*. New York: Leicester University Press, 1990.

de la Pena, Moisés T. *Veracruz económico*. Mexico City: n.p., 1946.

Domínguez Pérez, Olivia. *Política y movimientos sociales en el tejedismo*. Jalapa: Universidad Veracruzana, 1986.

_____, ed. *Agraristas y agrarismo*. Jalapa: Gobierno del Estado de Veracruz, 1992.

Dulles, John F. *Yesterday in Mexico: A Chronicle of the Revolution, 1919–1936*. Austin: University of Texas Press, 1961.

Eckstein, Susan. *The Poverty of Revolution: The State and the Urban Poor in Mexico*. Princeton: Princeton University Press, 1977.

_____, ed. *Power and Popular Protest: Latin American Social Movements*. Berkeley: University of California Press, 1989.

Escobar, Arturo, and Sonia Alvarez, eds. *The Making of Social Movements in Latin America: Identity, Strategy, and Democracy*. Boulder, CO: Westview Press, 1992.

Fagen, Richard, and William Tuohy. *Politics and Privilege in a Mexican City*. Stanford: Stanford University Press, 1972.

Falcón, Romana. *El agrarismo en Veracruz: La etapa radical, 1928–1935*. Mexico City: Colegio de México, 1977.

Falcón, Romana, and Soledad García Morales. *La semilla en el surco: Adalberto Tejeda y el radicalismo en Veracruz, 1883–1960*. Mexico City: Colegio de México, 1986.

Flores y Escalante, Jesús. *Imagenes del danzón: Iconografía del danzón en México*. Mexico City: Asociación Mexicana de Estudios Fonográficos, 1994.

Foweraker, Joe, and Ann Craig, eds. *Popular Movements and Political Change in Mexico*. Boulder, CO: Lynne Rienner, 1990.

Fowler-Salamini, Heather. *Agrarian Radicalism in Veracruz, 1920–30*. Lincoln: University of Nebraska Press, 1971.

French, William. *A Peaceful and Working People: Manners, Morals, and Class Formation in Northern Mexico*. Albuquerque: University of New Mexico Press, 1996.

Fritsche, L. F. *Mexico City and State Directory*. Mexico City: American Book and Printing Company, 1928.

Frost, Elsa Cecilia, Michael C. Meyer, and Josefina Zoraida Vázquez, eds. *El trabajo y los trabajadores en la historia de México*. Mexico City and Tucson: Colegio de México and University of Arizona Press, 1979.

García Auli, Rafael. *La unión de estibadores y jornaleros del puerto de Veracruz: Ante el movimiento obrero nacional e internacional de 1909 a 1977*. Veracruz: Author's edition, 1977.

García Cantú, Gastón. *El socialismo en México, siglo XIX.* Mexico City: Ediciones Era, 1969.

García Díaz, Bernardo. *Estado de Veracruz.* Jalapa: Estado de Veracruz, 1993.

———. *Puerto de Veracruz.* Jalapa: Archivo General del Estado de Veracruz, 1992.

———. *Textiles del valle de Orizaba, 1880–1925.* Jalapa: Universidad Veracruzana, 1990.

———. *Un pueblo fabril del porfiriato: Santa Rosa, Veracruz.* Mexico City: Sep-Setentas, 1981.

García Morales, Soledad. *La rebelión delahuertista en Veracruz, 1923.* Jalapa: Universidad Veracruzana, 1986.

García Morales, Soledad, and José Velasco Toro, eds. *Memorias e informes de jefes políticos y autoridades del régimen porfirista, 1877–1911.* Jalapa: Universidad Veracruzana, 1991.

García Mundo, Octavio. *El movimiento inquilinario de Veracruz, 1922.* Mexico City: Sep-Setentas, 1976.

Gilbert, Alan. *In Search of a Home: Rental and Shared Housing in Latin America.* London: UCL Press, 1993.

Gilbert, Alan, and Ann Varley. *Landlord and Tenant: Housing and the Poor in Urban Mexico.* New York: Routledge, 1991.

Gilbert, Alan, and Peter Ward. *Housing, the State, and the Poor: Policy and Practice in Three Latin American Cities.* Cambridge: Cambridge University Press, 1985.

Gill, Mario, ed. *México y la revolución de octubre (1917).* Mexico City: Ediciones de Cultura Popular, 1975.

Gilly, Adolfo. *The Mexican Revolution.* London: Thetford Press, 1983.

González Marín, Silvia. *Heriberto Jara: Un luchador obrero en la revolución mexicana, 1879–1917.* Mexico City: Sociedad Cooperativa Publicaciones, 1984.

González Navarro, Moisés. *Población y sociedad en México, 1900–1970.* 2 vols. Mexico City: UNAM, 1974.

González Sierra, José. *Monopolio del humo: Elementos para la historia del tabaco en México y algunos conflictos de tabaqueros veracruzanos, 1915–1930.* Jalapa: Universidad Veracruzana, 1987.

Gregory, Derek. *Geographic Imaginations.* Cambridge: Blackwell, 1994.

Gruening, Ernest. *Mexico and Its Heritage.* 1928. Reprint, New York: Greenwood Press, 1968.

Guzmán, Martín Luis. *La sombra del caudillo.* Madrid: Espasa-Calpe S.A., 1929.

Haber, Stephen. *Industry and Underdevelopment: The Industrialization of Mexico, 1890–1940.* Stanford: Stanford University Press, 1989.

Hall, Linda B. *Alvaro Obregón: Power and Revolution in Mexico, 1911–1920.* College Station: Texas A&M University Press, 1981.

———. *Oil, Banks, and Politics: The United States and Postrevolutionary Mexico, 1917–1924.* Austin: University of Texas Press, 1995.

Hamilton, Nora. *The Limits of State Authority: Postrevolutionary Mexico.* Princeton: Princeton University Press, 1982.

Hansen, Roger D. *The Politics of Mexican Development*. Baltimore: Johns Hopkins University Press, 1971.

Hart, John. *Anarchism and the Mexican Working Class, 1860–1931*. Austin: University of Texas Press, 1987.

_____. *Revolutionary Mexico: The Coming and Process of the Mexican Revolution*. Berkeley: University of California Press, 1987.

Harvey, David. *The Urban Experience*. Baltimore: Johns Hopkins University Press, 1989.

Hendricks, King, and Irving Shepard, eds. *Jack London Reports: War Correspondence, Sports Articles, and Miscellaneous Writings*. Garden City, NY: Doubleday, 1970.

Hobsbawm, Eric. *Primitive Rebels: Studies in Archaic Forms of Social Movement in the 19th and 20th Centuries*. Manchester: Manchester University Press, 1959.

Huitrón, Jacinto. *Orígenes e historia del movimiento obrero en México*. Mexico City: Editores Mexicanos Unidos, 1975.

Instituto Nacional de Estadistica Geografía e Informática. *Veracruz: Estado de Veracruz, cuaderno estadistico municipal*. Aguascalientes, 1993.

Johns, Michael. *The City of Mexico in the Age of Díaz*. Austin: University of Texas Press, 1997.

Joseph, Gilbert M. *Revolution from Without: Yucatán, Mexico, and the United States, 1880–1924*. Durham: Duke University Press, 1988.

_____, ed. *Land, Labor, and Capital in Modern Yucatán: Essays in Regional History and Political Economy*. Tuscaloosa: University of Alabama Press, 1991.

Joseph, Gilbert M., and Daniel Nugent, eds. *Everyday Forms of State Formation: Revolution and the Negotiation of Rule in Modern Mexico*. Durham: Duke University Press, 1994.

Katz, Friedrich. *The Secret War in Mexico: Europe, the United States, and the Mexican Revolution*. Chicago: University of Chicago Press, 1981.

_____, ed. *Riot, Rebellion, and Revolution: Rural Social Conflict in Mexico*. Princeton: Princeton University Press, 1988.

Kenny, Michael. *Inmigrantes y refugiados españoles en México (siglo XX)*. Mexico City: Instituto Nacional de Antropología e Historia, 1979.

Klunder, Juan, and Salvador Díaz Mirón. *La ciudad de Veracruz en 1858*. Mexico City: Editorial Citlaltépetl, 1972.

Knight, Alan. *The Mexican Revolution*. 2 vols. Lincoln: University of Nebraska Press, 1986.

_____. *U.S.-Mexican Relations, 1910–1940: An Interpretation*. San Diego: Center for U.S.-Mexican Studies, 1987.

Krauze, Enrique. *Mexico: Biography of Power, a History of Modern Mexico, 1810–1996*. New York: HarperCollins, 1997.

Lawson, Ronald. *The Tenant Movement in New York City, 1904–1984*. New Brunswick, NJ: Rutgers University Press, 1986.

Lerdo de Tejada, Miguel. *Apuntes históricos de la heroica ciudad de Veracruz*. Mexico City: Imprenta de Vicente García Torres, 1958.

Lida, Clara E., ed. *Una inmigración privilegiada: Comerciantes, empresarios y profesionales españoles en México en los siglos XIX y XX.* Madrid: Alianza América, 1994.

Link, Arthur S. *Woodrow Wilson and the Progressive Era, 1910–1917.* New York: Harper and Row, 1954.

Lomnitz-Adler, Larissa. *Networks and Marginality: Life in a Mexican Shantytown.* New York: Academic Press, 1977.

Loyola Díaz, Rafael. *La crisis Obregón-Calles y el estado mexicano.* Mexico City: Siglo Veintiuno Editores, 1980.

Lozano y Nathal, Gema. *Catálogo del Archivo Sindical del Puerto de Veracruz "Miguel Angel Montoya Cortés."* Mexico City: Colección Fuentes, Instituto Nacional de Antropología e Historia, 1990.

Magin, William, and James Clifton, eds. *Peasants in Cities: Readings in the Anthropology of Urbanization.* New York: Houghton Mifflin, 1970.

Mancisidor, José. *Frontera junto al mar.* Mexico City: Fondo de Cultura Económica, 1953.

_____. *La ciudad roja: Novela proletaria.* Jalapa: Editorial Integrales, 1932.

_____. *Veracruz recuperado.* Mexico City: Talleres Gráficos de la Nación, 1960.

Mancisidor Ortiz, Anselmo. *Jarochilandia.* Veracruz: Author's edition, 1971.

Maples Arce, Manuel. *El movimiento social en Veracruz.* Jalapa: Talleres Gráficos del Estado de Veracruz, 1927.

Martínez, Andrea. *La intervención norteamericana: Veracruz, 1914.* Mexico City: Secretaría de Educación Pública, 1982.

Martínez Verdugo, Arnoldo, ed. *Historia del comunismo en México.* Mexico City: Grijalbo, 1985.

McAdam, Doug. *Political Process and the Development of Black Insurgency, 1930–1970.* Chicago: University of Chicago Press, 1982.

McAdam, Doug, John D. McCarthy, and Mayer N. Zald, eds. *Comparative Perspectives on Social Movements: Political Opportunities, Mobilizing Structures, and Cultural Framings.* Cambridge: Cambridge University Press, 1996.

Melling, Joseph. *Rent Strikes: People's Struggle for Housing in West Scotland, 1890–1916.* Edinburgh: Polygon Books, 1983.

Melo de Remes, María Luisa. *Veracruz mártir: La infamia de Woodrow Wilson, 1914.* Mexico City: Imprenta Rúiz, 1966.

Méndez de Cuenca, Laura. *El hogar mexicano: Nociones de economía doméstica.* Mexico City: Herrero Hermanos, 1910.

Mexico, Dirección General de Estadística. *Estadísticas sociales del porfiriato.* Mexico City, 1956.

_____. *II Censo general de la República Mexicana, 1900.* Mexico City, 1904.

_____. *III Censo de población de los Estados Unidos Mexicanos, 1910.* Mexico City, 1918.

_____. *IV Censo general de población, 1921.* Mexico City, 1928.

_____. *V Censo de población, 1930.* Mexico City, 1936.

Meyer, Lorenzo. *Mexico and the United States, 1917–1942.* Austin: University of Texas Press, 1977.

Middlebrook, Kevin. *The Paradox of Revolution: Labor, the State, and Authoritarianism in Mexico.* Baltimore: Johns Hopkins University Press, 1995.

Moore, Barrington. *Injustice: The Social Bases of Obedience and Revolt.* Armonk, NY: M. E. Sharpe, 1978.

_____. *Social Origins of Dictatorship and Democracy.* Boston: Beacon Press, 1966.

Moreno Toscano, Alejandra. *Geografía económia de México, siglo XVI.* Mexico City: Colegio de México, 1968.

_____, ed. *Investigaciones sobre la historia de la ciudad de México.* Mexico City: Instituto Nacional de Antropología e Historia, 1974.

Moreno Toscano, Alejandra, and Samuel León González, eds. *75 años de sindicalismo.* Mexico City: Instituto Nacional de Estudios Históricos de la Revolución Mexicana, 1986.

Museo Nacional de Culturas Populares. *Obreros somos . . . expresiones de la cultura obrera.* Mexico City: Dirección General de Culturas Populares, 1984.

Norman, James. *Terry's Guide to Mexico.* Garden City, NY: Doubleday, 1962.

Nugent, Daniel, ed. *Rural Revolt in Mexico: U.S. Intervention and the Domain of Subaltern Politics.* Durham: Duke University Press, 1998.

Ochoa Contreras, Octavio, and Flora Velasquez Ortíz. *Volumen, dinámica y estructura de la población total del estado de Veracruz, 1793–1980.* Jalapa: Universidad Veracruzana, 1986.

Palomares, Justino N. *La invasión yanqui en 1914.* Mexico City: Author's edition, 1940.

Pani, Alberto J. *La higiene en México.* Mexico City: J. Ballescá, 1916.

Pasquel, Leonardo. *Biografía integral de la ciudad de Veracruz, 1519–1969: Colección suma veracruzana.* Mexico City: Editorial Citlaltépetl, 1969.

_____. *Cinquenta distinguidas veracruzanas.* Mexico City: Editorial Citlaltépetl, 1975.

_____. *La generación liberal veracruzana.* Mexico City: Editorial Citlaltépetl, 1972.

_____. *La invasión de Veracruz en 1914.* Mexico City: Editorial Citlaltépetl, 1976.

_____. *Manuel y José Azueta, padre e hijo, héroes en la gesta de 1914.* Mexico City: Editorial Citlaltépetl, 1967.

_____. *La revolución en el Estado de Veracruz.* 2 vols. Mexico City: Biblioteca del Instituto Nacional de Estudios de la Revolución Mexicana, 1971.

_____. *Obras del puerto de Veracruz en 1882.* Mexico City: Editorial Citlaltépetl, 1962.

_____. *Viajeros en el estado de Veracruz.* Mexico City: Editorial Citlaltépetl, 1979.

Paz, Octavio. *The Labyrinth of Solitude.* Translated by Lysander Kemp. New York: Grove Press, 1961.

Philip, George. *Oil and Politics in Latin America: Nationalist Movements and State Companies*. Cambridge: Cambridge University Press, 1982.

Piven, Frances Fox, and Richard A. Cloward. *Poor People's Movements: Why They Succeed, How They Fail*. New York: Vintage Books, 1977.

Plunz, Richard. *A History of Housing in New York City: Dwelling Type and Social Change in the American Metropolis*. New York: Columbia University Press, 1990.

Poblett Miranda, Martha, ed. *Cien viajeros en Veracruz: Crónicas y relatos*. 11 vols. Jalapa: Estado de Veracruz, 1992.

Poniatowska, Elena. *Nothing, Nobody: The Voices of the Mexico City Earthquake*. Translated by Aurora Camacho de Schmidt and Arthur Schmidt. Philadelphia: Temple University Press, 1995.

Quirk, Robert E. *An Affair of Honor: Woodrow Wilson and the Occupation of Veracruz*. New York: Norton, 1962.

Raat, W. Dirk. *Revoltosos: Mexico's Rebels in the United States, 1903–1923*. College Station: Texas A&M University Press, 1981.

Reina, Leticia. *Las rebeliones campesinas en México, 1819–1906*. Mexico City: Siglo Veintiuno Editores, 1983.

Reyna Múñoz, Manuel, ed. *Actores sociales en un proceso de transformación: Veracruz en los años veinte*. Jalapa: Universidad Veracruzana, 1996.

Rivière D'Arc, Hélène, and Claude Batallion. *La ciudad de México*. Mexico City: Sep-Setentas, 1973.

Roberts, Brian. *Cities of Peasants: The Political Economy of Urbanization in the Third World*. Beverly Hills: Sage, 1978.

_____. *Organizing Strangers: Poor Families in Guatemala City*. Austin: University of Texas Press, 1973.

Rodriguez, Hipolito, and Jorge Alberto Manrique. *Veracruz: La ciudad de mar, 1519–1821*. Veracruz: Instituto Veracruzano de Cultura, 1991.

Roy, M. N. *M. N. Roy's Memoirs*. Bombay: Allied Publishers, 1964.

Rúiz, Ramón Eduardo. *Labor and the Ambivalent Revolutionaries, 1911–1923*. Baltimore: Johns Hopkins University Press, 1976.

_____. *The Great Rebellion: Mexico, 1905–1924*. New York: Norton, 1982.

Salazar, Rosendo. *La casa del obrero mundial*. Mexico City: Editorial Costa Amic, 1964.

_____. *Las pugnas de la gleba*. Mexico City: Comisión Nacional Editorial, 1972.

Salinas Carranza, Alberto. *La expedición punitiva*. Mexico City: Ediciones, 1937.

Saragoza, Alex M. *The Monterrey Elite and the Mexican State, 1880–1940*. Austin: University of Texas Press, 1988.

Schmidt, Arthur P., Jr. *The Social and Economic Effect of the Railroad in Puebla and Veracruz, in Mexico, 1867–1911*. New York: Garland, 1987.

Schteingart, Martha. *Los productores del espacio habitable: Estado, empresa y sociedad en la Ciudad de México*. Mexico City: Colegio de México, 1989.

Scobie, James. *Buenos Aires: From Plaza to Suburb*. New York: Oxford University Press, 1974.

Scott, James. *Weapons of the Weak: Everyday Forms of Peasant Resistance*. New Haven: Yale University Press, 1986.

Secretaría de Economía, Dirección General de Estadística. *Estadísticas sociales del porfiriato, 1877–1910*. Mexico City: Talleres Gráficos de la Nación, 1956.

Secretaría de Industria, Comercio y Trabajo. *Documentos relacionados con la legislación petrolera mexicana*. Mexico City: Talleres Gráficos de la Nación, 1922.

Selbin, Eric. *Modern Latin American Revolutions*. Boulder, CO: Westview Press, 1993.

Siemens, Alfred H. *Between the Summit and the Sea: Central Veracruz in the Nineteenth Century*. Vancouver: University of British Columbia Press, 1990.

Sims, Howard Dana. *The Expulsion of Mexico's Spaniards, 1821–1836*. Pittsburgh: University of Pittsburgh Press, 1990.

Skocpol, Theda. *Social Revolutions in the Modern World*. Cambridge: Cambridge University Press, 1994.

_____. *States and Social Revolutions: A Comparative Analysis of France, Russia, and China*. Princeton: Princeton University Press, 1979.

Smith, Robert Freeman. *The United States and Revolutionary Nationalism in Mexico, 1916–1932*. Chicago: University of Chicago Press, 1972.

Southworth, John R. *El estado de Veracruz-Llave: Su historia, agricultura, comercio e industria en inglés y español*. Jalapa: Gobierno del Estado de Veracruz, 1900.

Spalding, Hobart. *Organized Labor in Latin America: Historical Case Studies of Urban Workers in Dependent Societies*. New York: Harper and Row, 1977.

Taibo II, Paco Ignacio. *Bolshevikis: Historia narrativa de los orígenes del comunismo en México, 1919–1925*. Mexico City: Editorial Joaquín Mortiz, 1986.

Tamayo, Jaime. *La clase obrera en la historia de México*. 17 vols. Mexico City: UNAM, Siglo Veintiuno Editores, 1987.

Tarrow, Sidney. *Power in Movement: Social Movements, Collective Action, and Politics*. New York: Cambridge University Press, 1994.

Thompson, E. P. *Customs in Common: Studies in Traditional Popular Culture*. New York: New Press, 1993.

Tilly, Charles. *From Mobilization to Revolution*. Reading, MA: Addison Wesley, 1978.

_____. *Popular Contention in Great Britain, 1758–1834*. Cambridge, MA: Harvard University Press, 1996.

Trens, Manuel B. *Historia de Veracruz*. Jalapa: Gráficos del Gobierno de Veracruz, 1957.

Tutino, John. *From Insurrection to Revolution in Mexico: Social Bases of Agrarian Violence, 1750–1940*. Princeton: Princeton University Press, 1986.

Ulloa, Berta. *Veracruz, capital de la nación, 1914–15*. Mexico City: Colegio de México, 1986.

_____. *Historia de la revolución mexicana, 1914–1917: La constitución de 1917*. Mexico City: Colegio de México, 1983.

Unikel, Luis. *El desarrollo urbano de México: Diagnóstico y implicaciones futuras.* Mexico City: Colegio de México, 1976

Valadés, José C. *Memorias de un joven rebelde: Mis confesiones.* México: University of Sinaloa, 1985.

———. *Revolución social o motín político.* Mexico City: Biblioteca de Partido Comunista, 1922.

Vanderwood, Paul. *Disorder and Progress: Bandits, Police, and Mexican Development.* Lincoln: University of Nebraska Press, 1981.

———. *The Power of God against the Guns of Government: Religious Upheaval in Mexico at the Turn of the Nineteenth Century.* Stanford: Stanford University Press, 1998.

Van Young, Eric, ed. *Mexico's Regions: Comparative History and Development.* San Diego: Center for U.S.-Mexican Studies, 1992.

Vasconcelos, José. *Ulysses criollo: La vida del autor escrita por el mismo.* Mexico City: Ediciones Botas, 1945.

Walton, John. *Reluctant Rebels: Comparative Studies of Revolution and Underdevelopment.* New York: Columbia University Press, 1984.

———. *Western Times and Water Wars: State, Culture, and Rebellion in California.* Berkeley: University of California Press, 1992.

Walton, John, and Alejandro Portes. *Urban Latin America.* Austin: University of Texas Press, 1976.

Ward, Peter. *Mexico City: The Production and Reproduction of an Urban Environment.* London: Belhaven Press, 1990.

Wasserman, Mark, and Thomas Benjamin, eds. *Provinces of the Revolution: Essays on Regional Mexican History, 1910–1929.* Albuquerque: University of New Mexico Press, 1990.

Williams García, Roberto. *Yo nací con la luna de plata: Antropología e historia de un puerto.* Mexico City: Costa-Amic Editores, 1980.

Womack, John. *Zapata and the Mexican Revolution.* New York: Vintage Books, 1968.

Articles and Book Chapters

Adleson, Lief. "Identidad comunitaria y transformación social: Estibadores y petroleros en Tampico (1900–1925)." *Historias* 7 (October–December 1982): 29–44.

Baer, James. "Tenant Mobilization and the 1907 Rent Strike in Buenos Aires." *The Americas* 49, no. 3 (January 1993): 343–69.

Bernstein, Harry. "Marxismo en México, 1917–1925." *Historia Mexicana* 7, no. 4 (April–June 1958): 497–516.

Berra-Stoppa, Erica. "Estoy en huelga y no pago renta." *Habitación* 1, no. 1 (1981): 33–39.

Bonilla, Frank. "The Urban Worker." In *Continuity and Change in Latin America*, ed. John J. Johnson, 186–205. Stanford: Stanford University Press, 1964.

Brading, David. "The City in Bourbon Spanish America: Elites and Masses." *Comparative Urban Research* 8, no. 1 (1980): 71–85.

Carr, Barry. "Marxism and Anarchism in the Formation of the Mexican Communist Party, 1910–1919." *Hispanic American Historical Review* 63, no. 2 (February 1983): 277–305.

———. "The Casa del Obrero Mundial, Constitutionalism, and the Pact of February 1915." In *Labor and Laborers through Mexican History*, ed. Elsa Cecilia Frost, Michael C. Meyer, and Josefina Zoraida Vázquez, 603–32. Mexico City and Tucson: Colegio de México and University of Arizona Press, 1979.

Cortes Rodríguez, Martha. "Bailes y carnaval en Veracruz, 1925." *Horizonte: Revista del Instituto Veracruzano de Cultura* 1, no. 1 (March–April 1991): 19–25.

Domínguez Pérez, Olivia. "El puerto de Veracruz: La modernización a finales del siglo XIX." *Anuario* 7 (1990): 87–102.

Durand Arp-Nisen, Jorge. "El movimiento inquilinario de Guadalajara, 1922." *Encuentro*, 1983, 7–28.

Fowler-Salamini, Heather. "Orígenes laborales de la organización campesina en Veracruz." *Historia Mexicana* 20, no. 2 (October–December 1970): 235–64.

García de León, Antonio. "Los patios danzoneros." *La Jornada Seminal* 223 (September 19, 1993): 33–40.

García Díaz, Bernardo. "Acción directa y poder obrero en la CROM de Orizaba, 1918–1922." *Historias* 7 (October–December 1984): 15–27.

García Morales, Soledad. "Manuel Peláez y Guadalupe Sánchez: Dos caciques regionales." *La Palabra y El Hombre* 67, no. 1 (January–March 1989): 125–36.

———. "Cotidianidad, cultura y diversión durante la ocupación delahuertista del puerto de Veracruz." In *Actores sociales en un proceso de transformación: Veracruz en los años veinte*, ed. Manuel Reyna Múñoz, 103–28. Jalapa: Universidad Veracruzana, 1996.

Gill, Mario. "Veracruz: Revolución y extremismo." *Historia Mexicana* 2, no. 8 (April–July 1953): 618–36.

Ginzberg, Eitan. "Ideología política y la cuestión de las prioridades: Lázaro Cárdenas y Adalberto Tejeda, 1928–1934." *Estudios Mexicanos/ Mexican Studies* 13, no. 1 (Winter 1997): 55–85.

———. "State Agrarianism versus Democratic Agrarianism: Adalberto Tejeda's Experiment in Veracruz, 1928–32." *Journal of Latin American Studies* 30, no. 2 (May 1998): 341–73.

González Sierra, José. "Revolución y derecho obrero: Veracruz, 1914–1916." *Anuario* 4 (1986): 117–41.

Goodwin, Jeff. "Toward a New Sociology of Revolutions." *Theory and Society* 23, no. 6 (December 1994): 731–66.

Jenkinson, Charles. "Veracruz." *The Survey* 2 (1914): 133–41.

Johns, Michael. "The Antinomies of Ruling-Class Culture." *Journal of Historical Sociology* 6, no. 1 (March 1993): 74–101.

Kaplan, Temma. "Female Consciousness and Collective Action: The Case of Barcelona, 1910–1918." *Signs: Journal of Women and Culture* 7, no. 3 (Spring 1982): 545–66.

Katz, Friedrich. "Pancho Villa and the Attack on Columbus, New Mexico." *American Historical Review* 83, no. 1 (February 1978): 101–30.

Knight, Alan. "Peasants into Patriots: Thoughts on the Making of the Mexican Nation." *Estudios Mexicanos/Mexican Studies* 10, no. 1 (Winter 1994): 135–61.

_____. "The Working Class and the Mexican Revolution, 1900–1920." *Journal of Latin American Studies* 16, no. 2 (May 1984): 51–79.

_____. "The Political Economy of Revolutionary Mexico." In *Latin American Economic Imperialism and the State: The Political Economy of the External Connection from Independence to the Present*, ed. Christopher Abel and Colin M. Lewis, 290–310. London: The Athlone Press, 1985.

Lear, John. "Mexico City: Space and Class in the Porfirian Capital, 1884–1910." *Journal of Urban History* 22, no. 4 (May 1996): 454–92.

London, Jack. "Stalking the Pestilence." *Collier's*, June 6, 1914. Reprinted in *Jack London Reports: War Correspondence, Sports Articles, and Miscellaneous Writings*, ed. King Hendricks and Irving Shepard (Garden City, NY: Doubleday, 1970).

Lozano y Nathal, Gema. "La negra, loca y anarquista federación local de trabajadores del puerto de Veracruz." *Antropología* 30 (April–June 1990): 10–19.

Machado, Manuel A., and James T. Judge. "Tempest in a Teapot? The Mexican-U.S. Intervention Crisis of 1919." *Southwestern Historical Quarterly* 74 (July 1970): 1–23.

Mayet, Sergio Florescano. "Las epidemias y la sociedad veracruzana en el siglo XIX." *Anuario* 8 (1992): 57–96.

Meade, Teresa. "Living Worse and Costing More: Resistance and Riot in Rio de Janeiro, 1870–1917." *Journal of Latin American Studies* 21, no. 2 (May 1989): 241–66.

Meyer, Jean. "Los obreros en la revolución mexicana: Los 'bataliones rojos.' " *Historia Mexicana* 21, no. 1 (July–September 1971): 1–37.

Moreno Toscano, Alejandra. "Cambios en los patrones de urbanización en México, 1810–1910." *Historia Mexicana* 22, no. 2 (October–December 1972): 160–87.

_____. "La 'crisis' en la ciudad." In *México hoy*, ed. Pablo González Casanova and Enrique Florescano, 152–74. Mexico City: Siglo Veintiuno, 1979.

Palmer, Frederick. "The American Spirit in Vera Cruz." *Everybody's Magazine* 30, no. 5 (May 1914): 806–20.

_____. "Watchful Perspiring at Vera Cruz." *Everybody's Magazine* 31, no. 1 (July 1914): 65–80.

Perlo Cohen, Manuel. "Política y vivienda en México, 1910–1952." *Revista Mexicana de Sociología* 41, no. 3 (July–September 1979): 769–835.

Perlo Cohen, Manuel, and Martha Schteingart. "Movimientos sociales urbanos en México." *Revista Mexicana de Sociología* 46, no. 4 (October–December 1984): 105–25.

Smith, Robert Sidney. "Shipping in the Port of Veracruz, 1790–1821." *Hispanic American Historical Review* 23, no. 1 (February 1943): 5–20.

Spenser, Daniela. "Workers against Socialism: Reassessing the Role of Urban Labor in Yucatecan Revolutionary Politics." In *Land, Labor, and Capital in Modern Yucatán: Essays in Regional History and Political Economy,* ed. Gilbert Joseph, 220–42. Tuscaloosa: University of Alabama Press, 1991.

Taibo II, Paco Ignacio. "Inquilinos del D.F., a colgar la rojinegra." *Anuario* 3 (1983): 99–126.

Tamayo, Jaime. "El Sindicato Revolucionario de Inquilinos y la huelga de rentas de 1922." In *Jalisco desde la revolución: Los movimientos sociales, 1917–1929,* ed. Jaime Tamayo, 129–40. Guadalajara: Universidad de Guadalajara, 1988.

Valencia Valera, Victor Hugo. "La influencia del movimiento urbano (los inquilinos) en la organización campesina: Veracruz, 1923." *Antropología* 32 (October–December 1990): 12–24.

Vanderwood, Paul. "The Picture Postcard as Historical Evidence: Veracruz, 1914." *The Americas* 45, no. 2 (October 1988): 201–55.

Van Young, Eric. "Islands in the Storm: Quiet Cities and Violent Countrysides in the Mexican Independence Era." *Past and Present* 118 (February 1988): 130–55.

Von Wobeser, Gisela. "La vivienda del nivel socioeconómico bajo en la ciudad de México entre 1750–1850." Paper presented at the 9th meeting of Canadian, U.S., and Mexican Historians, Mexico City, October 27–29, 1994.

Walton, John. "Guadalajara: Creating the Divided City." In *Latin American Urban Research,* Volume 6. *Metropolitan Change in Latin America: The Challenge and the Response,* ed. Wayne Cornelius and Robert Kemper, 25–50. Beverly Hills: Sage, 1978.

Whipple, George C. "The Broadening Science of Sanitation." *Atlantic Monthly* (May 1914): 630–41.

Wood, Andrew G. "Viva la revolución social! Postrevolutionary Tenant Protest and State Housing Reform in Veracruz, Mexico." In *Cities of Hope: People, Protests, and Progress in Urbanizing Latin America, 1870–1930,* ed. James Baer and Ronn Pineo, 88–128. Boulder, CO: Westview Press, 1998.

Dissertations, Theses, and Manuscripts

Adleson, Lief. "Historia social de los obreros industriales de Tampico, 1906–1919." Ph.D. diss., El Colegio de México, 1982.

Almanza García, Manuel. "Historia del agrarismo en el estado de Veracruz." Manuscript, Jalapa, 1952.

Berra-Stoppa, Erica. "Expansión de la ciudad de México y los conflictos urbanos." Ph.D. diss., El Colegio de México, 1982.

Calvo Cruz, Beatriz. "Historia social de Córdoba, Veracruz, 1915–1922." Bachelor's thesis, Universidad Veracruzana, 1986.

Contreras Utrera, Julio. "Los comerciantes del porfiriato: El puerto de Veracruz, 1880–1890." Bachelor's thesis, Universidad Veracruzana, 1989.

Hansis, Randall G. "Alvaro Obregón: The Mexican Revolution and the Politics of Consolidation." Ph.D. diss., University of New Mexico, 1971.

Landa Ortega, María Rosa. "Los primeros años de la organización y luchas de los electricistas y tranviarios en Veracruz, 1915–1928." Bachelor's thesis, Universidad Veracruzana, 1989.

Lear, John Robert. "Workers, *Vecinos*, and Citizens: The Revolution in Mexico City, 1909–1917." Ph.D. diss., University of California, Berkeley, 1993.

Mazzaferri, Anthony. "Public Health and Social Revolution in Mexico, 1877–1930." Ph.D. diss., Kent State University, 1968.

Schmidt, Arthur P. "The Social and Economic Effect of the Railroad in Puebla and Veracruz, Mexico, 1867–1911." Ph.D. diss., Indiana University, 1971.

Solorzano Ramos, Armando. "The Rockefeller Foundation in Mexico: Nationalism, Public Health, and Yellow Fever, 1911–1924." Ph.D. diss., University of Wisconsin, 1990.

Discography (Compact Discs)

Danzón, The Original Soundtrack. DRG Records, 1992.

Danzónes del porfiriato y la revolución. Testimonial/RCA/BMG, 1994.

Hot Music from Cuba, 1907–1936. Harlequin CD #23. 1993.

The Mexican Revolution: Corridos about the Heroes and Events, 1910–1920 and Beyond! Arhoolie Productions, 1996.

Toña La Negra: La Sensación Jarocha. Discos Peerless, 1991.

20 Exitos de Agustín Lara. RCA/BMG, 1991.

Index

Latin American Silhouettes
Studies in History and Culture

William H. Beezley and
Judith Ewell
Editors

Volumes Published

and the Mexican Revolution (2000).
ISBN 0-8420-2774-2

Mark T. Gilderhus, *The Second Century: U.S.-Latin American Relations since 1889* (2000). Cloth ISBN 0-8420-2413-1 Paper ISBN 0-8420-2414-X

Catherine Moses, *Real Life in Castro's Cuba* (2000). Cloth ISBN 0-8420-2836-6 Paper ISBN 0-8420-2837-4

K. Lynn Stoner, ed./comp., with Luis Hipólito Serrano Pérez, *Cuban and Cuban-American Women: An Annotated Bibliography* (2000). ISBN 0-8420-2643-6

Thomas D. Schoonover, *The French in Central America: Culture and Commerce, 1820–1930* (2000). ISBN 0-8420-2792-0

Enrique C. Ochoa, *Feeding Mexico: The Political Uses of Food since 1910* (2000). Cloth ISBN 0-8420-2812-9 (2002) Paper ISBN 0-8420-2813-7

Thomas W. Walker and Ariel C. Armony, eds., *Repression, Resistance, and Democratic Transition in Central America* (2000). Cloth ISBN 0-8420-2766-1 Paper ISBN 0-8420-2768-8

William H. Beezley and David E. Lorey, eds., *¡Viva México! ¡Viva la Independencia! Celebrations of September 16* (2001). Cloth ISBN 0-8420-2914-1 Paper ISBN 0-8420-2915-X

Jeffrey M. Pilcher, *Cantinflas and the Chaos of Mexican Modernity* (2001). Cloth ISBN 0-8420-2769-6 Paper ISBN 0-8420-2771-8

Victor M. Uribe-Uran, ed., *State and Society in Spanish America during the Age of Revolution* (2001). Cloth ISBN 0-8420-2873-0 Paper ISBN 0-8420-2874-9

Andrew Grant Wood, *Revolution in the Street: Women, Workers, and Urban Protest in Veracruz, 1870–1927* (2001). Cloth ISBN 0-8420-2879-X (2002) Paper ISBN 0-8420-2880-3

Charles Bergquist, Ricardo Peñaranda, and Gonzalo Sánchez G., eds., *Violence in Colombia, 1990–2000: Waging War and Negotiating Peace* (2001). Cloth ISBN 0-8420-2869-2 Paper ISBN 0-8420-2870-6

William Schell, Jr., *Integral Outsiders: The American Colony in Mexico City, 1876–1911* (2001). ISBN 0-8420-2838-2

John Lynch, *Argentine Caudillo: Juan Manuel de Rosas* (2001). Cloth ISBN 0-8420-2897-8 Paper ISBN 0-8420-2898-6

Samuel Basch, M.D., ed. and trans. Fred D. Ullman, *Recollections of Mexico: The Last Ten Months of Maximilian's Empire* (2001). ISBN 0-8420-2962-1

David Sowell, *The Tale of Healer Miguel Perdomo Neira: Medicine, Ideologies, and Power in the Nineteenth-Century Andes* (2001). Cloth ISBN 0-8420-2826-9 Paper ISBN 0-8420-2827-7

June E. Hahner, ed., *A Parisian in Brazil: The Travel Account of a Frenchwoman in Nineteenth-Century Rio de Janeiro* (2001). Cloth ISBN 0-8420-2854-4 Paper ISBN 0-8420-2855-2

Richard A. Warren, *Vagrants and Citizens: Politics and the Masses in Mexico City from Colony to Republic* (2001). ISBN 0-8420-2964-8

Roderick J. Barman, *Princess Isabel of Brazil: Gender and Power in the Nineteenth Century* (2002). Cloth ISBN 0-8420-2845-5 Paper ISBN 0-8420-2846-3

Stuart F. Voss, *Latin America in the Middle Period, 1750–1929* (2002). Cloth ISBN 0-8420-5024-8 Paper ISBN 0-8420-5025-6

Lester D. Langley, *The Banana Wars: United States Intervention in the Caribbean, 1898–1934*, with new introduction (2002). Cloth ISBN 0-8420-5046-9 Paper ISBN 0-8420-5047-7

Mariano Ben Plotkin, *Mañana es San Perón: A Cultural History of Perón's Argentina* (2003). Cloth ISBN 0-8420-5028-0 Paper ISBN 0-8420-5029-9

Allen Gerlach, *Indians, Oil, and Politics: A Recent History of Ecuador* (2003). Cloth ISBN 0-8420-5107-4 Paper ISBN 0-8420-5108-2

Karen Racine, *Francisco de Miranda: A Transatlantic Life in the Age of Revolution* (2003). Cloth ISBN 0-8420-2909-5 Paper ISBN 0-8420-2910-9